BEYOND THE POST-MODERN MIND

Cover design by *Anne Kilgore*

HUSTON SMITH

BEYOND THE POST-MODERN MIND

UPDATED AND REVISED

This publication is made possible with the assistance of the Kern Foundation

The Theosophical Publishing House
Wheaton, Ill. U.S.A.
Madras, India/London, England

This edition is published by arrangement
with The Crossroads Publishing Company,
370 Lexington Avenue, New York, NY 10017

First Quest Edition 1984
Second Quest Edition 1989. Quest Books are
published by the Theosophical Publishing House,
a division of the Theosophical Society in
America

Library of Congress Cataloging-in-Pubication Data

Smith, Huston.
Beyond the post-modern mind / Huston Smith. — 2nd
Quest ed. p. cm. — (A Quest book)
Includes bibliographical references.
ISBN 0-8356-0647-3 (pbk.) : $9.95
1. Philosophy, Modern—20th century. 2. Postmodernism.
I. Title.
B804.S576 1989
190'.9'04—dc20 89-40175
CIP

Printed in the United States of America

For Serena, Sierra, and Isaiah,
and the future they token

CONTENTS

PREFACE TO THE SECOND EDITION

"If, by some strange device, a man of our century could step backwards in time and mix with the people of a distant age," Gai Eaton wrote in *The King of the Castle*, "he would have good cause to doubt either their sanity or his own" (p. 7). The sun's daily cycle, a raven's flight, mossy oaks and water gushing from a glade would look familiar enough, but the meanings they carried for his new associates would be different. Each would think he knew what constitutes common sense and human normality, but their common sense would differ from his and their normality might seem to him abnormal. Questioning everything they took for granted and astonished that they did not see how much their conclusions were controlled by arbitrary assumptions, he would find everything he took for granted similarly called into question. His "Why?" would be met with their "Why?", and he would have no answer.

The essays here assembled attempt a move like the one just envisioned: they invite us to step outside our current Western outlook to see it in perspective. The limitations of earlier outlooks are so obvious that we forget that ours, too, is built on premises history will smile on. Science and the historical record we now possess may seem to exempt us from the perspectival character of human vision, but we know, of course, that they do not.

Like those who have lived before us, we too have fished certain objectives from the sea of human possibilities. These in turn have firmed up premises that support them, and from these premises an entire outlook has been spun—all this these essays try to show. To compare our world view with others is not to set light against shadow. It is to compare twilight zones; different kinds of limitations, "as though a man tunneling his way out of prison were to emerge within the perimeter, exchanging one cell for another. So it must always be," Eaton concludes, "unless the prisoner learns that freedom lies in quite another direction, never through the tunnel of time" (ibid.).

We shall encounter this other, atemporal and noncumulative dimension of knowledge in Part Two of this book, but here the point is that the stages peoples' outlooks pass through on the temporal continuum have led the West to one that has come to be called "Postmodern"* to distinguish it from the modernity that began in the seventeenth century and ended around the middle of our own. The Modern Mind took its cues from the new worldview that science introduced, but twentieth-century science has abandoned not just that worldview, but worldviews generally. From Aristotle to Dante the world was pictured as a series of concentric spheres. Newton replaced that with his clockwork universe, but quantum mechanics gives us, not a new picture of the world, but no picture at all. And philosophy has followed suit. Metaphysics died around the time that God died, Langdon Gilkey has observed, tying its death to the "death of God" movement that Nietzsche announced, but which took a half-century to come to public notice.

The essays in this book work toward bringing the world back into focus, and as the view that emerges resembles traditional ones more than it does either the Modern worldview or Postmodern lack thereof, the presumption

*Because this is not a new book, merely a new edition, the hyphen in "Post-Modern" has been retained in its title. Elsewhere, however, the hyphen has been dropped to conform to the growing convention regarding the word.

that these latter have permanently retired the way people used to see things needs to be questioned at the outset. The ways in which Modernity and Postmodernity have assumed that their perspectives were less limited than previous ones turn out to be diametrically opposed to each other. Whereas the Modern Mind assumed that it knew more than its predecessors because the natural and historical sciences were flooding it with new knowledge about nature and history, the Postmodern Mind argues (paradoxically) that it knows more than others did because it has discovered how little the human mind *can* know. "How well we now know how little we know," we shall find James Cutsinger noting in Chapter Two.

It is a good part of this book's intent to question these dual—and to repeat, contradictory—claims to superiority. The Modern Mind's mistake was to think that seeing further in a horizontal direction would compensate for loss of the vertical dimension. If we visualize a line that wanders upward and then downward again to silhouette the Himalayan range, it is as if Modernity grabbed hold of both ends of that line and stretched them apart. This collapsed the humps to a straight line along the base of the range, but Modernity reasoned that since that line could be indefinitely extended, it would enclose a volume greater than the one the line originally defined.

For the error of Postmodernism, we can visualize the same Himalayan range, but this time work with it differently. We are now inside a bungalow looking out on Mount Everest's awesome presence. The air is cold outside, so our breath begins to fog the window. Ventilation is poor, causing the moisture on the pane to condense until at some point it becomes difficult to determine whether the shapes we see are mountains or frosted textures of our own breath as it congeals on the pane. Visitors arrive. Not having gazed through the window when it was clear, they do not know what lies beyond it, so they fix on the foreground, assuming unthinkingly that shapes they see are on the windowpane only. Put straightforwardly, the mistake of Postmodernism is to assume that human beings look out on the world through windows so befogged that it would be unwise to assume that what they see is in the world itself.

Part One of the book is historical. It traces the course of Western civilization that has brought it to the Post-modern period.

Part Two establishes a vantage point for viewing the Modern/Postmodern scene.

Part Three attends to the facets of that scene that have engaged me most: higher education, the place of the humanities within that education, theology, science, and the place of social concerns. Although Modernity and Postmodernity can be clearly distinguished in principle, practically—in the actual ethos of our time—there is a great deal of overlap which the essays in this section of the book must sort out.

Part Four offers suggestions for moving into a twenty-first century that is less confused than ours at present is.

This second edition of the book differs from the first in three ways. Minor changes have been introduced throughout the book to position Modernism and Post-modernism in relation to each other more clearly and consistently. Chapter Two, on metaphysics, has been updated, and a new chapter (Eleven) on Postmodernism has been written to take account of recent developments in that area. Finally, statements on philosophy, science, and society have been added to Part Three to round out its survey of our prevailing ethos.

To try to step outside the perspective of one's own culture is a little like trying to step out of the shoes one is walking in. My talents for the move are no greater than the next person's, but circumstances have been in my favor. Born and raised as I was in a foreign and traditional society—China—the longest stretch of my career was at the Massachusetts Institute of Technology, a spearhead of the modern Western, scientific age. Two worlds were thereby joined. If the slant of these essays seems surprising at points, the reason may lie in that intersection.

Two "housekeeping" details:

All but two of these essays initially appeared elsewhere. I have edited them slightly to fit the book's trajectory, but I have not removed all the overlaps that occur in essays that approach different problems from a single angle and were written for different audiences. Doing so would have violated the integrity of the essays themselves, but another consideration also entered. When the reader comes upon an image or quotation that is being repeated, s/he will do well to take it as a signal. I am repeating myself to emphasize the point that is being made.

The slashed pronoun "s/he" that just appeared introduces the second stylistic point. In this awkward time respecting gender pronouns, I have not tried to be consistent in my use of them. Where I have not found uncumbersome ways to invoke gender-inclusive language, I have alternated between ideological and stylistic considerations.

ACKNOWLEDGEMENTS

Had it not been for the initiative of Richard Payne, then of The Crossroad Publishing Company, and his consultant Ewert Cousins, the first edition of this book would not have taken form. Had not Douglas Sloan, editor of the *Teachers College Record*, requested "Excluded Knowledge" and he and the Charles F. Kettering Foundation commissioned "Beyond the Modern Western Mindset," those essays would not have been written. Students at Syracuse University were stimulating, and my colleagues in philosophy and religion provided high-spirited criticism and basic support. My semester as visiting professor at Villanova University helped me to write Chapter Nine. My wife Kendra Smith's editorial eye improves with each successive book. A month when she and I were Teachers-in-Residence at Esalen Institute provided a serene setting for reworking the book into this second edition.

To all of these, my sincerest thanks.

Part One

DARK WOOD

If we think of contemporary Westerners from all walks of life, and the numberless directions in which their hopes and thoughts extend, we can only conclude what has become a truism: no comprehensive vision, no concerted sense of reality, informs our age. The opening lines of Dante's Divine Comedy *could have been written for our twentieth-century's Everyman:*

> *Midway this way of life we're bound upon*
> *I woke to find myself in a dark wood,*
> *Where the right road was wholly lost and gone.*

Near the century's start, John Dewey pointed to "despair of any integrated outlook and attitude [as] the chief intellectual characteristic of the present age," and every succeeding decade has borne him out. Heidegger believed that ages are powered by works of art that gather scattered practices into unified, persuasive models for behavior, and hold them before people who can then relate to each other along the lines they exemplify. Our age, though, he felt, is the first whose paradigm is a work, not of art but of technology: the hydroelectric power station. Being a technological construct, it is value-free. The power station converts the river's power into a grid that places it at the disposal of any purpose whatever. As electricity can be used to satisfy any desire we happen to have, this paradigm provides no directives or motivation for action at all. The consequence is a vacuum of meaning and purpose, as Saul Bellow, too, noted in his 1976 Nobel Laureate Lecture:

> *The intelligent public is waiting to hear from Art what it does not hear from Theology, Philosophy, Social Theory, and what it cannot hear from pure science: a broader, fuller, more coherent, more comprehensive account of what we human beings are, who we are, and what this life is for. If writers do not come into the center it will not be because the center is preempted. It is not.*

I used an invitation from The Saturday Evening Post *to contribute to its "Adventures of the Mind" series as occasion to trace the intellectual odyssey that has this empty center.*

1

THE REVOLUTION IN WESTERN THOUGHT*

Quietly, irrevocably, something enormous has happened to Western man. His outlook on life and the world has changed so radically that in the perspective of history the twentieth century is likely to rank—with the fourth century, which witnessed the triumph of Christianity, and the seventeenth, which signaled the dawn of modern science—as one of the very few that have instigated genuinely new epochs in human thought. In this change, which is still in process, we of the current generation are playing a crucial but as yet not widely recognized part.

The dominant assumptions of an age color the thoughts, beliefs, expectations, and images of the men and women who live within it. Being always with us, these assumptions usually pass unnoticed—like the pair of glasses which, because they are so often on the wearer's nose, simply stop being observed. But this doesn't mean they have no effect. Ultimately, assumptions which underlie our outlooks on life refract the world in ways that condition our art and our institutions: the kinds of homes we live in, our sense of right and wrong, our criteria of success, what we conceive our duty to be, what we think it means to be a man or woman, how we worship our

---

*Reprinted with permission and negligible changes from *The Saturday Evening Post*, 26 August 1961.

God or whether, indeed, we have a God to worship.

Thus far the odyssey of Western man has carried him through three great configurations of such basic assumptions. The first constituted the Graeco-Roman, or classical, outlook, which flourished up to the fourth century A.D. With the triumph of Christianity in the Roman Empire, this Graeco-Roman outlook was replaced by the Christian world view which proceeded to dominate Europe until the seventeenth century. The rise of modern science inaugurated a third important way of looking at things, a way that has come to be capsuled in the phrase "the Modern Mind."

It now appears that this modern outlook, too, has run its course and is being replaced by what, in the absence of a more descriptive term, is being called simply Postmodernism. What follows is an attempt to describe this most recent sea change in Western thought. I shall begin by bringing the Christian and modern outlooks into focus; for only so can we see how and to what extent our emerging thought patterns differ from those that have directly preceded them.

From the fourth-century triumph of Christianity in the Roman Empire through the Middle Ages and the Reformation, the Western mind was above all else theistic. "God, God, God; nothing but God"—in the twentieth century one can assume such an exclamation to have come, as it did, from a theologian. In the Middle Ages it could have come from anyone. Virtually without question all life and nature were assumed to be under the surveillance of a personal God whose intentions toward man were perfect and whose power to implement these intentions was unlimited.

In such a world, life was transparently meaningful. But although men understood the purpose of their lives, it does not follow that they understood, or even presumed to be capable of understanding, the dynamics of the natural world. The Bible never expands the doctrine of creation into a cosmology for the excellent reason that it asserts the universe to be at every point the direct product of a will whose ways are not man's ways. God says, "Let there be"—and there is. That is all. Serene in a blaze of lasting light, God comprehends nature's ways, but man sees only its surface.

Christian man lived in the world as a child lives in his parents' house, accepting its construction and economics unprobed. "Can anyone understand the thunderings of God's pavilion?" Elihu asks Job. "Do you know the ordinances of the heavens, how the clouds are balanced or the lightning shines? Have you comprehended the expanse of the earth, or on what its bases were sunk when the morning stars sang together and all the sons of God shouted for joy?" To such rhetorical questions the answer seemed obvious. The leviathan of nature was not to be drawn from the great sea of mystery by the fishhook of man's paltry mind.

Not until the high Middle Ages was a Christian cosmology attempted, and then through Greek rather than Biblical inspiration, following the rediscovery of Aristotle's Physics and Metaphysics. Meanwhile nature's obscurity posed no major problem; for as the cosmos was in good hands, it could be counted on to furnish a reliable context in which man might work out his salvation. The way to this salvation lay not through ordering nature to man's purposes but through aligning man's purposes to God's. And for this objective, information was at hand. As surely as God had kept the secrets of nature to himself, he had, through his divine Word and the teachings of his church, made man's duty clear. Those who hearkened to this duty would reap an eternal reward, but those who refused to do so would perish.

We can summarize the chief assumptions underlying the Christian outlook by saying they held that reality is focused in a person, that the mechanics of the physical world exceed our comprehension, and that the way to our salvation lies not in conquering nature but in following the commandments which God has revealed to us.

It was the second of these three assumptions—that the dynamics of nature exceed man's comprehension—

which the sixteenth and seventeenth centuries began to question, thereby heralding the transition from the Christian to the modern outlook. The Renaissance interest in the early Greeks revived the Hellenic interest in nature. For the first time in nearly two thousand years Western man began to look intently at his environment instead of beyond it. Leonardo da Vinci is symbolic. His anatomical studies and drawings in general disclose a direction of interest that has turned eye into camera, in his case an extraordinary camera that could stop the hawk in flight and fix the rearing steed. Once again man was attending to nature's details as a potential messenger of meaning. The rage to know God's handiwork was rivaling the rage to know God himself.

The consequence, as we know, was modern science. Under scrutiny, nature's blur was found to be provisional rather than final. With patience the structure of the universe could be brought into marvelous focus. Newton's exclamation caught the excitement perfectly: "O God, I think thy thoughts after thee!" Although nature's marvels were infinitely greater than had been supposed, man's mind was equal to them. The universe was a coherent, law-abiding system. It was intelligible!

It was not long before this discovery began to reap practical rewards. Drudgery could be relieved, health improved, goods multiplied and leisure extended. As these benefits are considerable, working with intelligible nature began to overshadow obedience to God's will as a means to human fulfillment. God was not entirely eclipsed—that would have entailed a break with the past more violent than history allows. Rather, God was eased toward thought's periphery. Not atheism but deism, the notion that God created the world but left it to run according to its own inbuilt laws, was the Modern Mind's distinctive religious stance. God stood behind nature as its creator, but it was through nature that his ways and will were to be known.

Like the Christian outlook, the modern outlook can be summarized by identifying its three controlling presuppositions. First, that reality may be personal is less certain and less important than that it is ordered. Second, man's reason is capable of discerning this order as it manifests itself in the laws of nature. Third, the path to human fulfillment consists primarily in discovering these laws, utilizing them where this is possible and complying with them where it is not.

The reason for suspecting that this modern outlook has had its day and is yielding to a third great mutation in Western thought is that reflective men are no longer confident of any of these three postulates. The first two are the ones that concern us here. Frontier thinkers are no longer sure that reality is ordered and orderly. If it is, they are not sure that man's mind is capable of grasping its order. Combining the two doubts, we can define the Postmodern Mind as one which, having lost the conviction that reality is personal, has come to question whether it is ordered in a way that man's reason can lay bare.

It was science which induced our forefathers to think of reality as primarily ordered rather than personal. But contemporary science has crashed through the cosmology which the seventeenth-to-nineteenth-century scientists constructed as if through a sound barrier, leaving us without replacement. It is tempting to attribute this lack to the fact that evidence is pouring in faster than we can throw it into perspective. Although this is part of the problem, another part runs deeper. Basically, the absence of a new cosmology is due to the fact that physics has cut away so radically from our capacity to imagine the way things are that we do not see how the two can get back together.

If modern physics showed us a world at odds with our senses, postmodern physics is showing us one which is at odds with our imagination, where imagination is taken as imagery. We have made peace with the first of these oddities. That the table which appears motionless is in fact incredibly "alive" with electrons circling their nuclei a million billion times per second; that the chair which feels so secure beneath us is actually a near vacuum—such facts, while certainly very strange, posed no permanent problem for man's sense of order. To accommodate them, all that was necessary was to replace the earlier picture of a gross and ponderous world with a subtle world in which all was sprightly dance and airy whirl.

But the problems the new physics poses for man's sense of order cannot be resolved by refinements in scale. Instead they appear to point to a radical disjunction between the way things behave and every possible way in which we might try to visualize them. How, for example, are we to picture an electron traveling two or more different routes through space concurrently, or passing from orbit to orbit without traversing the intervening space? What kind of model can we construct of a spece that is finite yet unbounded, or of light which is both wave and particle? It is such enigmas which have caused physicists like P. W. Bridgman of Harvard to suggest that "the structure of nature may eventually be such that our processes of thought do not correspond to it sufficiently to permit us to think about it at all. . . . The world fades out and eludes us. . . . We are confronted with something truly ineffable. We have reached the limit of the vision of the great pioneers of science, the vision, namely, that we live in a sympathetic world in that it is comprehensible by our minds."

This subdued and problematic stance of science toward reality is paralleled in philosophy. No one who works in philosophy today can fail to realize that the sense of the cosmos has been shaken by an encyclopedic skepticism. The clearest evidence of this is the collapse of what historically has been philosophy's central discipline: objective metaphysics, the attempt to discover what reality consists of and the most general principles which describe the way its parts are related. In this respect, Alfred North Whitehead marked the end of an era. His *Process and Reality: An Essay in Cosmology* is the last important attempt to construct a logical, coherent scheme of ideas that would blueprint the universe. The trend throughout the twentieth century has been away from faith in the feasibility of such undertakings. As a tendency throughout philosophy as a whole, this is a revolutionary development. For twenty-five hundred years philosophers have argued over which metaphysical system is true. For them to agree that none is true is a new departure.

The agreement represents the confluence of several philosophical streams. On one hand, it has come from the positivists who, convinced that truth comes only from science, have challenged the metaphysician's claim to extrascientific sources of insight. Their successors are the linguistic analysts, who have dominated British philosophy for the last several decades and who (insofar as they follow their pioneering genius Ludwig Wittgenstein) regard all philosophical perplexities as generated by slovenly use of language. For the analysts, "reality" and "being in general" are notions too thin and vapid to reward analysis. As a leading American proponent of this position, Professor Morton White of Princeton's Institute of Advanced Study has stated, "It took philosophers a long time to realize that the number of interesting things that one can say about all things in one fell swoop is very limited. Through the effort to become supremely general, you lapse into emptiness."

Equal but quite different objections to metaphysics have come from the existentialists who have dominated twentieth-century European philosophy. Heirs of Kierkegaard, Nietzsche, and Dostoevski, these philosophers have been concerned to remind their colleagues of what it means to be a human being. When we are thus reminded, they say, we see that to be human precludes in principle the kind of objective and impartial overview of things—the view of things as they are in themselves, apart from our differing perspectives—that metaphysics has always sought. To be human is to be finite, conditioned, and unique. No two persons have had their lives shaped by the same concatenation of genetic, cultural, historical, and interpersonal forces. Either these variables are inconsequential—but if we say this we are forgetting again what it means to be human, for our humanity is in fact overwhelmingly shaped by them—or the hope of rising to a God's-eye view of reality is misguided in principle.

The traditional philosopher might protest that in seeking such an overview he never expected perfection, but that we ought to try to make our perspectives as objective as possible. Such a response would only lead the existentialist to press his point deeper; for his contention is not just that objectivity is impossible but that it runs so counter to our nature—to what it means to be human—that every step in its direction is a step away from our humanity. (We are speaking here of objectivity as it pertains to our lives as wholes, not to restricted spheres of endeavor within them such as science. In these latter areas objectivity can be an unqualified virtue.) If the journey held hope that in ceasing to be human we might become gods, there could be no objection. But as this is impossible, ceasing to be human can only mean becoming less than human—inhuman in the usual sense of the word. It means forfeiting through inattention the birthright that is ours: the opportunity to plumb the depths and implications of what it means to have an outlook on life which in important respects is unique and will never be duplicated.

Despite the existentialist's sharp rebuke to metaphysics and traditional philosophy in general, there is at least one important point at which he respects their aims. He agrees that it is important to transcend what is accidental and ephemeral in our outlooks and in his own way joins his colleagues of the past in attempting to do so. But the existentialist's way toward this goal does not consist in trying to climb out of his skin in order to rise to Olympian heights from which things can be seen with complete objectivity and detachment. Rather it consists in centering on his own inwardness until he finds within it what he is compelled to accept and can never get away from. In this way he, too, arrives at what he judges to be necessary and eternal. But necessary and eternal for him. What is necessary and eternal for everyone is so impossible for a man to know that he wastes time making the attempt.

With this last insistence the existentialist establishes

contact with the metaphysical skepticism of his analytic colleagues across the English Channel and the Atlantic Ocean. Existentialism (and its frequent but not invariable partner, phenomenology) and analytic philosophy are the two dominant movements in twentieth-century philosophy. In temperament, interest, and method they stand at opposite poles of the philosophical spectrum. They are, in fact, opposites in every sense but one. Both are creatures of the Postmodern Mind, the mind which doubts that reality has an absolute order which man's understanding can comprehend.

Turning from philosophy to theology, we recall that the Modern Mind did not rule out the possibility of God; it merely referred the question to its highest court of appeal—namely, reality's pattern as disclosed by reason. If the world order entails the notions of providence and a creator, God exists; otherwise not. This approach made the attempt to prove God's existence through reason and nature the major theological thrust of the modern period. "Let us," wrote Bishop Joseph Butler in his famous *The Analogy of Religion*, "compare the known constitution and course of things . . . with what religion teaches us to believe and expect; and see whether they are not analogous and of a piece. . . . It will, I think be found that they are very much so." An enterprising Franciscan named Ramon Llull went even further. He invented a kind of primitive computer which, with the turning of cranks, pulling of levers, and revolving of wheels, would sort the theological subjects and predicates fed into it in such a way as to demonstrate the truths of the Trinity and the Incarnation by force of sheer logic working on self-evident propositions. Rationalism had entered theology as early as the Middle Ages, but as long as the Christian outlook prevailed, final confidence was reserved for the direct pronouncements of God himself as given in Scripture. In the modern period, God's existence came to stand or fall on whether reason, surveying the order of nature, endorsed it. It was as if Christendom and God himself awaited the verdict of science and the philosophers.

This hardly describes the current theological situation. Scientists and philosophers have ceased to issue pronouncements of any sort about ultimates. Postmodern theology builds on its own foundations. Instead of attempting to justify faith by appeals to the objective world, it points out that as such appeals indicate nothing about reality one way or the other, the way is wide open for free decision—or what Kierkegaard called the leap of faith. One hears little these days of the proofs for the existence of God which seemed so important to the modern world. Instead one hears repeated insistence that however admirably reason is fitted to deal with life's practical problems, it can only end with a confession of ignorance when confronted with questions of ultimate concern. In the famous dictum of Karl Barth, who has influenced twentieth-century theology more than anyone else, there is no straight line from the mind of man to God. "What we say breaks apart constantly . . . producing paradoxes which are held together in seeming unity only by agile and arduous running to and fro on our part." From the United States Reinhold Niebuhr echoed this conviction. "Life is full of contradictions and incongruities. We live our lives in various realms of meaning which do not cohere rationally."

Instead of "These are the compelling reasons, grounded in the nature of things, why you should believe in God," the approach of the church to the world today tends to be, "This community of faith invites you to share in its venture of trust and commitment." The stance is most evident in Protestant and Orthodox Christianity and Judaism, but even Roman Catholic thought, notwithstanding the powerful rationalism it took over from the Greeks, has not remained untouched by the postmodern perspective. It has become more attentive to the extent to which personal and subjective factors provide the disposition to faith without which theological arguments prove nothing.

It is difficult to assess the mood which accompanies this theological revolution. On one hand, there seems to be a heightened sense of faith's precariousness: as Jesus walked on the water, so must the contemporary man of faith walk on the sea of nothingness, confident even in the absence of rational supports. But vigor is present too. Having labored in the shadow of rationalism during the modern period, contemporary theology is capitalizing on its restored autonomy. Compensating for loss of rational proofs for God's existence have come two gains. One is new realization of the validity of Pascal's "reasons of the heart" as distinct from those of the mind. The other is a recovery of the awe without which religion, as distinct from ethical philosophy piously expressed, is probably impossible. By including God within a closed system of rational explanation, modernism lost sight of the endless qualitative distinction between God and man. Postmodern theology has reinstated this distinction with great force. If God exists, the fact that our minds cannot begin to comprehend his nature makes it necessary for us to acknowledge that he is Wholly Other.

These revolutions in science, philosophy and theology have not left the arts unaffected. The worlds of the major twentieth-century artists are many and varied, but none resembles the eighteenth-century world where mysteries seemed to be clearing by the hour. The twentieth-century worlds defy lucid and coherent exegesis. Paradoxical, devoid of sense, they are worlds into which protagonists are thrown without trace as to why—the world which the French novelist Albert Camus proclaimed "absurd," which for his compatriot Jean-Paul Sartre was "too much," and for the Irish dramatist Samuel Beckett is a "void" in which men wait out their lives for a what-they-know-not that never comes. Heroes driven by a veritable obsession to find out where they are and what their responsibility is seldom succeed. Most of Franz Kafka is ambiguous, but his parable, "Before the Law," closes with as clear a countermand to the modern vision of an ordered reality as can be imagined. "The world-order is based on a lie."

Objective morality has gone the way of cosmic order. Even where it has not been moralistic, most Western art of the past has been created against the backdrop of a frame of objective values which the artist shared. As our century has progressed, it has become increasingly difficult to find such a framework standing back of the arts.

A single example will illustrate the point. One searches in vain for an artistic frame of reference prior to the twentieth century in which matricide might be regarded as a moral act. Yet in Sartre's play *The Flies*, it is the first authentic deed the protagonist Orestes performs. Whereas his previous actions have been detached, unthinking, or in conformity with the habit patterns that surround him, this one is freely chosen in the light of full self-consciousness and acceptance of its consequences. As such, it is the first act which is genuinely his. "I have done my deed, Electra," he exults, adding "and that deed was good." Being his, the deed supplies his life with the identity which until then it had lacked. From that moment forward, Orestes ceases to be a free-floating form; his acquisition of a past he can never escape roots his life into reality. Note the extent to which this analysis relativizes the moral standard. No act is right or wrong in itself. Everything depends on its relation to the agent, whether it is chosen freely and with full acceptance of its consequences or is done abstractedly, in imitation of the acts of others, or in self-deception.

We move beyond morality into art proper when we note that the traditional distinction between the sublime and the banal, too, has blurred. As long as reality was conceived as a great chain of being—a hierarchy of worth descending from God as its crown through angels, men, animals, and plants to inanimate objects at the base—it could be reasonably argued that great art should attend to great subjects: scenes from the Gospels, major battles, or distinguished lords and ladies. With cubism and surrealism, the distinction between trivial and important disappears. Alarm clocks, driftwood, pieces of broken glass become appropriate subjects for the most monumental paintings. In Samuel Beckett and the contemporary French antinovelists, the most mundane items—

miscellaneous contents of a pocket, a wastebasket, the random excursions of a runaway dog—are treated with the same care as love, duty, or the question of human destiny.

One is tempted to push the question a final step and ask whether the dissolution of cosmic order, moral order, and the hierarchic order of subject matter is reflected in the very forms of contemporary art. Critic Russel Nye thinks that at least as far as the twentieth-century novel is concerned, the answer is yes. "If there is a discernible trend in the form of the modern novel," he writes, "it is toward the concept of the novel as a series of moments, rather than as a planned progression of events or incidents, moving toward a defined terminal end. Recent novelists tend to explore rather than arrange or synthesize their materials; often their arrangement is random rather than sequential. In the older tradition, a novel was a formal structure composed of actions and reactions which were finished by the end of the story, which did have an end. The modern novel often has no such finality." Aaron Copland characterizes the music of our young composers as "a disrelation of unrelated tones. Notes are strewn about like membra disjecta; there is an end to continuity in the old sense and an end of thematic relationships."

When Nietzsche's eyesight became too poor to read books, he began at last to read himself. The act was prophetic of the century that has followed. As reality has blurred, the gaze of postmodern man has turned increasingly upon himself.

Anthropological philosophy has replaced metaphysics. In the wake of Kierkegaard and Nietzsche, attention has turned from objective reality to the individual human personality struggling for self-realization. "Being" remains interesting only as it relates to man. As its order, if it has one, is unknown to us, being cannot be described as it is in itself; but if it is believed to be mysteriously wonderful, as some existentialists think, we should remain open to it. If it is the blind, meaningless enemy, as others suspect, we should maintain our freedom against it.

Even theology, for all its renewed theocentrism, keeps one eye steadily on man, as when the German theologian Rudolph Bultmann relates faith to the achievement of authentic selfhood. It is in art, however, that the shift from outer to inner has been most evident. If the twentieth century began by abolishing the distinction between sublime and banal subject matter, it has gone on to dispense with subject matter altogether. Although the tide may have begun to turn, the purest art is still widely felt to be entirely abstract and free of pictorial representation. It is as if the artist had taken the scientist seriously and responded, "If what I see as nature doesn't represent the way things really are, why should I credit this appearance with its former importance? Better to turn to what I am sure of: my own intuitions and the purely formal values inherent in the relations of colors, shapes and masses."

I have argued that the distinctive feature of the contemporary mind as evidenced by frontier thinking in science, philosophy, theology, and the arts is its acceptance of reality as unordered in any objective way that man's mind can discern. This acceptance separates the Postmodern Mind from both the Modern Mind, which assumed that reality is objectively ordered, and the Christian mind, which assumed it to be regulated by an inscrutable but beneficent will.

It remains only to add my personal suspicion that the change from the vision of reality as ordered to unordered has brought Western man to as sharp a fork in history as he has faced. Either it is possible for man to live indefinitely with his world out of focus or it is not. I suspect that it is not, that a will-to-order and orientation is fundamental in the human makeup. If so, the postmodern period, like all the intellectual epochs that preceded it, will turn out to be a transition to a still different perspective.

2

THE VIEW FROM EVERYWHERE: *Metaphysics and the Post-Nietzschean Deconstruction Thereof* *

Historically, philosophy has assumed responsibility for articulating worldviews systematically, metaphysics being its branch that dealt with them directly. This essay picks up on the story of metaphysics' collapse which the preceding selection began. As early as midcentury, R. G. Collingwood could describe our times as "an age when the very possibility of metaphysics is hardly admitted without a struggle," and not long afterwards Iris Murdoch was writing: "Modern philosophy is profoundly anti-metaphysical in spirit. Its anti-metaphysical character may be summed up in the caveat: There may be no deep structure."

The essay that follows argues against accepting our current metaphysical skepticism and disregard as a permanent state. Focusing as it does on a single academic discipline, philosophy, it is the most technical chapter in the book, and therefore one which the general reader may wish to skip.

What has come to be known as "the post-Nietzschean deconstruction of metaphysics" has been one of the important projects of our time. Its blows have been heavy;

---

*Excerpt from *Religion, Ontotheology and Deconstruction*, edited by Henry Ruf. Copyright © 1989 by Paragon House. A New Era Book, published by Paragon House.

some think lethal. " 'God' and metaphysics 'died' in the West in approximately the same half century," Langdon Gilkey has written.[1]

Has this assault on metaphysics been warranted? It is not likely that it could have enlisted assailants of the stature of Nietzsche, Heidegger, Wittgenstein, and Derrida—and in important ways before them Kierkegaard and Kant, to name only the representatives I shall be referring to—were there not something right in these assailants' polemics. The question is whether there is also something wrong with them. Are the charges that have been leveled against metaphysics in the last two centuries important half-truths, or are they, in aggregate, the full truth? Do they add up to caveats or to a death warrant? Has the time come for philosophy to close its books on the metaphysical enterprise?

I. What Metaphysics Is and Does

Much depends on definitions, so let me say what I see as at issue. By "metaphysics" I mean a worldview that provides a sense of orientation. The word "world" denotes inclusiveness: the view in question purports to embrace everything, including regions of being that are presumed to exist without their nature being known. The word "view" establishes an intentional analogy with eyesight: the landscape that metaphysics opens onto and spreads before the mind's eye is a topography, a lay of the land. If we shift our attention from the topography itself to the map of it, we see it as a "mattering map," a map that shows what matters, of the kind Rebecca Goldstein proposes in her book *The Mind-Body Problem*. Like the maps of demographers, regions that matter much to us are so crowded with dots that they look black, while other regions taper off in diminishing shades of gray into areas that are white, which is to say inconsequential.

These shadings tie in with the third pivotal word in our definition, namely orientation, for orientation always includes a sense of what is important and what is not: what we should emphasize and move towards and what we should avoid. The analogy with sight also notes that metaphysics is important. If it is difficult to walk the physical world while blindfolded, it is equally difficult to walk through life if "the eye of the soul" is closed. "Continued observations in clinical practice," William Sheldon tells us, "lead almost inevitably to the conclusion that deeper and more fundamental than sexuality, deeper than the craving for social power, deeper even than the desire for possessions, there is a still more generalized and universal craving in the human makeup. It is the craving for knowledge of the right direction—for orientation."[2] [a]

Now to be sure, this orientation not only can but does derive from sources other than metaphysics. Instinct supplies it for subhuman animals, and in tribal societies children acquire it unthinkingly—*cum lacte*, as the Romans used to say: with the mother's milk. "Unthinkingly" here means unquestioningly, but not mindlessly, for as human beings *have* minds, these inevitably get drawn into the act. In tribal societies the mind gets involved through myths that imprint individuals, causing them to internalize the tribe's orientation through stories of how things got started and what must be done to keep them on course. So far there is no metaphysics, for to the properties of metaphysics I have thus far mentioned—an inclusive, or more precisely unrestricted, vision that provides orientation—I must add one more. Metaphysics is abstract. That it is articulated goes without saying.

Here arises the first criticism of the project. Granted that life needs orienting and that in *homo sapiens* the mind figures in effecting it, isn't it better that the mind effect it concretely, through stories instead of abstractions?

---

[a]Need this importance of orientation, and the relevance of worldviews thereto, be argued? A review of a recent book on *Early Man and the Cosmos* that summarizes the hybrid field of archaeoastronomy emphasizes that "ancient astronomers were more than detached observers. They searched for the meaning of human existence in the ordered patterns of the stars. Their cosmologies encompassed the customs of entire civilizations, providing a unified vision that gave form and meaning to the actions of people on earth."

(Volumes of arguments extol narrative over philosophy, the Bible over theology, aesthetic *mythos* over logical *logos*, and the claims of rhetoric over the claims of reference.)

The answer is: yes, up to a point. The vividness, immediacy, and drama of stories, all made possible by their concreteness, give them the edge in every respect save one. When one foundational story collides with another that differs from it—which is to say: when one tribe or civilization encounters another, or when within a given civilization a story arises to challenge its original, founding one, producing thereby a crisis in the body politic—stories provide no court of appeal. When Biblical stories encountered those of Greece, Christian Platonism was born; when those stories collided with Koranic ones in the Middle Ages, someone had to write the *Summa Contra Gentiles*. Within Christendom itself, when the Darwinian account of human origins—we are the more who have derived from the less—arose to challenge the Bible's opposite contention, reason has again to enter the fray. The deepest definition of a civilization may indeed be that it is a form of life empowered by an embracing myth, but myths of this order cannot be created consciously. In some sense of the word, myths can only be revealed, which may be what Heidegger had in mind when toward the close of his life he said that "only a god can save us now." This leaves metaphysics as what we do till the Messiah comes.

II. Pitfalls: The Deconstructionists as Warners

Every project has its pitfalls, and the deconstructionists can be credited with spotting the principal ones that beset metaphysics. (I use lower-case "deconstruction" and its variants to refer to the deconstruction-of-metaphysics project in general. Capitalized, the word refers to Derrida's specific brand thereof. As this book aims at an audience beyond that of professional philosophers, let me note that Deconstruction is a movement of thought, growing out of the work of the contemporary French philosopher and critic Jacques Derrida, which calls into question the possibility of securely establishing the meaning of any human construction, including any text.)

Kierkegaard noted the complacency (through false security) that worldviews can engender. By purporting to disclose reality, worldviews can obscure how much of it remains a terrifying mystery—how dark the clouds of nescience that ring us round. Correlatively, in remaining stable—staying reliably in place—worldviews obscure life's precariousness and contingency, the ways in which we dangle by threads over seventy thousand fathoms. They also divert attention from what we do by leading us to suppose that we are saved by what we think.

Kant spotted the metaphysician's tendency to exaggerate the capacities of objective, autonomous reason. Metaphysics includes what lies beyond *physis*, the Greek word for nature, but outside the sensible world objective reason can disclose nothing directly. The most it can do is to hazard inferences.

Nietzsche made the historicist's point. The inclusiveness of worldviews tempts their authors to subsume even time within them. This inverts the actual situation, for time has the metaphysicians in *its* box, not vice versa. It affects their views of everything.

This leads directly to Wittgenstein, for his "forms of life" claim for language and praxis the suzerainity that historicism allots to time. Meaning derives from the interlocking complex of verbal and nonverbal practices that constitute society. To the extent that societies differ, the meanings they generate and legitimize likewise differ. How is it possible to get from the colloquialisms of actual speech to the universals that (metaphysicians would have us believe) hold cross-culturally?

Heidegger is exercised because metaphysical preoccupation with the way things are—for Heidegger the phenomenologist this always comes down to "a way they appear to us"—blocks Being from disclosing itself in alternative ways which a less assertive and willful attention might allow to surface. Derrida continues this point and focuses it on the interpretation of texts. To posit a

Signified to which signifiers refer, be the latter a name, an assertion, or (as in the case at hand) a metaphysical system, is to close the door on alternatives. Worldviews occlude, obscuring open vision.

If the thrust of deconstructionism were simply to point to problems and dangers of the sort just sampled, there would be no quarrel. Nor should we overlook the places where deconstructionists speak of metaphysics in tones of guarded respect. How they square this respect with their negative conclusions is not always clear, but traces of respect do obtrude, so let us take note of them.

III. Ambivalence towards Metaphysics: Deconstruction as a Lover's Quarrel

Kant deeply believed in the noumenal realm and even sought to address it directly. He simply concluded that we have no access to it either intuitively or through our categories of understanding. We each have our own reading of Nietzsche, but I read his call for the *ubermensch* as a cry in the dark—the only escape he could imagine from the nihilism that the collapse of metaphysics will bring in its wake, but an escape he doubted would occur.[b] For all of Heidegger's talk about the end of metaphysics, his call to "step back out of metaphysics into the essential nature of metaphysics"[3] seems to say explicitly that he is not against the project as such. His polemics seem invariably to be directed against constricting versions of the enterprises; specifically, ones tailored to "technological

---

[b]My reading of Nietzsche is heavily vectored by George Grant's 1969 Massey Lectures, "Time as History" (CBS Learning Systems, Box 500, Station A, Toronto M5W 1E6). I also take seriously Hanna Arendt's reading, as in this passage which I have cited on other occasions: "In *The Twilight of Idols*, [Nietzsche] clarifies what the word God meant. It was merely a symbol for the supersensual realm as understood by metaphysics; he now uses instead of God the word true world and says: 'We have abolished the true world. What has remained? The apparent one perhaps? Oh, no! With the true world we have also abolished the apparent one' " ("Thinking and Moral Considerations," *Social Research* 38 [Autumn 1971]: 240).

[modes of] description and interpretation" (*ibid.*) wherein all noetic components—all noetic "bits," as we might now say—are claimed to be explicitly in view; more on this later. Are we permitted to detect in Wittgenstein's contention that the mystical pertains not to "*how* the world is, but *that* it is" a deep feeling, at least, for something that transcends the sensible world? Does Derrida's call for us to write with both hands mean that we should write constructively—metaphysically?—with our right hands while our left hands cancel what our right hands have written; this to avoid fixations?

Here, as in their caveats, the deconstructionists merit attention: their ambivalences show them to be sensitive to problems that are inherent in their own critical program. It would be a mistake, though, and patronizing, to let fringe concessions and conciliatory asides obscure the deep iconoclasm of their mission—the respects in which they are all, like Nietzsche, men with hammers. The deconstruction-of-metaphysics movement would not have earned that name if its proponents were out simply to recondition and repair. At heart they are demolitionists—revolutionaries rather than reformers. Their conclusion is uncompromising, and it has two parts. Metaphysics is no longer possible, and the motives that engender it are suspect.

Kant pronounced the first half of this dual charge, Kierkegaard the second.[c] Nietzsche aligned the two, and most deconstructionists since him have pressed both its halves. Here, though, I shall consider them separately, and (in running our six philosophers past them) will confine myself to the single point that each philosopher is most commonly associated with. The diagram on the following page schematizes this agenda.

IV. Moral Objections

I begin with the contention that even if the metaphysical world were possible or retrievable, it is, as Richard Rorty

[c]As the earliest of our six deconstructers, Kant would say that metaphysics *as heretofore conceived* is no longer possible. His successors wax more categorical.

The Deconstructionists' Objections to the View from Everywhere

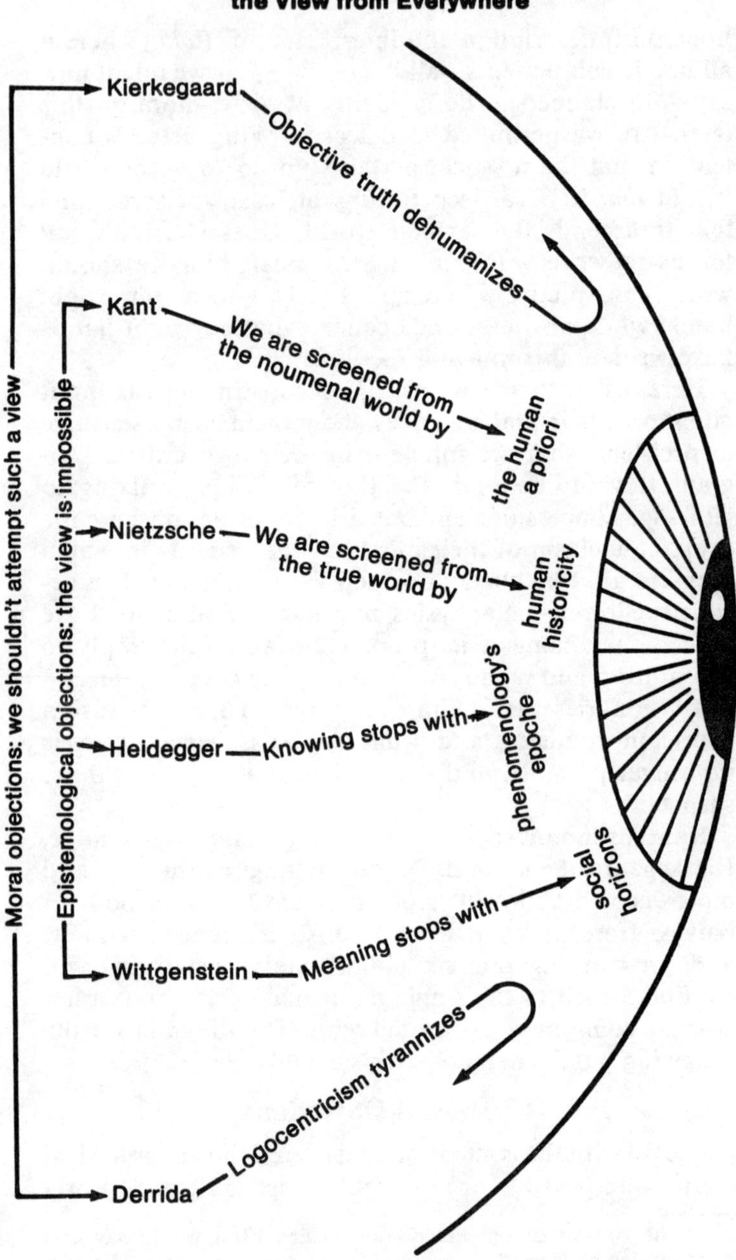

The diagram is intended to represent the human eye.

holds, a world well lost. Kierkegaard argued that the kind of truth he saw Hegel working with, objective truth, depersonalizes, for it distances us from ourselves and from the world. (Heidegger accepts this point completely.) To get the world explicitly before us and into the full light of consciousness, we must hold it at arm's length, so to speak. The analogy with vision serves existentialists perfectly, for we have to distance ourselves somewhat from objects to get them in focus, while concomitantly—here's the rub—distancing connotes disengagement. Insofar as we objectify our world by picturing it, it loses its power over us, for the move reverses our normal relation to it. Whereas formerly the world ruled us, beating on unconscious regions of our lives like waves on the shores they shape, now we rule the world, choosing which picture of it to affirm and which to reject. This may sound like gain, which in autonomy it is, but there remains the disturbing issue of motivation. Can a life be as empowered by a world it intentionally selects as by one that feeds it from unknown, subterranean springs? Existentialists think not. As someone, paraphrasing them, has quipped: "You can't get everything into your system [read "your metaphysical system"] until you get everything out of your system [your total, largely unconscious and even partly biological, system]." If an understanding of the causes of our neuroses helps to relieve *them*, might not an understanding of the causes of our lives—why we believe as we do and choose as we do—relieve us, this time in the ominous sense of that phrase, of life itself?

As was earlier acknowledged, Kierkegaard is on to something here, but it applies only to outlooks that purport to derive exclusively from reason. Versions that are anchored in an awesome source that grounds and orients reason itself—Anselm's "faith seeking understanding" is a famous formulation—are not candidates for Kierkegaard's concern; one can hardly charge the metaphysics of Anselm or Augustine with having distanced *them* from life. The issue of nihilism comes in here, for Nietzsche and Heidegger see the West as heading towards a condition wherein nothing seems better than anything else. If only metaphysical systems that aim for complete objectivity point towards this denouement, the project in its entirety need not be deterred by the prospect.

As for Derrida—and though we are reserving Heidegger for the next section, he belongs here as much as he did with the preceding point—his fear (as again noted in Section Two) is that Truth with a capital *T* marginalizes and occludes. It occludes, because if we think we *have* the Truth we will not be inclined to look further; it marginalizes, because the conviction that *we* have the Truth shuts out those who disagree. At best, their *reports* will not be taken seriously. At worst their persons will be hounded as heretics.

Here again, as moral warning the point is not only valid but important. It is also important, though, that we not let it derail us, for though we need to be reminded of it repeatedly, it hardly decommissions the metaphysical enterprise. In human behavior—in relationships between people—the word "discrimination" indicates a moral flaw, but with ideas the case is different. No idea is worth its salt if it doesn't discriminate, sifting truth from error, or at least relevance from irrelevance. In this respect every idea that asks to be taken seriously discriminates—yes, discriminates against: marginalizes is the preferred Derridaian word—its contrary, implying the irrelevance (if not invalidity) of the latter for purposes at hand. (For a generation, deconstructionist arguments have severely marginalized metaphysics and metaphysicians.) As for occluding—the charge that by focusing on Truth, logocentricism discourages consideration of potentially rewarding alternatives and supplements—this turns out to be the same as the charge of marginalizing, for to say *anything* diverts attention from (and thereby marginalizes) what is not being said. A further point crowds in here. How are we to decide where to turn our attention if we have no mattering map that grades regions in importance? Presumably the appearances we might experience in certain regions are so trivial that, given life's brevity, they scarcely *warrant* shepherding.

V. Epistemic Objections

Having used Kierkegaard and Derrida to introduce moral misgivings about the metaphysical enterprise, I turn now to epistemological misgivings. Primarily deriving, as they do, from the remaining four of our six philosophers, the misgivings issue from the domains those philosophers are associated with: critical philosophy, historicism, phenomenology, and linguistic philosophy. Together they all but box the recent philosophical compass.

Kant for critical philosophy. The mind doesn't mirror the order of nature; it constitutes that order. We see nature from the vantage point of, and as it conforms to, the structure of human reason. So argues the single most influential work in modern philosophy, Kant's *Critique of Pure Reason*. And because the categories of human understanding cope only with impressions that come to us from the world of nature, to try to deploy them elsewhere is like trying to cut the wind with a knife. There is no possibility of direct knowledge of suprasensible realities, or, for that matter, of nature as constituted of things-in-themselves. All we can directly know are phenomena: things as they present themselves to us; things as they appear to us, not things as they are. The world in its own right, the noumenal world, can only be inferred.

I cite the *Critique* that argues this epistemic posture as the most influential work in modern philosophy, and nothing so supports that judgment as Kant's lingering hold on the Modern Mind, despite the fact that there are no card-carrying Kantians anymore! There is an anomaly here. Why do we continue to accept Kant's conclusions when for some time now we have dismissed his arguments? This is partly because the cross-cultural findings, though they have shown his 'universal' categories of reason not to be such, *have* confirmed his underlying insight that the mind is constructive; its workings are variegated, but it is indeed agent, not only patient. This aspect of

Kant's heritage is an important legacy, a continuing gain. Its shadow side, however, is our continued acceptance of Kant's logically separate assumption that the mind's creativity (in affecting our knowledge of the natural world) is flanked by imbecility when it comes to understanding anything else. "With our lack of insight into supersensible objects . . . the *minimum* of knowledge must [there] suffice," Kant decreed.[4] We can appreciate why he did so. Alarmed by his associates' fascination with Swedenborg's "eye-witness" reports that heaven's antechambers resemble Stockholm in such detail that departed spirits have difficulty appreciating that they have died, Kant's rationalism recoiled in horror and laid down the law. This far may belief about the unseen world reasonably proceed, but no farther! To repeat: we can appreciate *why* Kant drew the line where he did, but must we, two hundred years later, be bound by that line against the combined evidences of Plato's "eye of the soul," the Vedantic *buddhi*, and the *intellectus* of the Middle Ages? Modesty has its place, but James Cutsinger has pointed out that we are not more modest than our precursors; we hang our arrogance in different quarters. Whereas our forebears strike us as arrogant in the amount they thought they knew, we are oppositely arrogant. "Virtually every contemporary [philosophical and] theological methodology takes as its starting-point how well we know how little we know." In this respect "fidelity to Kant [remains] the touchstone of our period."[5] Sociologists of knowledge would have no difficulty explaining this, but are there any *reasons* why we should keep our minds in this abject crouch?

Nietzsche for historicism. Nietzsche refuses to do our work for us; we have to be almost as shrewd as he was to impose on his corpus the reading that does most justice to his Rorschach blot. I have already tipped my hand. Agreeing with everyone about his enormous and continuing influence, I am also impressed by the clarity and alacrity with which he saw: first, that the whole realm of the supersensible and the transcendent has ceased to command Western credence; and second, how much that loss entails. These are the death-of-God and nihilism themes respectively. The rest is a very mixed bag, from which I shall extract only the single item that bears most on our topic, namely, Nietzsche's historicism.

History was Nietzsche's special field of study, and he never outgrew it. Accepting the "Copernican revolution" of Kant's first *Critique*, he turned the discussion away from the innate contributions the human mind brings to its knowing and towards the way it is conditioned by its historical milieu. "What separates us from Kant," he tells us in *Human, All Too Human*," is that we believe that becoming is the rule even in the spiritual things. We are historians from top to bottom.... [Philosophers] all to a man think unhistorically, as is the age old custom with philosophers."

What are we to think of this? That our times condition us is not in question; the question is whether the differences that successive periods introduce preempt the entire picture, thereby shutting out continuities. If the answer is no, historicism climbs down from its dogmatic perch and becomes a research program as we go to work sifting similarities and differences in each particular case. If, on the other hand, we preclude continuities by fiat, this dogmatic historicism self-destructs by its own weight; for the claim that historical horizons do not overlap at all is an ahistorical claim that purports to cover all historical horizons. Historicism also raises the question of whether our historicity conditions or determines us, and here too Nietzsche waffles. In his *Untimely Meditations* he is content to say that "since we are the outcomes of earlier generations... it is not possible *wholly* to free oneself from this chain" (emphasis mine). But in *The Twilight of Idols* he calls the notion of freedom itself into question. "In the beginning there is that great calamity of error that the will is something which is effective, that will is a capacity. Today we know that it is only a word" (3:5). It is one of the "phantoms and will-o'-the-wisps" that inhabit the imaginary "inner world" (6:3), a phantom that was "invented essentially for the purpose of punishment, that is, because one wanted to impute guilt" (6:7).

Heidegger for phenomenology. Husserl took the planks that Nietzsche pried up from Kant's boat and nailed them back together in a way that looked more like the original hulk. The task of philosophy is to understand the mind's a priori structures and workings. As Husserl's student, Heidegger began in this way, but sensing subjectivism and even solipsism waiting in the wings,[d] he shifted his weight to the other side of idealism's mind/world divide. *Dasein* is being-in-the-world. There is no need either to assume or to bracket the world, for there is no *dasein* without the world. Despite this radical shift, however, Heidegger remained a phenomenologist in retaining Husserl's *epoche*: he simply deployed it differently. Whereas Husserl excluded from consideration what might exist antecedent to the shaping influences of the human mind,[e] Heidegger excludes what might exist outside the shaping influences of historical epochs—influences that empower human knowledge, shape its character, and prescribe its limits. As historical horizons cannot be breached, only what appears within them—phenomena—can be countenanced. In the crucial case for metaphysics, since Being never presents itself within a horizon as a phenomenon, it is a procedural mistake to reify it and regard it as an agent that somehow produces or gives rise to phenomena. We must confine ourselves to the disclosures themselves as they appear in clearings that *Daseins* permit. Phenomenology's principle of principles, "to the things themselves," remains intact.

Because "the end of metaphysics" was central to

---

[d]Husserl could no more solve the problem of the "other" than could Kant,[6] whose premises (Strawson argues[7]) make the notion of a noumenal world incoherent from the outset.

[e]In his later years Husserl softened on this point and admitted into consciousness the life-world in which man is plunged before his intuition of essences congeals.

Heidegger's entire project, I shall say more about him than I have about my other philosophers. As a symptom-spotter, alerting us to the West's slope towards nihilism, calculative thought, and the manipulative arrangements its scientistic, technological social order impose on life, Heidegger is unsurpassed; he had a watchman's eye for danger signals. Equally impressive is the life-stance he advocates: a stance of openness, trustfulness, gratitude, and caring concern for the gifts of Being. So impressive are these virtues that I keep wondering if I am overlooking something in adding what I feel must be added; namely, that as diagnostician, in identifying the *causes* of the symptoms he so perceptively detects, Heidegger is unreliable.

I leave aside his controversial treatment of Plato. Friedlander and Gadamer called Heidegger on this in his own lifetime,[f] and I myself keep wondering why he: (a) typically cites the early rather than the later, more mature, Plato; and (b) neglects the overarching dramatic structure of the Dialogues, which conditions the meaning of their specific passages. Once and non-commitally, he mentions the Seventh Epistle which places Plato's entire project in a significantly different light.) Further, (c) I wonder if Aristotle would have broken with his mentor if Plato had been altogether the apodictic "metaphysician" (in Heidegger's pejorative sense of that word) that Heidegger makes him out to be? These points trouble me, but I leave them to better Plato scholars than I[8] in order to proceed to six points that loom larger.

[f]"Heidegger interprets [Plato's] doctrine of ideas as the beginning of that forgetfulness of being that peaks . . . in the technological age as the universal will to power. . . . But . . . the authentic dimension of the Platonic dialectic of ideas has a fundamentally different meaning. The underlying principle is a step beyond the simple minded acceptance of ideas and in the final analysis [is] a counter movement against the metaphysical interpretation of being as the being of existing beings" (Hans-Georg Gadamer, *Philosophical Apprenticeships* [Cambridge: MIT Press, 1985]). For Friedlander on Heidegger, see his *Plato: An Introduction* (Princeton University Press, 1969), *passim.*

1. Do we need to look earlier than the advent of modern science for the causes of our modern ailments that Heidegger so penetratingly perceives? In one of his illuminating articles on Heidegger, Hubert Dreyfus writes: "Science is our religion in the very important sense that we think science tells us what reality is." And what does it tell us? Dreyfus answers: reality "is meaningless physical reality."[9]

2. We *do* need to dig back further in our history, Heidegger's followers will answer, for we need to see that metaphysics prepared the way for science. That there is some connection between the two is probably the case—a civilization's worldview probably affects everything within it in some way. What has not been shown is that there is a tight, linear connection between metaphysics and modern science—Heidegger's claim that his "step back out of metaphysics . . . is the step out of technology and technological description and interpretation."[10] Shankara and Nagarjuna were metaphysicians or the word has no meaning, but modern science didn't issue from their labors.

3. There is one piece of historical evidence which single-handedly, alone and by itself it seems to me, demolishes Heidegger's charge that metaphysics engenders nihilism. Nihilism is sameness, the vanishing of significant differences between alternatives, and Heidegger argued that it began to rear its head with Plato and has kept pace thereafter with the advance of metaphysics. But until modern science dealt metaphysics what may yet prove to be a mortal blow—the patient remains in intensive care—metaphysics did not blur differences in the least. If anything, it pushed them to extremes, until at the peak of the Middle Ages it confronted Western man with the most momentous difference the mind can conceive: eternal salvation versus eternal damnation. It was not metaphysics as such but a specific version thereof, the scientistic version, that collapsed the infinite distance between heaven and hell by dismissing their referents.

4. All of the foregoing points come down, in the end, to whether Heidegger's definition of metaphysics does justice to the enterprise, which is why I gave my opening section to indicating how I think the enterprise should be conceived. Heidegger presents metaphysics as working exclusively with objective, autonomous reason. "Reason" here is the mind working logically with clear and distinct ideas. To prefix it with the word "objective" is to claim for such reason rights over the human mind *per se*; people whose minds are normal and informed must, on pain of forfeiting their rationality, bow to its claims. "Autonomous" (in all this) means that to deliver its binding judgments, reason has no need of promptings from any extra-rational source. If Heidegger is right and this is what metaphysics is—objective, autonomous reason purporting to produce a definitive printout of the way things finally are—the sooner its brittle pretentions are punctured, the better.

To be sure, this *is* what metaphysics looks like if we squint primarily at its modern expressions, severed by choice not only from religion but from tradition generally. These versions are also disdainful (if even cognizant) of the great Asian systems which regularly open onto the ineffable and draw their profundities therefrom—Nirguna Brahman, Sunyata, and the Tao that cannot be spoken. But the Enlightenment Project is not the sum of metaphysics, or even its signature. Because Heidegger writes as if in signature it were, his criticisms are usually well-taken; they simply do not apply—not (I would argue) to metaphysics' most mature and impressive models. For Heidegger defines, simply defines in a mode that approaches pure legislation, metaphysics as the exercise that "thinks about beings as beings";[8] since the pre-Socratics it has been forgetful of the Being from which

[8] "The Way Back into the Ground of Metaphysics," in Walter Kauffman (ed.), *Existentialism from Dostoevsky to Sartre* (New York: New American Library, 1956), p. 207. Or alternatively, "metaphysics begins by recognizing the difference between Being and beings, but then takes Being to be that highest being which is the ground

they issue. Deflated thus by definition—severed from its higher reaches and in this sense decapitated, it is not too much to say—metaphysics, or rather in a very real sense its corpse, becomes for Heidegger easy prey.

The living species is different. Until modern science placed it on the defensive and skewed its course, metaphysics was seldom unaware of Being's ineffable source. Nor did its reason presume to function autonomously, as we are reminded by the medieval characterizations of philosophy as the handmaiden of theology. In Christian philosophy it was fed by theology, which was based on stories, which in turn derived from events, while in Greece it drew on intuitive discernments (Plato's "eye of the soul") and a legacy of myths that motored reason powerfully and directed it aright. It is of course the apophatic or mystical tradition, with its distinction between *ratio* and *intellectus*, that recognizes the dependent character of reason most explicitly. Pythagoras, Plato, Plotinus, Dionysus, and Augustine; medieval philosophy where it inclines towards Plato rather than Aristotle (though the mysticism in Aquinas and even Aristotle is coming to be reappreciated); and Gregory of Palamos and Meister Eckhart—these I see as Western instances of metaphysics in a mode that the deconstruction of metaphysics movement leaves unscathed.

5. Is Heidegger historian only, purporting to do no more than interpret the odyssey of Western philosophy? Or does he slant his interpretation from a metaphysical stance of his own—a "view from everywhere" which,

---

of the possibility and actuality of all beings" (Henry Ruf's paraphrase of Heidegger in the book from which this essay is reprinted). To indicate how inadequate these definitions are, I must content myself here with a single instance. In describing Plato's metaphysics, Paul Friedlander writes: "At last still another dimension becomes visible above the level of being. As the cause of becoming is not in itself becoming, so the source of being is not in itself being. Then we encounter the highest paradox: not itself being, but beyond being. While there is still knowledge about being . . . there can be no knowledge about what is beyond being" (*Plato: An Introduction* [Princeton University Press, 1969], p. 63.

though unacknowledged, is metaphysical by Heidegger's own definition of metaphysics as that which "thinks . . . what is indifferently valid everywhere"? I see him doing the latter. Acknowledged or not, did he not in fact believe that, not just in our Western clearing but wherever there are human beings, unconcealing (*aletheia*) occurs through "clearings in the forest darkness" that human linguistic, social, and cultural practices open up and provide? This unconcealing is, for Heidegger, of Being, a term which (in its ineffability, unconditionedness, and presumed infinitude) I am unable to distinguish from Sunyata, Nirguna Brahman, the Beyond-Being of Iambicus, or even the Plotinian One, save in two respects. Heidegger's Being is not an agent or cause, and it cannot be presumed to be good. By my lights both these lacks are defects,[h] but the issue here is not the worth of Heidegger's metaphysics or its affinity with positions to which it seems cognate in ways. Rather, it is whether his position should be seen as metaphysical in its own right. It appears to me that it should be.

6. Because metaphysics for Heidegger is the heart of philosophy, he sees the end of one as the end of the other. Within his historicist framework this makes sense in a certain way, for it is difficult to see where the trajectory of modern philosophy might yet lead. But that simply reraises the problematics of untempered historicism.

Confining himself to the West, and defining metaphysics

[h]On the issue of causality, I have it from Norris Clarke that on an occasion when Heidegger was pushed in a seminar on why he would not countenance causality from a God beyond our finite horizons, he replied: "I am still too much of a Kantian to believe in causality. Participation, metaphysical causality—these are past mittences of Being to the medieval world. They are lost to us now."

But as Father Clarke rightly continues in the letter to me that reported this confession: "How does one pretend to know and proclaim what Being is up to at a given time—what cards it is currently dealing from its deck? Could it not be that the signals have already changed, and that *Kantianism* with its suspicion of causality has had its day?" A danger in historicism is the abject posture it can induce toward time, leading us to assume that we are trapped in our historical moment and can do little to affect its character.

(the heart of philosophy, remember) idiosyncratically, Heidegger lays philosophy to rest by sundering body from soul. His own position emerged from his life-long wrestle with philosophy, but he emerged from that *aganon* bent on patricide. For if (as he concludes) the soul of philosophy is Being and its body reason, with the passing of the centuries the two factor out and part company. Displaying with increasing clarity its *telos* towards calculative, manipulative mentation, reason splays out into the positive sciences, while Being, having delivered reason to *its* destined home, checks in with the poets. "This is the point in Heidegger's philosophy to which I take exception," writes one of its staunchest admirers, John Caputo:

> Heidegger rejects the possibility of philosophy as a *tertium quid*, that is, as a thinking which is neither will-less non-representational "meditation" (*Besinnung*) nor a calculative, mathematical science.... That leaves us with a whole host of problems for which I do not see that there would be, in Heidegger's view, any place to turn in order to find a solution. I believe that there is a whole network of difficulties which are not merely technical problems and with which the methods of the technological sciences are simply unsuited to deal. Nor are they questions from which we can expect an answer from the (poets).[11]

Wittgenstein for linguistic philosophy. The philosophical cold war of the middle third of this century—between continental existentialism and phenomenology east of the English Channel, and Anglo-American analytic and linguistic philosophy to its west—has ended, thanks to a concept that has drawn the antagonists together. It is the concept of human beings as social functionaries. For Heidegger's socio-historical horizons in the preceding section, we need only substitute Wittgenstein's "forms of life," and we have the same basic epistemology, one that sees knowing as socially generated and restricted to its generating crucible.[i] Heidegger favors thinking that

---

[i]"Probably nothing has had greater impact on the way philosophers today understand the human mode of life than the acceptance... of

is meditative while Wittgenstein inclines toward thought that is instrumental—rationality *is* practical reason for him—but the sources and ceilings of knowing are the same in both cases. "It makes [no] sense to talk about getting outside all social schema of concepts, beliefs and ideals of truth [to see them] as so many views of how things 'really' are," says Henry Ruf, speaking for Wittgenstein in the paper cited in the preceding footnote. If Saul Kripke is correct,[12] Wittgenstein held that even mathematical truth is socially conjured, for *all* truth is "intrasystematic"; as Richard Rorty puts the point jauntily, it is "what our peers will let us get away with saying."[13] Cross-cultural consensus in arithmetic doesn't derive from the compelling power of concepts and reason. It is the other way around. Social consensus is what makes concepts compel, while producing those concepts in the first place.

What is a metaphysician to think of this? That thought —all thought—is socially mediated presents no problem. The question is: where do the worlds that are socially mediated (a) differ incommensurably, (b) overlap, thanks to cross-cultural correspondences in human nature and the physical world, and (c) differ in ways that can be hermeneutically reconciled. Piaget reports that in the course of human development, individuals normally reach a stage of "decentration" wherein they can adopt increasingly universal standpoints, giving up particular egocentric or sociocentric ways of understanding and acting to move towards the "universal human community." Have Wittgenstein and Heidegger discovered any uncircumventable barriers beyond which this movement cannot proceed?[j]

---

the idea that we are social beings, that human language, thought, knowledge and morality are social and historical. Introduced in the West as a viable hypothesis by Hegel, Marx and Dewey, the idea that we are social beings was diffused through every area of philosophy by Heidegger, the later Wittgenstein and Quine" (Henry Ruf in an unpublished paper).

[j]Richard Bernstein is only one who has criticized "the type of . . . fashionable . . . pluralism . . . that thinks of different perspectives,

Wittgenstein was so burned by his youthful effort to produce specifications for a universal "ideal" language that, when he realized that such a language would be unable to register the idioms and other idiosyncrasies of disparate communities, he went to the opposite extreme, arguing that language is capable of virtually nothing but colloquialisms. Ernest Gellner pinpoints the consequence:

> Language was, and [for Wittgenstein] would only be, a set of multi-purpose customs enmeshed in an inevitably idiosyncratic 'form of life'—cultures. *Gemeinschaft* thereby . . . became the only possible form of society, and the possibility of anything else was excluded. The closed community carried meanings, and the meanings sustained it. Meaning was *only* possible in community, and it alone made community possible. . . . Transcendence of social bounds, by private and independent thought, was declared impossible.[14]

VI. Rejoinder

Differences among these four epistemologies should not obscure from us their collective drift, which is from the one to the many, from the absolute to the relative, from objectivity to subjectivity, from realism to idealism-in-Kant and pragmatism-elsewhere, and from correspondence and representational thinking to instrumental, heuristic thinking as this alternates with aesthetic immediacy. This characterization will be resisted, and,

---

paradigms, language-games, etc., as incommensurable—as windowless monads where there is no possibility of communication among them. This fortress-like pluralism," he contends, "subscribes to what Karl Popper calls the 'Myth of the Framework' where we are presumably 'prisoners caught in the framework of our theories; our expectations; our past experiences; our language' and are so locked into these frameworks that we cannot communicate with those encased in 'radically' different frameworks or paradigms. But while proponents of the incommensurability thesis do call into question naive assumptions about fixed, transcendental standards and criteria, . . . they fail to show that we cannot rationally communicate, confront, and argue with what is different and other" (1988 Presidential Address to the Metaphysical Society of America).

stated thus baldly, it can be faulted in details. But no amount of squirming can relieve the ultimate disjunctions in the decisions that are being made. To take just the realism/pragmatism option, Timothy Jackson is quite right in saying that "the competing intuitions behind the realism-pragmatism debates [are] entirely basic and mutually exclusive. . . . Realism and pragmatism are contradictories, not contraries; there is no third alternative, [for] once all theory-independent reality is denied, some form of pragmatism [is] inevitable."[15] Jackson is right, too, in adding that "waiting at the end of this road is a fideism in which theology [and philosophy are] indeed, 'just talk'."

What about the objective-subjective disjunction—Kant with his human subjectivity, Nietzsche with his historical subjectivity, and Heidegger and Wittgenstein with their self-enclosed, cultural-linguistic, social subjectivities? We can come straight to the point and ask if subjectivity has any *meaning* apart from objectivity. If not, is not our ability to understand the very concept "subjectivity" evidence of our mind's objective capacity? (A dog's knowing *is* subjective, the proof being that it doesn't know that it is such.) What the deconstructionists seem to overlook is that objectivity, in some form of adequation to the given, is the mind's *raison d'etre*, its distinctive talent.[k]

The trouble is that, with the rise of modern science, the given has for all practical purposes been reduced to empirical reality and objectivity to knowledge thereof. Human life cannot be reduced to this dimension, and the deconstructionists, standard-bearers in part for Kierkegaard's and Nietzsche's existentialism, see that clearly. Fighting desperately for the rights of the human, they have selected a different "object" for thought, the human *subject*, and sought to fashion a different kind of

---

[k]Someone has written that it would be quite false "to assume with the subjectivists, that there is no adequate knowledge, for that is to forget that adequation constitutes the sufficient reason for the intelligence and thus its very essence; even a limited knowledge is adequate to the exact degree that it is a knowledge and not something else."

truth to deal with it. Kierkegaard went so far as to call it "truth as subjectivity." In protesting the encroachment of scientific objectivity on humanity's understanding of itself, the deconstructionists are right. Where they go wrong is in faulting the second word in the phrase "scientific objectivity" rather than the first; they mistakenly suppose that knowledge suffers when we require it to be *objective*, whereas in fact it suffers only if we require that, to be knowledge in the full sense of the word, it must be objective *by the canons of science*, including proof. That small slip opened the sluice-gates to subjectivism and its associate, relativism, and the "human sciences" have been floundering in their tide ever since.[1] Historicism and hermeneutics, deconstruction and the extolling of narrative truth over its metaphysical counterpart—all, at root, are ways of trying to keep one's nose above water, trying cognitively to *breathe*, while sloshing around in the subjectivist bog. We know that solipcism, however logically invincible its die-hard version may seem, is wrong. What we do not see, having been thrown off balance by the power of science which is at the same time stupendous and radically limited, is that subjectivism and relativism are halfway houses down solipsism's slope. They are social or collective solipsisms, we might say; not quite as absurd as solipsism's strict, individualistic version, but in the end no more workable or true.

As for the ceilings to which deconstructionist epistemologies all (in their various ways) subject human knowing, I have room here for no more than a single rhetorical question: are many things more futile than trying to use the mind to limit the mind? Many *modes* of mental functioning are indeed limited, but to indicate these the mind must shift to a different register, proving

[1]"While the problem of objective worth for the physical or natural sciences is an absence of value in the world described by them, the problem of objective worth for the social science and hermeneutics is just the opposite, *too much value*—too many cultures, forms of life, language games, too many competing systems of value, and no way to tell which is the right one" (Robert Kane, "Metaphysical Ends," an unpublished paper).

thereby the existence of that register. In India the most developed distinction is between *manas* and *buddhi*, in the West between *ratio* and *intellectus*. Heidegger's *alethia* and Wittgenstein's "showing" gesture towards these noetic distinctions, but inadequately, being hobbled by assumptions that rule out important possibilities.

VII. The View from Everywhere

Bouncing off from Thomas Nagel's *The View from Nowhere* which holds that, though we can think about the world as it transcends our own interests and experience, we cannot really know anything about it, this essay urges a return to more hopeful expectations.

True, a "view from everywhere" should be read as "everywhere human," for there is no reason to think that our view is much like a caterpillar's—or God's, though it *is* claimed that (in a way analogous to the way relativity theory leaves Newtonian mechanics intact) God sees that things are objectively positioned *towards us* in the way we see them. As finite selves, we are set amidst other objects and selves whose existence does not depend on us. Some of those objects and selves conspired to bring us into existence; hence metaphysical realism.[m] A correspondence theory of truth, not a pragmatic one, is both natural and required toward those independent-of-us objects. Pragmatism can be folded into the correspondence theory as useful in places, but it cannot replace that theory. (Tell a man who is falling in love that "She loves me" means no more than "Given the evidence, steps that will deepen our relationship are appropriate"—not that "She feels towards me the way I feel towards her"—and

[m]" 'Realism' . . . is the view that truth is radically non-epistemic, that truth is not determined solely by consciousness, linguistic conventions, conditions of evidence, verifiability, or warranted assertibility, even in the long run. It is determined by the way the world is and this is independent in some sense of our ways of knowing that world" (Robert Kane, in the paper previously cited). Kane goes on to point out that realism in this sense is intimately related to the fallibilism its opponents so vociferously defend, for it is realism that insists most emphatically that truth is underdetermined by the conditions of belief and evidence of knowing subjects.

he is likely to hit you.) In some sense correspondence calls for representation, so it is unfortunate if Foucault is right in saying that "everywhere representational thinking is at an end."[n] Representational thinking need not be naive, though. In subtle gradations it can range all the way from almost picture postcard depictions of tables and chairs to the claims of mathematicians that they "see" logical objects and their relationships. A sand dune would not have to think of the wind as granular to be right in representing it as a force that exists apart from dunes and impacts them to shape their contours.

It may be the case that at some ultimate level, duality and correspondence *do* disappear as knowing phases into direct apprehension; if it is mysticism, immanent or transcendent, that the deconstructionists have in mind, it would help if they said so more explicitly. It is not my present object, though, to press the question of what a fitting metaphysics for our time might be; that is the concern of the next section. Believing with Jacques Maritain that "a loss or weakening of the metaphysical spirit is an incalculable damage for the general order of intelligence and human affairs," I have sought here only to argue for the continued importance of the metaphysical quest.

Two rhetorical questions can round off my case.

First. In reviewing favorably Jean-Luc Marion's *Dieu sans l'etre (God without Being)*, yet another in the seemingly endless torrent of books that catalogue the sins of metaphysics, Harvey Cox nevertheless concedes that "eventually, of course, all these antimetaphysical critics will have to face the contention that no one ever really escapes metaphysics, that its derogators end up hiding it, obscuring it, or doing it badly."[16] To which it seems sensible to ask: if eventually, why not now?

---

[n]Even Derrida concedes that "language is marked through and through by referential . . . assumptions. . . . What he seeks[s] to show . . . is that classical ideas of this referential function have greatly simplified its nature" [Christopher Norris, *Derrida* (Cambridge: Harvard University Press, 1987), p. 54.] This could be so.

That seems obvious, but this second question I do not find as frequently raised. Do the deconstructionists accurately assess what our times require? Within the freedom-form polarities between which life has no choice but to shuttle, this century's deconstructionists side invariably with freedom. "Unmasking" is the word the following characterization of the "postmodern movement" uses for this predilection.

> It is an antinomian movement that assumes a vast unmaking in the Western mind. . . . I say 'unmaking' though other terms are now *de rigeur*: deconstruction, decentering, disappearance, dissemination, demystification, discontinuity, *difference*, dispersion, etc. Such terms . . . express an epistemological obsession with fragments or fractures, and a corresponding ideological commitment to minorities in politics, sex and language. To think well, to feel well, to act well, to read well, according to the *episteme* of unmaking, is to refuse the tyranny of wholes; totalization in any human endeavor is potentially totalitarian.[17]

Pointing to the "deep suspicion, hostility and ridicule of any aspiration to unity, reconciliation, harmony, totality, the whole, the one" in this movement, Richard Bernstein, in his 1988 Presidential Address to the Metaphysical Society of America, goes on to note also its reason: a "widespread bias that these signifiers mask repression and violence; that there is an inevitable slippage from totality to totalitarianism and terror."[18]

What is needed, Bernstein argues, is a questioning of this bias, an inquiry into whether the slippage is inevitable or, alternatively, a danger to be guarded against. "When we are told that 'to think well, to feel well, to act well, to read well' is to refuse 'the tyranny of wholes,'. . . what is secreted is an ideal of what constitutes the good life. . . . We need to question this ideal of living well and why it should be affirmed."[19]

Notes

1. *Religion and the Scientific Future* (New York: Harper and Row, 1970), p. 22.
2. *Psychology and the Promethean Will* (New York: Harper and Row, 1936).
3. *Identity and Difference* (New York: Harper and Row, 1969), p. 52.
4. *Religion Within the Limits of Reason Alone* (New York: Harper and Row, 1960), p. 142n.
5. "Toward a Method of Knowing Spirit," *Sciences Religieuses/ Studies in Religion*, 14/2 (Spring 1985), pp. 149, 152.
6. See J.-P. Sartre, *Being and Nothingness* (New York: Harper and Row, 1960), pp. 315-18.
7. P. F. Strawson, *The Bounds of Sense* (London: Methuen, 1959), p. 42.
8. Chapter Two of Robert Bernasconi, *The Question of Language in Heidegger's History of Being* (New Jersey: Humanities Press, 1985) is especially deserving of study in this connection. I am indebted to Jason Wirth for calling my attention to this work.
9. "Knowledge and Human Values," *Teachers College Record*, 82/3 (Spring 1981), p. 519.
10. *Op. cit.*, p. 52.
11. *The Mystical Element in Heidegger's Thought* (New York: Fordham University Press, 1978), p. 266.
12. *Wittgenstein on Rules and Private Language* (Cambridge: Harvard University Press, 1983).
13. *Philosophy and the Mirror of Nature* (Princeton University Press, 1979), p. 176.
14. "The Stakes in Anthropology," *The American Scholar* (Winter 1988), p. 19.
15. *Religious Studies Review*, Vol. 11, No. 3/July 1985.
16. *Christianity and Crisis*, April 15, 1985, p. 140.
17. Ihab Hassan, as cited by Albrect Wellmer, "On the Dialectic of Modernism and Postmodernism," *Praxis International* 4:338.
18. "Metaphysics, Critique, Utopia," in *Review of Metaphysics*, XLII/2, p. 259.
19. *Ibid.*, p. 260.

Part Two

A CLEARING

Part One of this book traced the intellectual odyssey that has led to the West's current despair over the possibility of overviews—or even their desirability, some think—and was historical. It was also abstract in that it focused on the fate of the metaphysical enterprise as such.

Part Two turns a corner on both those counts. Putting history aside, it becomes constructive. And it becomes concrete, for we get further (I believe) if instead of indefinitely arguing the fate of worldviews abstractly, we put forward the best one we know and see how it fares.

This next essay—the only one that was written expressly for this book in its first edition—makes that move. If the outlook it introduces appears to have more in common with ones that predated the rise of modern science, I ask the reader not to judge that fact prematurely. What may at first glance seem conservative can in fact be "radically conservative" if it cuts back on the tree trunk to a point below where its limbs begin to branch, that being the point where sap flows strongest.

In the mnemonic device we use for remembering how to reset our clocks in relation to Daylight Saving Time, Part Two "falls back" in order to "spring forward."

3

PERENNIAL PHILOSOPHY, PRIMORDIAL TRADITION

An indication of how the outlook to be described broke over me may help to highlight some of its features, so I shall use this way of moving into it.

Early resonance to the writings of Gerald Heard had led me to his friend Aldous Huxley and the mosaic of mysticism the latter had put together under the title *The Perennial Philosophy*. In his introduction to that book Huxley notes that though it was Leibniz who coined the phrase *philosophia perennis*, the thing itself—"the metaphysic that recognizes a divine Reality substantial to the world of things and lives and minds; the psychology that finds in the soul something similar to, or even identical with, divine Reality; the ethic that places man's final end in the knowledge of the immanent and transcendent Ground of all being—is immemorial and universal. Rudiments of the Perennial Philosophy," he continues,

> may be found among the traditionary lore of primitive peoples in every region of the world, and in its fully developed forms it has a place in every one of the higher religions. A version of this Highest Common Factor in all preceding and subsequent theologies was first committed to writing more than twenty-five centuries ago, and since that time the inexhaustible theme has been treated again and again, from the standpoint of every religious tradition and in all the principal languages of Asia and Europe.[1]

For twenty-five years I had known of this position and even sensed theoretically that it pointed in the right direction, but it took a sequence of concrete events to bring me face to face with it, whereupon it quickly took over. I had known that certain contemporary thinkers such as Ananda Coomaraswamy and René Guénon stood in direct line with the writers Huxley had anthologized, but it was Frithjof Schuon's books that caused the familiar to jump to my attention as if I were seeing it with new eyes. I tell the story in my introduction to the revised edition of Schuon's *Transcendent Unity of Religions*, but retell it here for purposes at hand.

It was the autumn of 1969, and I was embarking on an academic year around the world. Of the decisions as to what to include in my forty-four-pound luggage limit, the final one concerned a book that had just crossed my desk: *In the Tracks of Buddhism* by Frithjof Schuon. I barely recognized his name, but the book's middle section, entitled "Buddhism's Ally in Japan: Shinto or the Way of the Gods," caught my eye. Two weeks later, at our first stop, Japan, I would have to be lecturing on Shinto and I had little feel for its outlook. I badly needed an entrée, so I wedged the book into my bulging flight bag.

It proved to be the best decision of the year. Before the sacred shrine at Ise, symbolic center of the nation of Japan, under its giant cryptomeria and at low tables in its resthouse for pilgrims, the Way of the Gods opened before me. Ise's atmosphere itself could not be credited with the unveiling, but only if I add that it was Schuon's insights that enabled me to sense within that atmosphere—its dignity, beauty, and repose—an intellective depth. I came to see how ancestors could appear less fallen than their descendants and thereby serve, when revered, as doorways to transcendence. I saw how virgin nature—especially in its grand phenomena: sun, wind, moon, thunder, lightning, and the sky and earth that are their containers—could be venerated as the most transparent symbols of the divine. Above all, I saw how Shinto, indigenous host for "the Japanese miracle," could be seen as the most intact instance of an archaic hyperborean shamanism that swept from Siberia across the Bering Straits to the Native Americans.

Two months later, in India, the same thing happened. Perusing a bookstore in Madras, my eye fell on a study of the Vedanta entitled *Language of the Self*, again by Frithjof Schuon. This time I didn't hesitate. The remaining weeks in India were spent with that book under my arm, and I was happy. A decade's tutelage under a swami of the Ramakrishna Order had familiarized me with the basic Vedantic outlook, but Schuon took off from there as if from base camp, while showing at each step, through a stunning series of cross-references, how the Vedantic profundities were Indic variations on themes that are universal because grounded in man's inherent nature as related to his Source.

Would one believe a third installment? In Iran the leading Islamicist pointed me to Schuon's *Understanding Islam* as "the best work in English on the meaning of Islam and why Muslims believe in it." I had been to East Asia, South Asia, and West Asia, and in each the same personage had surfaced to guide and illumine. The point, though, is not the person or the particular books that crossed my path but rather the position they articulated.

The feature of that position that grasped me was the way it joined universality to final truth. Of these two, truth is the more important, but the position's insistence that no human collectivity has been without it (an insistence so strong that the words "primordial" and "perennial" are built into its very name) made me listen intently to what was being said, for I was caught up in the cross-cultural issue. As missionaries to China, my parents and grandparents had given their lives to taking truth to those who lacked it, whereas my cross-cultural eyes had accommodated better to the truths of others that were relevant to myself as well.[a] How much my

[a]This sentence is not intended to disown the missionary enterprise. In 1982 I attended a service of worship in a church my family frequented in the 1920s and 30s when we passed through

upbringing in another culture set the stage I do not know, but what was clear was that, though I had delighted in cultural differences, I had not been able to absolutize them. Training under swamis, Zen masters, and Sufi shaikhs; encountering Tiwis and Aruntas in the Australian bush; sitting in total harmony with Thomas Merton, the Dalai Lama, and a remarkable Native American chief on the nearby Onondaga reservation, I had felt the same still presence.

What I did not know was how to articulate that presence, and the perennial philosophy showed me how. Because the words were in "esperanto," so to speak, their claimed universality merits another two paragraphs.

I think we can now see that the radical existentialist claim that man has no nature ("existence precedes essence") was an exaggeration to make a point; the givens in human existence cannot be discounted this easily. By definition we all partake of these givens—we are all more human than otherwise, someone has remarked—and as intelligence is one of them, it stands to reason that in pondering our commonalities, thoughtful persons everywhere would have gravitated toward similar conclusions. If we approach the point by way of revelation instead of human discovery, the result is the same. That God, while desiring the well-being of his children, should have left the vast majority of them (including the most gifted) to stagnate for thousands of years, practically

Shanghai. Two thousand parishioners were in attendance. In addition to the sanctuary which was packed, sixteen amplified Sunday school rooms were overflowing and the minister pled with the congregation not to attend church more than once on a Sunday because doing so deprived others of the privilege. To gaze on the faces in that congregation, many streaming with tears, while remembering the twenty-eight years of persecution the church in China had suffered before its doors had been permitted to reopen two years before my visit, was to know that Christianity was providing at least these people with something their indigenous tradition did not, and perhaps to them could not. This is to say nothing of the incalculable debt I myself owe to dedicated Indian, Japanese, Tibetan, and Islamic teachers who have made America their mission field.

without hope, in the darkness of mortal ignorance until he chose to disclose his truth to a rivulet of humanity concentrated in a tiny locale, this "scandal of particularity" (if I have rightly stated its essence) is too monstrous to abide. "To suppose that God could act in such a manner... flagrantly contradicts [his] nature, the essence of which is Goodness and Mercy. This nature, as theology is far from being unaware, can be 'terrible' but not monstrous."[2] Saint Augustine's doctrine of "Wisdom uncreate, the same now as it ever was and ever will be," is more generous and becoming, as is his conclusion that this Wisdom came to be called Christianity only after the coming of Christ. According to an esoteric exegesis of Genesis 11:1, the primordial or unanimous tradition goes back to the single spiritual language which, with the Tower of Babel, splintered into multiple but parallel dialects.

The obvious problem the claim of unanimity must face is the differences that traditions also display. Some thinkers are so occupied with these differences that they dismiss claims of commonality as simply sloppy thinking, yet identity *within* difference is as common an experience as life affords. Green is not blue, yet both are light. A gold watch is not a gold ring, but both are gold. Women are not men, but both are human. Everything turns on which foot one comes down on. And as that cannot be decided by logic, we need to bring in content to determine which "foot" deserves to be emphasized. That the truth in question has been ubiquitous—"the living God . . . in . . . all nations . . . left not himself without witness" (Acts 14:15-17)—is in its favor, but it is not that which makes it either important or true.

I have already quoted Aldous Huxley's characterization of the perennial philosophy as

> the metaphysic that recognizes a divine Reality substantial to the world of things and lives and minds; the psychology that finds in the soul something similar to, or even identical with, divine Reality; the ethic that places man's final end in the knowledge of the immanent and transcendent Ground of all being,

and as I cannot imagine a better brief summation, I shall let my own exposition take the form of a commentary on these three basic themes.

1. Metaphysics

The Metaphysic that recognizes a divine Reality substantial to the world of things and lives and minds.

The perennial philosophy is emphatically ontological, which is to say that its overriding concern is with being (*on* in Greek). Heidegger says that the West has forgotten the question of being, and on the whole he is right. The collapse of metaphysics which Part One of this book describes is the clearest sign of this forgetting, along with the concomitant rise to preeminence of topics which, though important, should rightfully remain ancillary: epistemology, language, and questions of method. "A loss or weakening of the metaphysical spirit is an incalculable damage for the general order of intelligence and human affairs," I have already quoted Jacques Maritain as writing,[3] and so it is. As our fate is totally dependent on the matrix that produced and sustains us, interest in its nature is the holiest interest that can visit us.

A key feature of that nature, according to the perennial philosophy, is its hierarchical character.[b] In outlining his own notion of the universe as a "holarchy," a hierarchy of holons or self-maintaining entities that are parts of larger wholes, Arthur Koestler admits that "hierarchy is an ugly word. Loaded with ecclesiastical and military associations, [it] conveys to some people a wrong impression of a rigid or authoritarian structure." But misunderstandings and possible abuses, he goes on to say, should not blind us to the fact that "all complex structures and processes of relatively stable character display hierarchic organization, and this applies regardless whether we are considering inanimate systems, living

[b]"The ability to see the Great Truth of the hierarchic structure of the world, which makes it possible to distinguish between higher and lower Levels of Being, is one of the indispensable conditions of understanding" (E. F. Schumacher, *A Guide for the Perplexed*, p. 14).

organisms, social organizations, or patterns of behavior."[4] "The almost universal applicability of the hierarchic model" that Koestler points to (p. 291) is obvious in the empirical world,[c] but the metaphysical point is that it is not likely that it would figure so prominently there if it were not embedded in the structure of reality itself.

> The conception of the universe as . . . ranging in hierarchical order from the meagerest kind of existents . . . through "every possible" grade up to the *ens perfectissimum* . . . has, in one form or another, been the dominant official philosophy of the larger part of civilized mankind through most of its history.[5]

The different grades that are mentioned in this quotation are analogous to the levels of size in inanimate matter (as encountered in quantum mechanics, chemistry, daily life, and astronomy) and the degrees of complexity in organic life (plant, animal, and human). In each domain or kingdom we find distinctive properties and laws that hold for its population but not others; they define the region in question and distinguish it from its neighbors. In philosophy categories are used to sort out classes of things that need to be distinguished, and the phrase "category mistake" has caught on to signal the confusion that results when their differences are neglected. The distinctive claim of the perennial philosophy, as the quotation from Lovejoy brings out, is that the categories of existents—the classes of kinds of things that exist—are hierarchically ordered. Reality is tiered; being increases as the levels ascend. Ascent is used here figuratively, of course. No literal up, or spatial move whatever, is involved.

We must attend carefully here, for this is the step in

---

[c]To cite a single compelling example, "there is some principle of organization of living matter that is shared with no other natural assemblage of atoms. . . . Despite a knowledge of the structure of protein molecules down to the very placement of their atoms in exact three-dimensional space, we do not have the faintest idea of what the rules are for folding them up into their natural form" (R. C. Lewontin, in *The New York Review* [April 27, 1989], p. 18).

the argument which, though it was commonplace to the point of being universal in the past, is the most difficult for modern consciousness to grasp. What can it mean to say that X has more being than Y; or in ordinary parlance, that it is more real?

Plato's allegory of the cave is the classic effort to tell us. The shadows its chained prisoners see are certainly real in that they exist in some sense and to some degree, but the objects that cast them are more substantial and, in this sense, embody more existence. In possessing three dimensions rather than two, in outlasting their shadows and manifesting more independence generally, three-dimensional objects possess in greater abundance properties that things must possess to some extent if they are to exist at all. When one of the prisoners manages to escape from Plato's cave, the privative character of shadows becomes even more evident, for shadows are nothing but the relative absence *of* light—the light that can then be directly seen.

To ring a change on Plato's allegory: I enter a room and see my wife. No, it turns out not to be her; it is her reflection in a wall-size mirror. The reflection exists, but it is certainly not my wife. And it is manifestly less than my wife. If it be objected that it is less real as wife but not as reflection, the answer is that it is the former that is at issue. That her reflection falls short of her full selfhood is (we are asked to think) analogous to the ways some beings fall short of others. The difficult part, of course, is to imagine things that are more real than the three-dimensional objects that stand before us in clear daylight. Perhaps it will help if, staying with the example of my wife, we try to imagine a perception that could encompass her entire history—each moment exactly as she lived it but collapsed in a way that enabled me to take them all in in an instant. If in some magical way the dimension of time were thus added to the three that are now evident, the wife I now see would by comparison seem abstract in the way her two-dimensional reflection is abstract now. To my newly endowed eyes her three-dimensional self would be only the surface of her complete, longitudinal self that the added time dimension placed before me like a four-dimensional "block."

The point of fanciful moves like these is to try to breathe life into the possibility that we are not the highest octave in being's register. There are things that exceed us, and the things our senses report, in the way objects exceed shadows and wives their mirror images. Obviously we are surrounded by objects that exceed us *in certain respects* —mountains outlast us in duration and lightning packs more power—but the claim of the great chain of being, which can be taken as the perennial philosophy's ontological spine (or better, spire), is that positive attributes go together: increase one and the others burgeon concomitantly. That the longevity of mountains does not make them wise any more than lightning's power makes it long-lasting is no refutation of that claim, for the claim concerns deep structures only. Lightning and mountains belong to the same level of reality, the physical, and on any single level qualities group and regroup in all manner of ways to allow for variety. It is only in crossing ontic lines, in ways analogous to passing from the quantum to the atomic level in physics, that qualities keep step with one another. And we can see why this lockstep is important. To Ernst Haeckel's question of questions, "Is the universe friendly?", religion answers, finally yes; in William James's formulation, "religion says that the best things are the more eternal things, the things in the universe that throw the last stone, so to speak, and say the final word."[6] Three categories are aligned in this statement, all in their exemplary modes: value (the best things), time (the more eternal things), and power (the things that throw the last stone). In a completely meaningful world they *must* thus converge, for the only fully satisfactory explanation for the way things are is that they should be that way. The charge that attention to teleological considerations of this sort reduces the perennial philosophy to a rationale for wishful thinking will be dealt with in the "Flakes of Fire" essay in Part

Three, but we can anticipate what will be said there to the extent of a single sentence. As the hypothesis that this is a good world and that fuller understanding will carry us beyond appearances to the contrary is the most fruitful working hypothesis there is; it is the metaphysical counterpart of science's working premise that cancer has a cause even if it is not yet known. To explore this hypothesis energetically is a sign of health rather than pathology as long as facts are not blinked along the way.

Thus far the claim of a tiered reality has been broached through images, but it can be stated literally if we are willing to accept abstractions. To have more being, or be more real, is to possess more of the properties of being per se. These include:

a. Power. It may be miniscule, but it is present. Plato seems to have been the first to have said that to exist is to exert influence. If there were something to which nothing responded, it would not register at all and we would have no reason to assume it exists. "What is it to be 'real'?" William James asked, and answered, "The best definition I know is: 'Anything is real of which we find ourselves obliged to take into account in any way.' "[7] It has the power to make its presence felt.

b. Duration.

c. Locale.

d. Unity. What exists can have parts and usually does, but unless these cohere in a way that gives it an identifiable integrity, *it* cannot be said to exist; only the components do.

e. Importance. Again this may be small, but to exist to any degree is to count for something.

f. Worth. If nothing is better than something, there is no basis for discussion. *Esse qua esse bonum est;* being as being is good.

Other properties may be required, but these suffice for our purpose. We have been asking what it would mean for X to possess them in higher degree than Y, but to sharpen the contrast we can change "higher" to "highest." If X's power were infinite, it would be *omnipotent.* If its duration had no cutoff, it would be *eternal.* If its locale were without bounds, it would be *omnipresent*. If its unity were uncompromised, it would be *simple* in the technical sense of harboring no divisions whatever. If its importance were utter, it would be *absolute*. If its worth were categorical, it would be *perfect*.

These are, of course, the attributes of God, and all theists will subscribe to a hierarchy of two levels (God and the world), as will metaphysicians who distinguish in some way between the absolute and the relative. A simple dichotomy, though, is inadequate for the distinctions that are needed; both God and the world must be qualified, God by separating his knowable from his unknowable aspects, the world by distinguishing its invisible from its visible features. For to repeat the criteria that require levels to be demarcated in the first place, each of the four we now have in view—God manifest, God unmanifest; world visible, world invisible—has an importantly distinct population and distinctive ways in which its members interact. The number four oversimplifies—the number may actually be indefinite—but these four broad divisions, appearing as they do explicitly in all known civilizations and implicitly in virtually every studied tribe, appear to be the minimum that collectivities must respect if their outlooks are to mesh reasonably with the way things are. Individuals can get along with less than four, but not societies if they are to accommodate the full range of spiritual personality types that surface everywhere. My *Forgotten Truth* takes the description of the four levels as its primary task; here they can only be identified. A supplementing identification appears in the essay "Excluded Knowledge" on pages 93-95. The reader may wish to glance ahead to it, for both descriptions are brief and together they may deepen the view like a stereopticon.

Listed in the order of diminishing reality as the eye moves down the page, the four principal levels of existence are the following:

God unmanifest: Godhead or the Infinite.

God manifest: the celestial plane.

The world in its invisible aspects: mind and the vital principle; the intermediate plane.[d]

The world as (in principle) visible: space, time, and matter; the terrestrial plane.

As the God/world distinction is relatively standard, I shall ride on it and identify the four levels by the additional cuts that are needed on each side of that initial divide. In *Forgotten Truth* I distinguished God from the Godhead (Boehme's *ungrund*; Tillich's God-above-God; Eckhart's *Gottheit*) by defining the former as personal and the latter transpersonal, but this now strikes me as a tactical mistake. It is not wrong, but we have so much difficulty imagining anything superior to persons that, whatever is actually said, the impression that is conveyed in denying the attribute "personal" to the Godhead is that it must be subpersonal, rather than suprapersonal as the distinction intends. This misunderstanding can be avoided if we draw the line instead between aspects of divinity our minds can grasp—its personal aspect included—and ones that outdistance comprehension categorically. When, two paragraphs above, the pinnacle of being was said to be omnipresent, eternal, and the like, God was in focus. In the Godhead these superlatives are not withdrawn; they are, rather, advanced beyond the range of our imaginings and fused into a unity reason

[d]Obviously the terms "visible" and "invisible" refer here not merely to the ocular sense but to all of our senses of outward observation. The powers of life, consciousness, and self-awareness are entirely invisible (without color, sound, taste, or smell) while being—this is important—what we are mainly interested in. All our thoughts, emotions, feelings, imaginations, reveries, dreams, fantasies, are invisible, and this has implications that are more startling than we normally realize. As it is these interior features that we identify with most—take ourselves at heart to be—we are invisible; we live in a world of invisible people. I have not chosen that way of putting the matter for its shock value. No verbal legerdemain is involved; only the insistence that we face the implications of the way we actually, workingly, think of ourselves. It would be an oversimplification to say that we are completely invisible, for we do have bodies; but as between oversimplifications, it is literally more accurate to say that we are invisible than to say the opposite.

cannot penetrate. There is an age when a child may look at you earnestly and deliver a long, pleased speech in which the inflections of spoken English are perfectly reflected, yet not a single syllable is intelligible. There is no way you can tell the child that she has done marvels with the melody but, since language also makes sense, she has not gotten very far with it. Something like this is involved in the God to Godhead move; the language of theism gets God's melody right, but the sense that is hidden in his final depths eludes it. In technical terms, God is the object of kataphatic theology, the *via affirmativa*, whereas Godhead is the object of apophatic theology, the *via negativa*. The line is not hard and fast, but priests and prophets tend to focus on God, mystics on the Godhead. And the latter tell us that in those rare, supernatural moments when the Godhead is directly disclosed to man, what man then sees is that he cannot understand its nature at all. It is not that depths of its nature remain opaque and ineffable; its simplicity precludes ladling things out this way. Its entire *nature* reposes in depth unfathomable. So the incomprehensibility of the Godhead becomes evident at the precise moment that its nature is most clearly apprehended—there is no way to state the point less paradoxically. In the light of mystical vision the Godhead's hiddenness is not dispelled; it appears. Not that there are two Gods, of course. It is just that his/her single nature does not stop where our minds do.

As we turn from God to the world, its material countenance greets us most emphatically, yet we need only close our eyes to find ourselves in a totally different medium: the world of direct, immediate, inner awareness. Idealists have tried to reduce matter to mind and materialists the opposite, but neither has carried the day. The difference between inner and outer, subjective and objective, the living and the dead, cannot easily be argued away. I shall not try to say here where the line should be drawn between the terms in these pairs; a small run on the point appears on pages 93-94 below. Those who wish to pursue it further can turn to chapters three and four in *Forgotten Truth*. It is enough to say that the great chain of being places mind ahead of matter not only in its worth but in its power and extent as well; thereby it runs counter to current suppositions. The essays that follow argue that these suppositions derive from modernity's having tailored its outlook excessively to science which sees how far things can be (a) explained in terms of ones that are simpler, and (b) controlled by altering these simpler components. The attention to "upward causation" that results from this approach has rubbed off onto the modern outlook as a whole, causing it to assume that influence per se flows predominantly from less to more. Yet even in science we sometimes catch glimpses of the opposite possibility.

Item. Together with time and mass/energy, size (space) is a property of matter; things in the upper three realms do not have to conform to it. Yet power stands in inverse ratio to size. The well-founded law that the shorter the wavelength the larger the energy that is compressed into it, produces the conclusion that "in a thimbleful of vacuum there is more . . . energy than would be released by all the atomic bomb fuel in the universe."[8] Stated in terms of particles instead of waves,

> the amount of energy associated with light corpuscles increases *as the size is reduced*. . . . The energy necessary to create a proton is contained in a light pulse only about 10^{-13} centimeter in diameter. And the energy of a million protons would be contained in a light pulse a million times smaller.[9]

As the principle has "no theoretical limit" (Arthur Young), speculation races toward the prospect that the energy of something that has no size at all—God?—might be infinite.

Item. Turning from physics to biology, we find the Gaia Hypothesis suggesting that causation descends from the animate to the inanimate in ways we had not suspected. Standard evolutionary theory depicts life as threading its way upward in an environment that is its opposite in being dead. The Gaia Hypothesis reverses this, suggesting that the remarkable life-supporting stability and coherence of the biosphere make it more plausible to think of it as some sort of enormous developing embryo. The earth is itself a form of life, "a complex entity involving the Earth's biosphere, atmosphere, oceans and soil; the totality constituting a feedback or cybernetic system which seeks an optimal physical and chemical environment for life on this planet. The physical and chemical condition of the surface of the Earth, of the atmosphere, and of the oceans has been and is actively made fit and comfortable by the presence of life itself."[10] Lewis Thomas notes that this hypothesis

> is beginning to stir up a few signs of storm, and if it catches on, as I think it will, we will soon find the biological community split into fuming factions, one side saying that the evolved biosphere displays evidence of design and purpose, the other decrying such heresy (ibid.).

The underlying question is whether the less or the more has the greater influence, and I have included these two items from science because major shifts in perspective are difficult and help from every quarter is useful.

In essential (if barest) outline, the primordial metaphysics is now before us. Before proceeding to the psychology and ethics that follow from it, let me state five features which, once this metaphysics had come to focus for me, I found impressive.

1. There is the sheer quantity of material it "gestalts" into a meaningful pattern. Its hierarchical character deserves much of the credit for this achievement, for chains of command are a proven way of introducing order into large numbers. An army without staff and line would be a mere rabble, and something of the same can be said of worldviews. The computer scientist Herbert Simon has described, in a parable, the efficiency that hierarchies make possible, and because it applies in its own way to the hierarchy in the great chain of being, the parable is worth inserting. Two watchmakers, Hora and

Tempus, both make watches composed of a thousand parts each. Hora assembles his watches piece by piece, so when he drops a watch he is working on it falls to pieces and he must begin from scratch. Tempus, for his part, assembles subassemblies of ten parts each, joins ten of these to make a larger subassembly of a hundred units, and then joins ten of these to make a complete watch. If he drops a part he is working on he will have to repeat at most ten assembling operations and possibly none. If we assume a ratio of one mishap in a hundred operations, it will take Hora four thousand times longer to assemble a watch; if Tempus can do it in a day, it will take Hora eleven years. And if for mechanical parts we substitute amino acids, protein molecules, organelles, and so on, the ratio between time scales becomes astronomical.

The levels of reality in the great chain of being form an analogue to the assemblies and subassemblies of Hora's watch. Each can be studied separately, after which only a manageable number of moves are required to bring them into an ordered whole. The marvels of the *terrestrial* plane are being unveiled at an astonishing rate by the physical sciences. The *intermediate* realm adds life and consciousness; biology helps with the former, and for light on the latter we can turn to the durable findings of phenomenology, depth psychology, and parapsychology, as well as aspects of shamanism and folk religion. The theologies of the great traditions describe God's knowable nature (the *celestial* plane) from a variety of cultural angles, and the literature of mysticism carries the mind as far as it can journey into God's absolute and infinite depths. Is anything of importance omitted in this ontic list? All worldviews must take account of everything in some way, but many do so by denying the existence of things their rivals consider important. Is it only because the perennial philosophy strikes me as true that it seems more generous in this regard? It validates so much that peoples have lived by. Many philosophies have no place for parapsychology, Jungian archetypes, or even phenomenology; many theologies no place for mysticism, other religions, or what falls under the rubric of folk religion. In the perennial philosophy these are all accorded a respectful place; science too, of course. It is as if the perennial philosophy were to say to the others: You are right in what you affirm. Only what you deny needs rethinking.

2. Not that it is all things to all people. If "a place for everything" shows its generous side, the sequel it appends, "and everything in its place," reveals its uncompromising, adamantine edge. That the lesser things (the lower rungs of being) really are inferior—to say nothing of not being the whole story—is, in its eyes, true and therefore not finally negotiable. Those who do not believe that higher realms exist will naturally not accept this. Such disagreements are unavoidable—worlds were not made for one another—but better serious controversy than a flabby tolerance that places agreement ahead of truth. The point is: the perennial philosophy is not relativistic, and this is a second thing that feels right about it. In calling his epochal discovery "relativity" Einstein all but named our age, which is riddled with relativities of unbelievable variety,[e] but what he actually unearthed was its opposite: invariance—the constancy of light's speed despite the apparent confusions, illusions, and contradictions produced by the relative motions or actions of gravity. It would have been better if Einstein had called his discovery "the invariance theory," as he considered doing, for not only is invariance more fundamental than the relativities it explains, it signals better what truth is after. "Timeless truth" sounds almost like a contradiction in terms today, but we need to believe that the truth we seek is rooted in the unchanging depths of the universe. For were it not, would it be worth the cost of the search, to say nothing of the cost it exacts once the discovery is made? More on the latter point in the section on ethics that follows.

---

[e]See, below, the section titled "The Possibility of Certitude" in Chapter 10.

3. Absolutes can lock one into a limited perspective, and as all perspectives *are* limited, some thinkers now nominate iconoclasm—the smashing of ideologies and all conceptual schemes—for the ruling virtue. This sounds a little like trying to run a farm by careful weeding and no planting, but the danger that prompts it is real, and the third thing that appeals to me in the perennial philosophy is the way it handles the issue. The problem—our need to believe while remaining open to better beliefs and what lies beyond belief altogether[f]—must be resolved existentially, through living it, but the guidelines the perennial philosophy proposes seem right. In insisting that the final reality, the infinite, is radically ineffable, it relativizes all concepts, formulations, and systems vis-à-vis *it*—the finger pointing at the moon is not the moon itself; "all things pass save for the face of God" (the Koran). Meanwhile the confident orientation life needs if it is to be lived well is met by saying that *within* the ballpark of outlooks and theories—at the human level the game of life must in part be played in that park—this outlook carries the day and will yield tomorrow only to fresh and perhaps improved expressions that continue its general trajectory.

4. This last statement may confirm a suspicion that could have been germinating for some time; namely, that the unchanging character of this philosophy—its static quality, if you will, as embossed in its very name, "perennial"—gives it a somewhat stagnant air. Where is the sense of intellectual excitement, the prospect of new worlds to discover? The answer brings us to the fourth feature of the perennial philosophy that I find convincing. No more in this philosophy than in any other is there

---

[f]What lies beyond belief altogether! "The starkness of . . . an incommensurable split between, on the one side, *language and the world included in language*, and, on the other side, *the unsayable and the world as unsayable* (sheer existence, immediacy of content, voiceless physiognomies, confronting the *I*)" was Wittgenstein's central vision and lifelong obsession (Henry Le Roy Finch, *Wittgenstein: The Later Philosophy* [Atlantic Highlands, N.J.: Humanities Press, 1977], p. 242).

the prospect of a stopping point in this life. The questions are *where* one wants to go and *with what*, one's mind only, or one's total self. In the domain of mind a distinction must be drawn between cumulative and noncumulative truth; we find the first kind in history and science where information snowballs, and the second kind in metaphysics, religion, and art where it does not. In the latter triumvirate a restless, insatiable appetite for novelty is like compulsive eating—fed by a disordered drive. What, twenty-five hundred years later, do we know about evil that Job did not know? That the question is rhetorical in no way means that adventure and discovery disappear. Their place in noncumulative knowledge is as lively as anywhere, but they face in a different, more important, direction: toward a deeper understanding of truths that are inexhaustible, and beyond this—here we move from mind to the total self—to the seasoning of one's being so understanding may phase into realization. The reservoir of noncumulative knowledge no more needs augmenting than, in the eyes of Robert Coles, Research Professor of Psychiatry at Harvard University, the data bank of psychiatry requires increase. Fully aware that to question the need for more research in that field is the gravest heresy one can risk, Coles proceeds to ask:

> What will psychiatry ever know that it does not know now about the damage done by thoughtless, cruel parents to vulnerable children? What further "frontiers" do we really have to conquer, when it comes to such subjects as despair, brutality, envy?

His answer:

> There is not much left for us to discover about man's fantasies, dreams, wishes, and doubts. The dynamics are all on the table, and in a way were there before Freud ever came along, as he acknowledged more than once. . . . We know all there is to know.[11]

When this statement is placed beside the following for the perennial philosophy, the similarity on the underlying point is striking.

> Few topics are so unrewarding as conventional laments about the "researches of the human mind" never being satisfied; in fact everything has been said already, though it is far from being the case that everyone has always understood it. There can therefore be no question of presenting "new truths"; what is needed in our time . . . is to provide some people with keys fashioned afresh—keys no better than the old ones but merely more elaborated—in an eternal script in the very substance of man's spirit.[12]

5. A fifth feature of the perennial philosophy I found compelling will complete this list: its ontic exuberance. Today it is mostly the sciences that are exuberant as they unveil a nature extravagant beyond belief. A million suns bursting into being each hour—it has been some time since a claim in contemporary philosophy knocked me down like that one did, yet it is no more than the latest sample to have chanced my way. What is hard to realize concretely is that the perennial philosophy upstages the best show science can manage. For without backing off in the slightest on numbers, it makes, as it were, a right-angle turn into a wholly new dimension: that of quality—qualitative experience, we might say, to make sure that it is not abstractions that we are talking about. To see what this involves, we might try to imagine the qualitative difference between the experience of a wood tick and ourselves, and then, continuing on in the same expanding direction, introduce orders of magnitude that science has accustomed us to: 10^{23} or whatever. Or collapse to the size of a drop the degree of reality in the terrestrial plane and then imagine the intermediate plane as an ocean—not oceanically large, but oceanically more real—balanced on top of it, repeating the operation (intermediate plane reduced to a drop, celestial plane the supervening ocean) until the infinite is reached. If our imaginations could concretely effect such moves we would have no difficulty understanding Plato's exclamation: "First a shudder runs through me, and then the old awe creeps over me."

To speak of upper planes as more real does not imply that lower ones are unreal or illusory, only less real. Nor does it impugn their worth, for not only does each have its place in the entire scheme; matter anywhere, hosting its master, can become a temple of its Lord. Though I have tried to offset the suspicion that higher and lower on the chain of being involve spatial separation, it may help if we convert the chain into concentric circles with the lower, lesser realms located inside the higher ones in which they "live and move and have their being." Always the less is permeated by the more; the problem is to see this. But it can be seen. "There is no rung of being on which you cannot find the Holiness of being," said Martin Buber. "God's is-ness (*istigkect*) is my is-ness, neither less nor more," said Meister Eckhart. And Hakuin:

> *This earth where we stand is the Pure Lotus Land,*
> *And this very body the body of Buddha.*
> ("Chant in Praise of Zazen")

With the metaphysics of the perennial philosophy in place, the essentials of its psychology and ethics can be dubbed in quickly.

2. Psychology

"The psychology that finds in the soul something similar to, or even identical with, divine Reality." I know of no more efficient way to elucidate Huxley's summary here than through a commentary on the diagram from *Forgotten Truth* on the following page:

In his *Religio Medici* Sir Thomas Browne wrote, "Man is the great amphibian whose nature is disposed to live, not only like other creatures in diverse elements, but in divided and distinguished worlds." These "divided and distinguished worlds" are the multiple levels of reality the preceding section set forth, and in the perennial psychology the human self intersects them all. That they erupt in inverse order, the lesser now appearing above the greater (body above mind, etc.) is appropriate, for microcosm mirrors macrocosm (man mirrors the universe), and mirrors invert. Envisioned externally, the good dons metaphors of height; but when we reverse our gaze and look inward, our value-imagery transposes: it turns over. Within us the best lies deepest; it is basic, fundamental, the ground of our being. The way *body* and *mind* correlate with the terrestrial and intermediate planes is obvious; the former swim, as it were, in the latter. Theists will have no difficulty recognizing the *soul*—final locus of our individuality—as engaged in I-Thou relation with the knowable God. More controversial is the contention that (in Huxley's formulation) there is "in the soul

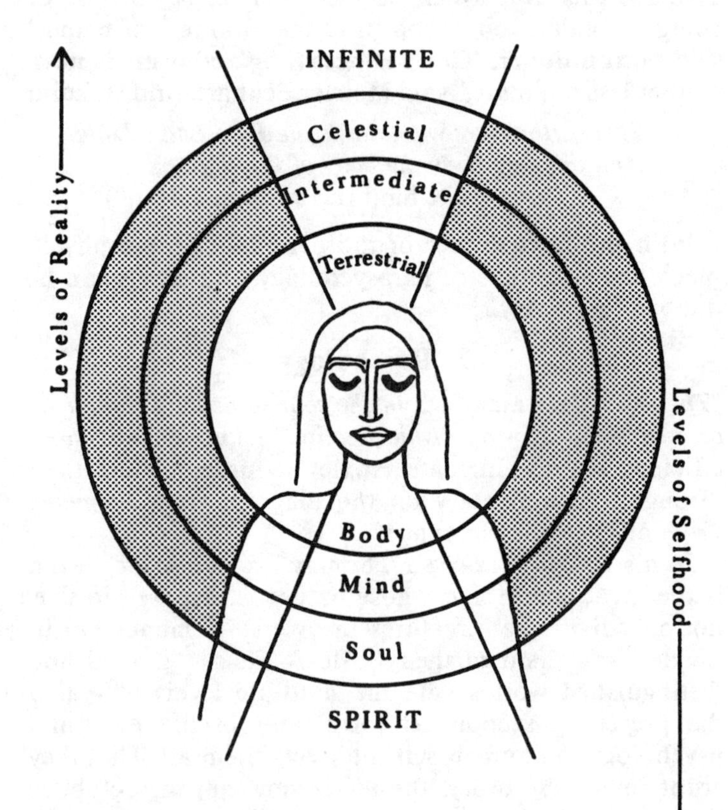

something similar to, or even identical with, divine Reality." In the diagram this something is named *spirit.*

The lines of the dispute have, in the course of the centuries, become recognizable. If you persist in walking north, there comes a moment when, though you think you are still headed north, you are actually moving south, for in the preceding step you unwittingly crossed the pole. Theists use this analogy to argue that though mystics think they are entering deeper into God's nature with their notions of spirit and infinite, they are actually departing from the living God who is Lord of history, particularity, community and decision. This is not the place (even were there wish) to argue the mystic's reply to this objection. The issue is rich in subtleties; what, for example, is one to make of Saint Paul's assertion that "the word of God is quick and powerful, and sharper than any two-edged sword, piercing even to *the dividing asunder of soul and spirit*" (Hebrews 4:12, emphasis added; see preceding diagram where soul and spirit are demarcated)? But as the perennial psychology obviously allows an important place for the mystic, reasons must be given for its doing so.

No feature of our nature is more undeniable than its duality: we have a "me" that is circumscribed, and an "I" which, in its awareness of this circumscription gives evidence of being itself exempt from it. The mystic is drawn to this "I"; s/he fixes on it, labors to develop his/her sense of its reality, and generally tries to identify with it as much as possible. And as noncircumscription is its essence, there is nothing that separates it in principle from the infinite. Unconsciously dwelling at our inmost center; beneath the surface shuttlings of our sensations, precepts, and thoughts; wrapped in the envelope of soul (which too is finally porous) is the eternal and the divine, the final Reality: not soul, not personality, but All-Self beyond all selfishness; spirit enwombed in matter and wrapped round with psychic traces. Within every phantom-self dwells this divine; within all creatures incarnate sleeps the Infinite Sentience—unevolved, hidden, unfelt, unknown, yet destined from all eternity to waken at last and, tearing away the ghostly web of sensuous mind, break forever its chrysalis of flesh and pass beyond all space and time.

In the language of the great affirmations, spirit is the Atman that *is* Brahman, the Buddha-nature that appears when our finite selves get out of its way, my *istigkect* (is-ness) which, once we stop standing in our own light, we see is God's is-ness. Back of every wave stands the entire ocean; "the deeper I go within myself, the more I find that which is beyond myself," as Gabriel Marcel said. We catch glimmers of this unbounded "I" in moments when we are so totally engrossed in a task that no attention for our finite self remains—in I/me terms, no "me" appears at all. The need, though, is not to try to anticipate what this desideratum would be like, but rather to see that life's ballast can lodge at any of the four levels of selfhood our diagram depicts; all are present in everyone, but they are actualized to different degrees. In a catalogue that would sound elitist and self-righteous if it were not read as a project for oneself:

> a life that identifies primarily with its physical pleasures and needs ("getting and spending we lay waste our days") is superficial;
>
> one that advances its attention to mind can be interesting;
>
> if it moves on to the heart (synonym for soul) it can be good;
>
> and if it passes on to spirit—that saving self-forgetfulness and egalitarianism in which one's personal interests loom no larger than those of others—it would be perfect.

How far life can move in this direction may be left an open question. It is the direction that is indicated, not the distance covered, that counts.

What needs to be added is the epistemological bearing of this "ballast lowering," if we may continue to use this metaphor for the deepening of self that results as its center of gravity settles progressively into the arms of being and becomes more stable in consequence. The perennial epistemology respects reason, but in the way one respects a fine tool; what it accomplishes depends more on who uses it than its own perfection. If it is a power tool, we can visualize outlets on the various levels of being, but now let science fiction enter. The power that increases as the outlets ascend is magical in enabling the tool (reason) to accomplish qualitatively greater marvels as it passes from one to the next; the higher the socket into which reason is plugged, the greater the wonders it can effect. In this somewhat cumbersome image, the outlets represent an intellective capacity that empowers reason and provides the degree of luminosity it enjoys but which must be clearly distinguished *from* reason. Call it the intuitive intellect and see that, while it is always fully present in everyone in the way spirit is—in the end it *is* spirit, but that's a different story—it is actualized to different degrees as the differently powered sockets suggest. If it is not too awkward to join the power-tool image to the earlier one of ontological ballast, the picture that results is as follows: reason plugged in to a life that is fixated on the bodily level will detect little more than matter and will spin a materialistic worldview. Things other than matter will be evident to someone who takes his mind seriously, and *his* reason will fashion an outlook that ranges from animism in traditional societies to naturalism in the contemporary West. To those who, their hearts having been opened, can see with *its* eye (the Sufi's "eye of the heart"; Plato's "eye of the soul"), spiritual objects will be discernible and a theistic metaphysics will emerge. The final "night vision" which can detect the awefilled holiness of everything is reserved for those whom, in this essay, I have called mystics.

A section that has already become something of a junk yard for metaphors can stand one more. The divisions between the levels of reality are like one-way mirrors. Looking up, we see only reflections of the level we are on; looking down, the mirrors become plate glass and cease to exist. On the highest plane even the glass is removed, and immanence reigns. To anticipate the sentence that begins the next section: looking up from planes that are lower, God is radically transcendent (*ganz anders*; wholly other); looking down, from heights that human vision (too) can to varying degrees attain, God is absolutely immanent.

3. Ethic

"The ethic that places man's final end in the knowledge of the immanent and transcendent Ground of all being."

A few years ago the *Review of Metaphysics* published an essay by Jacob Needleman with the arresting title, "Why Philosophy is Easy." In the past, Needleman noted, philosophy was thought to be anything but easy. Only the ablest citizens were expected to undertake it, and even they, only after training not only their minds but their bodies, their emotions, and their wills as well. This has of course changed. Today everyone is encouraged to try his or her hand at the art, even high school students. The switch has occurred because rational abilities are now considered the only prerequisites. The reason the others have been dropped, Needleman goes on to say, is that the wisdom the modern philosopher seeks through his philosophy is no longer a new state of being. "The abandonment of this [former] objective more than any single conceptualized point of view," he concludes, is what "distinguishes modern philosophy from so much of ancient and medieval philosophy."[13]

The difference becomes apparent when we note the kinds of experience the two philosophies appeal to. Modern philosophy's touchstone is *generic* experience: experiences of perception, linguistic usage, moral decisions, and the like, that are familiar to us all. Because Ernest Gellner is unique in being not only a philosopher in his own right but also a sociologist who studies philosophers and their discipline professionally, I shall refer to his findings more than once in these essays. His report on the present point is that beliefs, if they are to be considered legitimate today, must pass "the empiricist insistence that [they] be judged by . . . something reasonably close to the ordinary notion of experience."[14] This comes close to being the exact opposite of philosophy's former goal, which was to realign the components of the soul in ways that would enable it to experience the world in an *un*ordinary way—a way so *extra*ordinary, in fact, that from its perspective, passion-and-ignorance-laden ordinary experience seems almost psychotic. It is the abandonment of this former, exalted objective that makes contemporary philosophy relatively easy.

I have used Needleman's point to introduce this brief section on ethics because it helps us to position that enterprise in the primordial outlook. An ethic is an assemblage of guidelines for effecting the self-transformation that enables the world to be experienced in a new way. In doing so, it is integrally related to anthropology on the one hand and epistemology and ontology on the other: revised, reformed conduct (ethics) leads to a new condition of self (anthropology) which includes as its principal yield the capacity to see and know (epistemology) the world (ontology) more truly as it is.[g]

As for the content of the primordial ethic—which in *The Abolition of Man* C. S. Lewis refers to as the *Tao*, meaning by that the value system in which the moral imperatives of

---

[g]Occasionally we find a modern philosopher echoing this claimed link between ethics and outlook, as in this statement by William James: "Practice may change our theoretical horizon, and this in a twofold way: it may lead into new worlds and secure new powers. Knowledge we could never attain, remaining what we are, may be attainable in consequence of higher powers and a higher life, which we may morally achieve." (Quoted in Aldous Huxley, *Perennial Philosophy*, p. viii.)

There are also Wittgenstein's famous assertions: "The philosopher's treatment . . . is like the treatment of an illness. . . . Sickness . . . is cured by an alteration in the mode of life of human beings. . . . Pretensions are a mortgage which burdens a philosopher's capacity to think." (Compiled from *Philosophical Investigations*, p. 225; *Remarks on the Foundations of Mathematics*, p. 57; and *On Certainty*, p. 549.) Well and good, but what does modern philosophy do with such occasional asides? What is the altered "mode of life" that is intimated? How is it achieved?

all the major traditions coalesce—it condenses (in Western idiom) in the virtues of humility, charity, and veracity; alternatively (expressed negatively and in Asian idiom), it focuses on the three poisons that work against those virtues, the poisons being greed, aversion, and ignorance. Humility has nothing to do with low self-esteem. It is the capacity to distance oneself from one's private, separate ego to the point where one can see it objectively and therefore accurately, as counting for one, but not more *than* one, even as charity sees one's neighbor as counting fully *for* one. Both these initial virtues, which pertain to the human order, announce the arrival into that order of the third virtue, veracity—the capacity to see things in what Buddhists call their *suchness*; the way they actually, accurately, objectively *are*. With self and other made interchangeable through this objective, numerical "one," humility is seen as looking on oneself as if one were another (and as severely as truth allows, but not more), while charity is to look on the other as if he were oneself (as indulgently as truth allows, but again not more). These terse pronouncements show that the primordial ethic in no way neglects the interpersonal, but as its attention never strays far from the whole, what comes through most strongly in its ethical discussions is the cosmic alignment that the virtues effect. To pick up again with humility: to be freed of self is to become emptied and hollow; in this hollow, as Annie Dillard says, you catch grace as a man fills his cup under a waterfall. Or to tie the hollowness to sound, for our ears to hear the music of the spheres its amplitude must be raised. We must turn ourselves into resounding songboxes, carving out careful emptinesses like those in cellos and violins.

To return to epistemology, if wisdom, the capacity to see things as they truly are, is a correlate of virtue,[h] it

[h] "Virtue . . . is necessary, for light does not go through an opaque stone and barely illuminates a black wall; so man must become like crystal or like snow, but without pretending that snow is light" (Frithjof Schuon, *Spiritual Perspectives and Human Facts* [London: Perennial Books, 1969], p. 178).

requires methods for *acquiring* that virtue. It is not necessary here to detail those methods, the spiritual exercises and "eightfold paths" of the various historical traditions; only the general point need be noted. The perennial philosophy is a path to be walked as much as it is a map that charts that path. Knowing and doing, wisdom and method, work together; they walk hand in hand. Close from the start, they draw increasingly so, to the point where it becomes difficult to tell them apart. In Marco Pallis's formulation, wisdom comes to look increasingly like static method (counsels as to how to live) and method like dynamic wisdom (the way wisdom would appear were it enacted).

Two final points:

First. Against the current tendency to glorify one's own inner promptings—the state of "Saint Ego" wherein nothing seems quite so wonderful and worth heeding as some aspect of one's own self—the primordial outlook notes that if those promptings were reliable we would be at the end of our journey, not its start. The most useful service they can perform is to guide one to a tradition that contains the winnowed wisdom of a civilization or culture. It is difficult to imagine a verdict that favors that wisdom over private judgment more categorically than this one by the social psychologist Donald Campbell—that he arrives at it through scientific considerations only augments its force. "On evolutionary grounds," Campbell writes,

> it is just as rational to follow religious traditions which one does not understand as it is rational to continue breathing air before one understands the role of oxygen in bodily metabolism. If modern psychology and social science disagree with religious tradition on ways of living one should, on rational and scientific grounds, choose the traditional recipes for life for these are the better tested. Priests who narrow the precious tradition which they transmit to that pittance which they themselves can understand and agree with are neglecting their duty and are guilty of hubris or pretension of omniscience.[15]

Second. I have spoken here only of ethics' personal dimension. Social ethics is more complicated, and is reserved for essay number nine, in Part Three.

Notes

1. New York: Harper and Brothers, 1945, p. vii.
2. Frithjob Schuon. *The Transcendent Unity of Religions* (Wheaton, IL: Theosophical Publishing House, 1984), p. 20.
3. *The Degrees of Knowledge* (New York: Charles Scribner's Sons, 1959), p. 59.
4. *Janus: A Summing Up* (New York: Vintage Press, 1979), pp. 289-90.
5. Arthur Lovejoy, *The Great Chain of Being* (Cambridge: Harvard University Press, 1936), pp. 59, 26.
6. *The Varieties of Religious Experience* (New York: Longmans, Green & Co., 1902).
7. *Some Problems of Philosophy* (New York: Longmans, Green & Co., 1911), p. 101.
8. Quoted in Harold Schilling, *The New Consciousness in Science and Religion* (Philadelphia: United Church Press, 1973), p. 110.
9. Arthur Young, *Which Way Out?* (Berkeley: Robert Briggs Associates, 1980), p. 2. In David Bohm's formulation: "If one computes the amount of energy that would be in one cubic centimetre of space, with . . . the shortest wavelength that should be considered as contributing to the 'zero-point' energy of space . . . it turns out to be very far beyond the total energy of all the matter in the known universe" (*Wholeness and the Implicate Order* [London: Routledge & Kevan Paul, 1980], pp. 190-91).
10. Quoted in Lewis Thomas, "Debating the Unknowable," *Atlantic Monthly,* July 1981, p. 51. See J. E. Lovelock, *Gaia* (Oxford University Press, 1979).
11. "The Limits of Psychiatry," *The Progressive,* May 1967, pp. 32-33.
12. Frithjof Schuon, *Understanding Islam* (Baltimore: Penguin Books, 1972), p. 7.
13. Jacob Needleman, "Why Philosophy Is Easy," *Review of Metaphysics* 22, no. 1 (September 1968): 3-4.
14. *The Legitimation of Belief* (Cambridge: Cambridge University Press, 1974), p. 206.
15. From the prospectus of a seminar on "Social Evolution and the Authority of Religious Tradition."

Part Three

LOOKING AROUND

An Angle on Our Times

When the primordial tradition first jumped seriously to my attention, my mind had evidently reached a stage of saturated solution which needed but the shock of the right contact to recrystallize in forms that were a revelation. The world they brought to view was not categorically different; it was rather that it glistened in sharp focus.

When invitations came my way to comment on several aspects of contemporary culture—higher education, the humanities, theology, science, and the place of social concern—I found I now had things I wanted to say. The essays that register those thoughts form the third section of this book, beginning with the current state of higher education.

4

EXCLUDED KNOWLEDGE

A Critique of the Modern Western Mind-Set *

> ***The learning of the imagination can remain an excluded knowledge only so long as the premises of material science remain unquestioned and their exclusions undetected.***
>
> Kathleen Raine

The editor of this journal has done something unusual. He has invited me to present my thoughts precisely because they "are not shared by most educators today," which is to say not shared by most readers of this journal. I have been eager to get on with some other work, but I find this concern to get at fundamental issues compelling. I shall write in a personal vein because I think that an indication of how I came to the atypical views that have impressed themselves on me will help throw into relief what those views are. And if (beginning with my title) I sound brash and argumentative, I hope the reader will understand that this is to get huge issues into sharp focus in small compass.

I begin with the journey that brought me to where I now am.

I. Preliminaries

My first book chanced to be on education.[a] It was well received. Robert Ulich, perhaps the grand old man of

*Reprinted with permission from *Teachers College Record*, vol. 80, 3 November 1979.

[a]Huston Smith, ***The Purposes of Higher Education*** (New York: Harper & Brothers, 1955). "Chanced" is the exact word here, for the book

educational philosophy at that time, rated it above the famed 1945 "Redbook," Harvard University's *General Education in a Free Society*.

Thanks to this early and, as the preceding footnote indicates, almost fortuitous venture into educational theory, the professionals in that field seem for twenty years to have considered me one of them—at least I have felt included. When teaching encountered the new medium of television, the American Council on Education asked me to consider the implications.[1] The American Broadcasting Company included me in its 1962 "Meet the Professor" series. I was invited to deliver the 1964 Annual Lecture to The John Dewey Society,[2] and in that same year to assess the state of the humanities for the fiftieth anniversary issue of Liberal Education.[3] When T-groups and "encounter" came along, the National Training Laboratories, an arm of the National Education Association, invited me to Bethel, Maine, to consider the role of group dynamics in the learning process;[4] and when political rumbles broke out on college campuses in the late 1960s, Phi Beta Kappa asked me for an analysis of the traumas Vietnam and other factors were occasioning higher education.[5] I have lost count of the educational conferences I have participated in, but find that at least two produced printed fallout.[6]

I have included these autobiographical paragraphs to make the point that in education theory I have not been an outsider. For the bulk of my career I have been emphatically "in." Why, then, am I now out?—"out," I

---

almost did not get written. Had I not run into a professor of speech who said he had been meaning to tell me that he was using a committee report I had written in his choral reading class, that report would have remained buried in my files until discarded. As it was, the idea of a committee report being intoned as art was so bizarre that I unearthed the document and reread it. It was the report of a committee that had been appointed to define the aims of liberal education at the university where I was then teaching (Washington University, St. Louis), and finding that it did read passably, I dispatched it to a publisher. The reply was back in a week. The contents had to be expanded tenfold, but a contract was enclosed.

want to stress, only in that my views have grown atypical, not that my feelings are estranged. The shape of my ideas may have taken a curious turn, but my interests in ideas themselves has never been livelier. I remain a teacher,[b] and I have never doubted that given the vocational slots of the modern world, the university is my home.

As for the content of my thoughts, which (as has been indicated) now run rather counter to the prevailing academic mindset, they are spelled out in the book that brought the invitation to write this essay. Titled *Forgotten Truth: The Primordial Tradition,* it was published by Harper and Row in 1976; the Colophon paperback appeared a year later. I shall be itemizing the book's key claims and arguing their validity, but before doing so let me enter a final propaedeutic. I want to note how the opposition between truth as I now see it and the prevailing contemporary mindset broke upon my awareness.

It came into view through the conjunction of two elements that, once I got them sorted out, bounced off each other like antagonists. Even so, they had no choice but to keep on interacting—honing my perceptions of each; getting their outlines into clearer and clearer focus—because both were locked within me. Call the components East and West or past and present, the facts are that I was born and raised in China and sometime later found myself teaching at M.I.T. A more unlikely conjunction of opposites would be difficult to imagine. China (the China of my boyhood at least) represented tradition and the past, whereas M.I.T. stood for "the future in microcosm," as we liked to say. China was religious (folk religion, mostly, but religious all the same), whereas M.I.T. was secular—its chapel has no windows, as if the architect were saying, "No hope for transcendence here unless

[b]I almost wrote "born teacher," for when my father built his children a workshop I lost no time in converting it into a schoolroom. Tools were shelved, benches brought in, and my younger brother and the servants' children—we were in China—impressed for pupils. And I? I assumed the podium as if authorized by the Mandate of Heaven, if not the Tao itself. The sensation has never left me. Imprinting is too weak. It is enough to make one consider reincarnation.

you blot out the Institute completely." And China was humanistic whereas M.I.T. was scientific.

Pulled in these opposite directions, my fifteen years in Cambridge were tumultuous. They were also exhilarating, absorbing, and above all instructive. As they progressed I discovered, first, an organic connection between the three terms on each side of the divide: optimally defined, it seemed to me, "traditional," "religious," and "humanistic" have more in common than I had realized, as do "modern," "secular," and "scientific." But then came the surprise. I found that if I stayed with the problem instead of capitulating to accepted ways of construing things—giving in to Bacon's "idols of the theater"—there was no way I could avoid the conclusion that truth sides more with the first of these two sets of triumvirates than with the second.

Before I say why that conclusion seemed forced on me, let me introduce the two antagonists—the two contenders for truth—more properly. For simplicity's sake I shall refer to the first triumvirate as tradition and the second as modernity. The gist of their differences is that modernity, spawned essentially by modern science, stresses quantity[c] (in order to get at power and control) whereas tradition stresses quality (and the participation that is control's alternative). That's the nub of the matter, but the assertion is compact, so I shall amplify it.

The point is this. Before the rise of modern science in the seventeenth century, the entire world, humanly speaking,[d] was wrapped in an outlook that had embraced

---

[c]Cf. René Guénon. *The Reign of Quantity* (Baltimore, Md.: Penguin Books, 1972), and this statement by Gerald Holton: "The difficulty has perhaps been not that this new way [of separating primary quantifiable properties from secondary qualitative ones] was too hard, but that it turned out to be all too easy. Once the scientists of the seventeenth century had found the key to this particular gate, the road that opened beyond led more speedily and deeply into remote and fascinating territory, further from the original ground of understanding the world" (*Thematic Origins of Scientific Thought* [Cambridge: Harvard University Press, 1973], p. 440).

[d]"Entire" overstates the case slightly, but not much. Mary Douglas tells us in *Natural Symbols* that every type of society, from the most secular to the most religious, can be found in the tribal world, but my point concerns proportions.

it from its start, the outlook that in the subtitle to *Forgotten Truth* I designate "The Primordial Tradition." I must describe that outlook of course, but let me back into doing so. As it was science that unhorsed tradition, if we understand what science is we shall be on our way toward understanding the soul of the perspective it dislodged.

II. The Nature of Science

I agree with those who say that science is not one thing, but to conclude that its multiple facets are joined by no more than "family resemblances" gives up the hunt too quickly.[e] There is a discernible thrust to these facets, which this diagram from my just mentioned book is designed to identify.

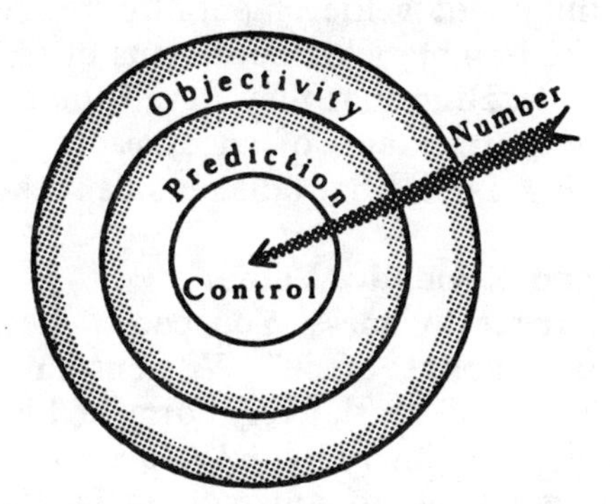

[e]A quick review of the signification that led up to the current meaning of our word "science" can help orient us for what follows. *Scientia* in the classical world meant reasoned disclosure of something for the sake of the disclosure itself. Up to the seventeenth century such disclosure consisted largely of classifications of things that were qualitatively different, but after Galileo it became the search for nature's quantitative laws. The German *Wissenschaft*, however, continues to carry broader denotations than our English "science" and includes all scholarly disciplines; it is in this German sense, for example, that Marxism claims to be scientific. It is my contention that our English word has come to refer basically to what goes on in the natural or empirical sciences and their mathematical underpinnings. In saying that "physics is a science," no one feels it necessary to warn his hearer that he means that it is a natural science, whereas "sociology is a science" will provoke dispute if the qualifying adjective "social," functioning here as a diminutive, is not added.

No knowledge deserves to be called scientific unless it is objective in the sense of laying claim to intersubjective agreement. Many things meet this initial requirement, however, without being scientific in any rigorous sense—court testimony, for example. We move closer to science proper when we come to truths that enable us to predict[f]—what cannot be falsified is not scientific—and closer still when we reach truths that facilitate control. Each move we make toward the center finds our knowing increasingly locked into mathematics, number being (as is often remarked) the language of science. Numbers lend themselves to the objectivity and precision science seeks because, unlike words, they are unambiguous—more on this later.

The achievements of this thrust toward truth—I am thinking of the noetic achievement of pure science quite as much as the pragmatic achievements of technology—have been so dazzling that they have blinded us to the fact that they are products of an exceedingly restricted kind of knowing. Look what falls outside its ken:

1. Intrinsic and Normative Values

"Values. A terrible business. You can at best stammer when you talk about them," Wittgenstein remarked, illustrating his point by the very form of his utterance. Science can deal with instrumental values but not intrinsic ones. It can tell us that nonsmoking is conducive to health, but whether health is intrinsically better than somatic gratification it cannot adjudicate. Again, it can determine what people do like (descriptive values) but not what they should like (normative values). Market

[f]B. F. Skinner stands as a parody of the lengths to which science's concern for predictability can drive a man. When it was suggested to him sometime back that it would be a mistake for psychology to take a position on determinism that the Heisenberg Principle had shown to be unsupportable in physics, Skinner replied that the "muddle of physics" was physics' worry, not psychology's. From the fact that electrons are unpredictable, he seemed to be saying, it doesn't follow that human behavior cannot be predicted. See T. W. Mann, ed., *Behaviorism and Phenomenology* (Chicago: University of Chicago Press, 1964), pp. 139-40.

research and opinion polls are sciences but there can be no science of the *summum bonum*.

2. Purposes

To attribute an intentional character to what happens in nature is anthropomorphic, and anthropomorphic explanations are the opposite of scientific ones. For science to get down to work seriously, Aristotle's final causes had to be banished and the field left free for explanation in terms of efficient causes only. "The cornerstone of scientific method is . . . the *systematic* denial that 'true' knowledge can be got at by interpreting phenomena in terms of final causes—that is to say, of 'purpose.' "[7]

3. Global and Existential Meanings

Science itself is meaningful throughout, but there are two kinds of meaning it cannot get at. One of these is global meanings—what is the meaning of it all? It is as if the scientist were inside a large plastic balloon; he can shine his torch anywhere on the balloon's interior but cannot climb outside the balloon to view it as a whole, see where it is situated, or determine why it was fabricated. The other kind of meaning science cannot handle is existential: it is powerless to force the human mind to find its discoveries meaning*ful*. Let the discovery be as impressive as you please; the knower always has the option to shrug his shoulders and walk away. Having no handle on meanings of these two specific kinds, science "fails in the face of all ultimate questions" (Jaspers) and leaves "the problems of life . . . completely untouched" (Wittgenstein).

4. Quality

This is basic to the lot, for it is their qualitative dimensions that give values, meanings, and purposes their pride of place in life. Yet it is precisely this qualitative dimension that eludes the quantitative measuring grid that science must try, at least, to impose on events if they are to become precise data. Certain qualities (such as tones or colors) are connected with quantifiable substrates (light waves of varying lengths), but quality itself is unmeasurable. Being a subjective experience, it cannot be laid out on a public chopping block; being a simple experience, it cannot be dissected even introspectively. In consequence, it is "refractory to measurement"—not just provisionally, but in principle.

> We cannot say that in experience one light has twice the brightness of another. The terms in which we measure experience of a sound are not terms of experience. They are terms of the stimulus, the physical sound, or of the nervous or other bodily action concomitant with the experience. . . . The search . . . for a scale of equivalence between energy and mental experience arrives at none.[8]

Qualities are either perceived for what they are or they are not so perceived, and nothing can convey their nature to anyone who cannot perceive it directly. The most that one can do is to compare things that have a quality with things that do not, and even then the comparison is meaningful only to persons who know from experience what the quality in question is. Science's inability to deal with the qualitatively unmeasurable leaves it dealing with what Lewis Mumford called a "disqualified universe."

This account of what science cannot deal with is certain to encounter resistance. Not, as far as I have been able to discover, because it is untrue. All that would be required to show that it is untrue would be a counterexample—a single instance in which science has produced precise and provable knowledge concerning a normative value, a final cause, an existential or global meaning, or an intrinsic quality. Considering the importance of these four domains for human life—for three hundred years mankind has all but held its breath waiting for science to close in on them—the fact that it has made no inroads whatever would seem to be a clear sign that science is not fashioned to deal with them. The reason we resist science's limitations is not factual but psychological—we don't want to face up to them. For science is what the modern world believes in. Since it has authored our world, to lose faith in it, as to some extent we must if we admit that its competence is limited, is to lose faith in our kind of world. Such loss of faith would be comparable to the crisis that would have visited the Middle Ages had it suddenly discovered that God was only semicompetent—that he was not God but just another god. The fall of a God is no small matter.

The moves to avoid admitting the limitations of science take two turns. It is argued either that science is not as I depict it; or that it is, but its character will change.

1. *First objection:* Science is not as I depict it. It is more flexible, more human, and more humane than I make it appear.

a. First version: Scientists are as human as the rest of us. Their idealism, warmth, and natural piety—a quotation from Einstein on his mystical feeling for the universe can be expected—is as well developed as the next man's.

Answer: I have said nothing to the contrary. I am talking neither about the persons who discover scientific truths nor about the ends to which their truths are directed—ends that obviously can be either helpful or destructive. I am talking about the character of scientific truth itself.

b. Second version: I make it sound as if there were a single scientific method that delivers discoveries almost on command, whereas in fact that method—insofar as there is a method in the singular—is as "human" as any other. It is human both in the noble sense of pivoting on distinctively human capacities for inspiration and imagination, and in the less noble, "all too human" sense of being subject to pitfalls. Science is fallible. False starts, blind alleys, inhouse vendettas, and dishonesty all figure in its record. (Citations from Michael Polanyi, Thomas Kuhn, Abraham Maslow, and James Watson's *The Double Helix*.)

Answer: If the preceding confusion lay in failure to separate scientific truth from the persons who discover it on the one hand, and from the ends to which it is put on the other, the confusion here lies in conflating such truth with the processes by which it is reached—the psychology and sociology of scientific discovery. The routes by which scientists arrive at their discoveries may be as inspired, diverse, and fallible as one pleases—I personally think Feyerabend's *Against Method* goes too far, but I agree that the scientific method can never be completely formalized. But again, that is not what I am talking about. My eye is not on how science is acquired. It is on the truth its acquisition-process arrives at. Or more precisely, it is on the defining features of such truth—the kind of truth science tries to get at.

c. Third version: I make objectivity the minimum requirement of scientific knowledge just when we are coming to see that there is no such thing.

Answer: Here the confusion is between two meanings of objectivity. Science need not be objective in the sense of claiming to mirror the way things are in themselves—the so-called camera theory of knowledge. One can even go so far as to say that in its frontier reaches science says very little about what nature itself is like; mostly it tells us how it responds to the experiments we direct toward it, with the result that these experiments must themselves figure in our conclusions as to what has been disclosed. Knowing of this kind is indeed subjective in the sense of conforming to a knowing subject. But this kind of subjectivity does not touch the objectivity science demands as its admissions ticket, which (to repeat) is consensual agreement. Man may be as implicated in his knowing as you please; science asks only that he be implicated generically rather than idiosyncratically—that he be implicated as physicist, say, rather than as Jones or Smith.

2. So much for the first objection, that science is not as I have depicted it. The *second objection* accepts my account as applicable for today's science but not necessarily for tomorrow's.

Answer: Obviously science will change in many respects; the question is: Will its changes be of the sort that enable it to deal with the values, purposes, meanings, and qualities it has thus far neglected? (The change from classical to relativity physics was momentous, but it changed nothing in physics' stance toward the four lacunae I keep citing.) If science is to deal with these lacunae, it will have to relax the demands for objectivity, prediction, control, and number that have excluded it from qualitative domains while producing its power in quantitative ones. We are free, of course, to turn science in this new direction, a direction that is actually old in that it points back to the preseventeenth-century, partly-alchemical notion of what science should be. What we must realize is that every step taken toward humanizing science in the sense of moving it into the four fields it has thus far ignored will be a step away from its effectiveness in the sense of its power-to-control. For it is precisely from the narrowness of its approach that the power of modern science derives. An effective and restricted science or one that is ample but does not enable us to control the course of events much more than do art, religion, or psychotherapy—we can of course define the word as we wish. What is not possible is to have it both ways.

As this issue of the *Record* focuses on values that include religion, this section on science should perhaps be rounded off by noting that the stress I place on the differences between science and religion runs counter to the prevailing trend, which is to accent their similarities, a trend that has led theologians to appreciate Teilhard de Chardin, Michael Polanyi, and Thomas Kuhn (for all their merits) perhaps extravagantly. I think this bedfellows approach holds dangers. We see, I think, what prompts the approach. If it can be shown that science resembles religion, perhaps the credibility of the first will rub off onto the second. The kicker, however, is this: the similarities that are being made so much of in the current science/religion discussions concern person (the scientist who does science), method (how science is done), or application (the uses to which science is put), none of which, taken individually or even collectively, rival in importance a fourth issue, namely, the kind of knowledge science seeks. Science has advanced to the unrivaled respect it now enjoys by virtue of the kind of knowledge it has discovered and the control to which such knowledge lends itself. It is with reference to this kind of knowledge, therefore, that it deserves to be defined and by our society will be defined—alternative proposals by theologians or philosophers are not going to change this. The result is that any credibility rub-off from science onto religion that may derive from associating the two will be outweighed by the pull to conform religious truth to scientific: the more religion is linked with top-dog science, the greater will be the expectation that its truth conform to the top dog's successful mold. The process is subtle but very strong. It is at work in the academic study of religion where objectivity has already become an almost undisputed norm.

III. The Traditional, and in Effect Primordial, Outlook

I hope that the preceding section has not cast scientists in the role of white-coated bad guys. I do not know if science has brought more harm or good even to date, much less what the long-term balance will show. Pointing fingers nowhere save at ourselves—at us, denizens of the modern world in general, and even here there is no finger pointing really; we would have had to have been prescient demigods for what has happened not to have happened—I am occupied with a single phenomenon, quite a simple one really. When attention turns toward something it turns away from something else. The triumphs of modern science—all in the material world, remember—have swung our attention toward the world's material aspects. The consequence—could anything be more natural?—has been progressive inattention to certain of the world's other properties. Stop attending to something and first we forget its importance; from there it is only a matter of time till one begins to wonder if it exists at all.[g] But let me invoke another voice to make my point more graphically.

---

[g]An example at hand: The item I wrote just before starting this present essay was a review of Bollingen's two-volume posthumous

In his posthumous *A Guide for the Perplexed*, a book that appeared a year after *Forgotten Truth* and parallels it to the point that it can be read as the same book for a different audience, E. F. (*Small Is Beautiful*) Schumacher tells of being lost while sight-seeing in Leningrad. He was consulting his pocket map when an interpreter stepped up and offered to help. When he pointed on the map to where they were standing, Schumacher was puzzled. "But these large churches around us, they aren't on the map," he protested. "We don't show churches on our maps," he was informed. "But that's not so," Schumacher persisted. "That church over there—it is on the map." "Oh, that," the guide responded. "That's no longer a church. It's a museum."

Comparably, Schumacher goes on to say, with the philosophical map his Oxford education provided him: Most of the things that most of mankind has considered most important throughout its history didn't show on it. Or if they did, they showed as museum pieces—things people used to believe about the world but believe no longer.

The anecdote provides an ideal entrée to the traditional world view in suggesting modernity omits something—as the title of my just cited book puts the matter, it has forgotten something. This something, which constitutes the ontological divide that separates tradition and modernity, is higher realms of being—domains of existence that begin precisely where science stops. "Higher" functions metaphorically here, of course—the additional realms are not spatially removed. But if we discount this literal, spatial sense of higher, they are superior in every (other) way. They are more important. They exert more power. They are less ephemeral. They are more integrated. They are more sentient and therefore more beneficent. And

---

compilation of the writings of A. K. Coomaraswamy, so I looked up John Kenneth Galbraith's review of the set in *The New York Times Book Review*. It was delightful, of course, but he dismissed the second volume of the set, which contains Coomaraswamy's metaphysical writings, with a single sentence: "It worries me in stating as true what can only be imagined" (12 March 1978).

they enjoy more felicity, a felicity that in the highest octaves phases into beatitude. Ontologists fuse these various facets of worth by saying that the higher regions have more being. They are more real.

If the reader finds such notions incredible, his response is completely understandable; the truth I have come to think they represent would not be forgotten, again as in *Forgotten Truth*, if they pressed the "of course" button within us. Theodore Roszak voices the typical incredulity of today's intellectual toward the primordial vision when, in reviewing the Schumacher book just alluded to, he writes: "It does no good at all to quote [Aristotle, Dante, and Thomas Aquinas], to celebrate their insight, to adulate their wisdom. Of course they are wise and fine and noble, but they stand on the other side of the abyss" (*Los Angeles Times*, 11 September 1977). But capacity to believe (or disbelieve) has never been a reliable index of whether the belief in question is true; innumerable social, historical, and psychological factors affect what people are able to believe. I do not argue that the primordial vision continues today to seem self-evident or even (to our practical, workaday sensibilities) plausible. What has escaped me, if it is around, is anything modernity has discovered that shows it to be mistaken. In searching for negative evidence I naturally turned first to science, only to find that when its discoveries are freed of interpretations the facts themselves do not require, they slip into the folds of tradition without a ripple. Only when negativism intrudes and the successes of science are wittingly (as in positivism) or unwittingly (as in modernity generally) used to erode confidence in realities other than those science can handle—when, in a phrase, science phases into scientism—does opposition appear. Tradition (a word I try never to pronounce with contempt) incorporates science, whereas scientism excludes tradition by fiat. The fact that tradition has the more generous, inclusive purview stands for me as at least an initial count in its favor.

Were I to say in detail what the higher reaches of reality are, there would be no room to suggest before I close some possibilities they hold for education. So, accenting their primordial, near-universal character, I shall say briefly that in addition to practical life, which is grounded in (1) the material or *terrestrial* plane, every known culture has allowed a place for religion, which, to accommodate important differences in spiritual personality types, proceeds on three levels: folk religion, theism, and mysticism. Folk religion is involved with what Plato calls (2) the *intermediate* plane (*to metaxy*); theism with (3) the *celestial* plane (Wilhelm Schmidt's "High God," a supreme divinity manifesting personal attributes, classical theism), and mysticism with (4) the *Infinite*—God in his ineffable mode: the Tao that cannot be spoken, nirvana, sunyata, and Godhead. "The Great Truth about the world," as Schumacher says, "is that it is a hierarchic structure of four great 'Levels of Being.' "[9]

To amplify only slightly:

1. The matrices of the terrestrial plane are space, time, and matter. Science seems to be developing nearly ideal procedures for understanding it. We are so into the scientific way of seeing things that we tend to think of this physical stratum as foundational; we assume that it could exist without the others, but not vice versa. In point of fact, however, from our human point of view, matter (primary qualities, "vacuous actuality") is far from our starting point—it is with experience, not matter, that we begin. Phenomenology has come forward to make this point painstakingly and, as counterpoise to the reductionism that results when we forget it, is an important movement.

2. Human life is so obviously psyche and soma, body and mind, that the terrestrial and intermediate planes are usually best considered together. Nevertheless, the intermediate plane does contain ingredients that exceed its manifestly human ones that phenomenology attends to. These additional ingredients have the looks of a hodgepodge, a grab bag—they constitute the world of tarot cards, tea leaves, and premonitions, as someone has characterized it. The animate denizens of this world are

gods, ghosts, and demons; the "little people" of various description; the "controls" of spiritualists, mediums, and amanuenses; departed souls in limbo, purgatory, and the Tibetan bardos—in a phrase, discarnates generally. Some of these are so suspect that I am embarrassed even to list them, but one man's mush is another man's meaning, so in view of the difficulty of producing reliable criteria for sorting out what has at least some factual basis, it is best at this point to be egalitarian. So much nonsense goes on in the name of this intermediate or psychic plane that it takes courage to say, as did anthropologists Margaret Mead and Gregory Bateson, that something does go on. The courage can be less if we depersonalize the contents of the intermediate plane, for as we have now come to assume that the universe that wraps us round is by and large impersonal, it is easier for us to countenance forces or entities that fit this description. Regarded as impersonal, the contents of the intermediate plane turn up as psi phenomena of parapsychology, "coincidences" (as in Arthur Koestler's *The Roots of Coincidence*), Jungian archetypes, and astral influences—again, much winnowing is needed to separate the wheat from the chaff. Dreams seem to have some sort of privileged access to this plane, and Theodore Roszak's *Unfinished Animal* is lush witness that interest in it is not confined to traditional cultures or unsophisticated minds in ours. A leading analytic philosopher recently observed that whereas Freudianism has a marvelous theory but no facts, parapsychology has facts but no theory. The second half of his statement holds pretty much for the intermediate plane generally. Enigmatic energies of some kind seem to be at work, but, as we have noted, it is the very mischief to verify them or identify what they are. And let me repeat that it is usually best to think of the terrestrial and intermediate planes together, for on the one hand the terrestrial cries out for infusion from the intermediate to account for the difference between life and nonlife, while the intermediate for its part resembles the terrestrial in being a maelstrom of forces that threaten as much as they sustain us.

3. Impersonally, the celestial plane consists in Western idiom of the Platonic archetypes as integrated in the Idea of the Good. Personally, as we have said, it is the God of classical theism.

4. The Infinite is everything, integrated to the unimaginable point of excluding separations. It can be intuited, but words can depict it only paradoxically, for univocal assertions (being definite) necessarily exclude something, which the Infinite (by definition) cannot.

It bears repeating that the higher planes are not more abstract. Quite the contrary, each ascending plane, in addition to being incredibly vaster, is more concrete, more real, than the ones below. Only on superior levels are the contents of lower levels revisioned to make the way they first appeared seem, like dreams on awakening, relatively unreal. This last phrase, "relatively unreal," should be glossed to read, "not totally unreal, but requiring revision from the way they appear on planes that are more restricted."

The disappearance of the higher planes of reality from our contemporary philosophical maps—or, to speak more carefully, the decline in our confidence in such planes—is, as I say, the change that separates modernity from tradition most decisively.[h] In common parlance, our outlook has become more this-worldly, "this world" being the one that connects with our senses. And it is clear from what I have said that I think the change has impoverished our sense of what the world includes and what it means to be fully human—in giving "ultimate authority to the worldview of a slightly sleepy businessman right after lunch," to invoke G. K. Chesterton's wry formulation, we have lost our grip on the innate immensity of our

[h]"If anything characterizes 'modernity,' it is a loss of faith in transcendence, in a reality that encompasses but surpasses our quotidian affairs," we read in "Review of *Facing Up to Modernity* by Peter Berger," *The Chronicle of Higher Education*, 9 January 1978, p. 18. Because this quotation spots the exact phenomenon that prompted the writing of these essays, it will be cited several times in the course of this book.

true nature.[i] It stands to reason that a new ethos has emerged to fit this reduced onto-anthropology, and before I turn to saying a thing or two about education I need to dub in that ethos. My sketch holds, I think, for our culture as a whole, but again especially for today's university.

IV. The Ethos of the Modern West

The most pertinent way to characterize the modern ethos briefly is to say that it is a blend of naturalism and control. The two terms are related, for it is our wish to control that has brought our naturalism. By way of a new epistemology, we can add, so we actually have three things going: our will to power, its attendant epistemology, and the metaphysics this epistemology brings in its train.

1. Promethean Motivation

Can anyone doubt that science has enlarged man's power incalculably,[j] or that this is the primary reason we are so invested in it? Life by its very nature is beset with problems, and problems cry out to be solved. Since science, via technology, is the most effective problem solver we have developed, it is natural that in trying to solve the problems that beset us we have come to look increasingly in science's direction.

This much seems clear. What we are only beginning to see is that Prometheanism breeds a distinctive epistemology.

2. Promethean Epistemology

Let me introduce Ernest Gellner here, for as a philosopher-sociologist who brings his sociological equipment to bear

---

[i] "We are the only people who think themselves risen from savages; everyone else believes they descended from gods," Marshall Sahlins tells us in *Culture and Practical Reason* (Chicago: University of Chicago Press, 1976). And from Saul Bellow's 1976 Nobel Prize address: "We do not think well of ourselves; we do not think amply about what we are. . . . It is the jet plane in which we commonplace human beings have crossed the Atlantic in four hours that embodies such values as we can claim."

[j] It has also rendered us as a species more vulnerable, but that has only recently come to light.

on analyzing philosophy, his conclusions are more than personal opinions; they claim, at least, to report on the conditions of philosophy in general. In his *Legitimation of Belief* he tells us that underlying the seeming variety, chaos even, of twentieth-century philosophy, an "emerging consensus" can be discerned. Having for some time accepted that epistemology is philosophy's current central task, philosophers are now coming to agree, broadly speaking, that to be recognized as legitimate, beliefs must pass certain tests. "There is the empiricist insistence that faiths . . . must stand ready to be judged by . . . something reasonably close to the ordinary notion of 'experience.' Second, there is the 'mechanistic' insistence on impersonal . . . explanations."[10]

Without dropping a word, Gellner proceeds to acknowledge that it is our Prometheanism that has established this twofold requirement:

> We have of course no guarantee that the world must be such as to be amenable to such explanations; we can only show that we are constrained to think so. It was Kant's merit to see that this compulsion is in us, not in things. It was Weber's to see that it is historically a specific kind of mind, not human mind as such, which is subject to this compulsion. What it amounts to is in the end simple: if there is to be effective knowledge or explanation at all, it must have this form, for any other kind of "explanation" . . . is *ipso facto* powerless.
>
> We have become habituated to and dependent on effective knowledge, and hence have bound ourselves to this kind of genuine explanation. . . . "Reductionism," the view that everything in the world is really something else, and that something else is coldly impersonal, is simply the ineluctable corollary of effective explanation.[11]

Gellner admits that this epistemology our Prometheanism has forced upon us carries "morally disturbing" consequences:

> It was also Kant's merit to see the inescapable price of this Faustian purchase of real [sic] knowledge. [In delivering] cognitive effectiveness [it] exacts its inherent

> moral, "dehumanizing" price. . . . The price of real knowledge is that our identities, freedom, norms, are no longer underwritten by our vision and comprehension of things.[12] On the contrary we are doomed to suffer from a tension between cognition and identity.[13]

Even so, Gellner concludes, we must accept this tension, for the only alternative to "effective knowledge" is "meretricious styles of thought" aimed at "restoration of the moral order within a cozy world in which identities and moral norms were linked in a closed circle of definitions."

3. Naturalistic Metaphysics

Given the way Promethean reason imposes itself on the objects it works with, the world it presents to us can be viewed as the product of a vast display of ventriloquism in which the so-called external world is a dummy; if this comparison, which I take from Philip Sherrard, leans too far in the direction of science-as-construct, it at least gets us past the simplistic model of the archeologist who discovers through straightforward acts of uncovering. Empiricism and mechanism being ill suited to deal with transcendence and the unseen, the epistemology of Prometheanism necessarily conjures for us a naturalistic world. Hannah Arendt stressed this toward the close of her life. "What has come to an end," she wrote, "is the . . . distinction between the sensual and the supersensual, together with the notion, at least as old as Parmenides, that whatever is not given to the senses . . . is more real, more truthful, more meaningful than what appears; that it is not just beyond sense perception but above the world of the senses."[14] Emphasizing that "what is 'dead' is not only the localization of . . . 'eternal truths' but the [temporal/eternal, sensual/supersensual] distinction itself," Dr. Arendt continues with some sentences that are serious enough, perhaps even momentous enough, to be quoted in full:

> Meanwhile, in increasingly strident voices, the few defenders of metaphysics have warned us of the danger of nihilism inherent in this development; and although

they themselves seldom invoke it, they have an important argument in their favor: it is indeed true that once the supersensual realm is discarded, its opposite, the world of appearances as understood for so many centuries, is also annihilated. The sensual, as still understood by the positivists, cannot survive the death of the supersensual. No one knew this better than Nietzsche who, with his poetic and metaphoric description of the assassination of God in Zarathustra, has caused so much confusion in these matters. In a signigicant passage in *The Twilight of Idols*, he clarifies what the word God meant in Zarathustra. It was merely a symbol for the supersensual realm as understood by metaphysics; he now uses instead of God the word true world and says: "We have abolished the true world. What has remained? The apparent one perhaps? Oh no! With the true world we have also abolished the apparent one."[15]

V. Import for Education

Education has so much to learn. It needs to learn, needs to see, what is happening to it, and what it should do in the face of this happening.

What is happening to it is that it is being pressed increasingly into the service of the kind of knowing that facilitates control. Inasmuch as our will-to-control has cut our consciousness to fit its needs—tailored our awareness to fit its imperatives—our educational attempts naturally conform to this tailoring. I shall not attempt to document this assertion systematically—only to note a few straws in the wind.

Philosophy

The place where philosophy intersects science is of course logic, and the growth of logical concern in twentieth-century philosophy has been dramatic. It is going too far to suggest, as someone recently has, that philosophy departments have in effect now become departments of applied logic, but the trend to "do philosophy" via the formal arguments of symbolic logic is unmistakable. Even in the philosophy of language, Chomsky's mildly metaphysical (Cartesian) interests have been overtaken by Donald Davidson's efforts to apply symbolic logic to natural languages. The other side of the coin is, of course, the "melancholy, long, withdrawing roar" of philosophy's retreat from metaphysics; where worldviews cannot be avoided entirely, the species that is usually admitted is a brand of mechanism, materialism, or empiricism—a recent *New York Times* report refers to "the materialism that is overwhelmingly predominant in current analytic philosophy."[16] Yet neither Quine nor Kripke—the senior and junior "Mr. Logics" of our times—thinks that empiricism or materialism are themselves empirically grounded.[17] They have been instated—I am speaking for myself now—because they are the premises that support most forthrightly the kind of knowledge that facilitates control.[18]

Economics

"Contemporary economics thinks of itself as a science, heavily quantitative, using mathematics and statistics as its vocabulary. Paul Samuelson and Wassily Leontief are its giants."[19] In *Small Is Beautiful*, E. F. Schumacher contends that its quantitative orientation has become so excessive, so totally devoid of qualitative understanding, that even the quality of "orders of magnitude" ceases to be appreciated.

Political Science

"The profound option of mainstream social scientists for the empiricist conception of knowledge and science makes it inevitable that they should accept the verification model of political science," Charles Taylor, Professor of Social and Political Theory at Oxford University, tells us. "The basic premise [of this approach is] that social reality is made up of brute data alone," data that is objective in requiring no interpretation and being in principle recordable by machines. The consequence, Professor Taylor concludes, is that a "whole level of study of our civilization . . . is ruled out. Rather [it] is made invisible."[20]

History

A member of the external examining committee that was appointed a year or two back to review the graduate history program at my university happened to belong to the new breed of quantitative historians. At one point in the committee's deliberations he was reported to have said, "If you can't count it, you might as well be playing football." Granted that his statement was extreme, it says something about our times that a responsible academic could have said it at all.

Anthropology

"English-speaking anthropology over the last half century has been and continues to be passionately scientistic in its hopes and claims, and methods. One consequence—and it shares this trait with other sciences—is a built-in positivism and an aversion to history, both general and its own."[21]

Psychology

Insofar as there is a model of man in academic psychology, it seems still to be basically Freudian, and "classical psychoanalytic theory is based quite explicitly on a specific, highly materialist view of man's nature."[22]

The Social Sciences Generally

Charles Taylor generalizes the point we quoted him as making about political science as follows:

> The progress of natural science has lent great credibility to this [verificationist] epistemology, since it can be plausibly reconstructed on this model. . . . And, of course, the temptation has been overwhelming to reconstruct the sciences of man on the same model; or rather to launch them in lines of inquiry that fit this paradigm, since they are constantly said to be in their "infancy." Psychology, where an earlier vogue of behaviorism is

> being replaced by a boom of computer-based models, is far from the only case.[23]

May Brodbeck notes that there are

> two factors within the social disciplines. One of them exuberantly embraces the scientific idea; the other [introducing the distinction between *Verstehen* and explanation], exalts its own intuitive understanding as being superior in logic and in principle to scientific explanation,[24]

but Thomas Lawson of Western Michigan University says that recent scholarly critiques of the nonscientific faction have "been so powerful and penetrating that [it is] bankrupt."[25] This seems to justify the following overview in the September 1978 issue of *The Atlantic Monthly:*

> The social sciences are, or aspire to be, sciences; they have a scientific methodology. . . . The majority of social sciences have adopted a form of radical empiricism. According to this doctrine, the only sentences that are scientifically acceptable are those that are directly verifiable by experiment. . . .
>
> This methodology was borrowed from the teachings of the logical positivists. . . . Logical positivism was given up long ago by most scientists and philosophers, including many of the positivists themselves. Yet this positivistic doctrine . . . has taken firm root in the social sciences. It has done so because it provides a simple (if oversimple) distinction between fact and value which allows social scientists to make the (sometimes bogus) claim of scientific objectivity.[26]

The Arts

I shall let the poet Kathleen Raine describe the situation here.

> Poets of the imagination write of the soul, of intellectual beauty, of the living spirit of the world. What does such work communicate to readers who do not believe in the soul, in the spirit of life, or in anything that can be (unless the physically desirable) called "the beautiful"? For in René Guénon's "reign of quantity" such terms

> of quality become . . . "meaningless," because there is nothing for which they stand. . . .
>
> What can be saved from a culture whose premises are of a spiritual order in an iron age peopled by Plato's "men of clay" (the human primate of the scientist) is the quantifiable; the mechanics of construction, in whatever art. And the engineering element in the making of a poem is negligible in comparison with that of the most impressive and typical work of the reign of quantity, the space-ship. What meaning is there, in materialist terms, to the word "poet"; or the essence—the "poetry"—and the quality—the "poetic"—of works of art?[27]

Geography

I save for last a field that shows some signs of a turning tide. Following World War II, geography's classic concern with place lost ground to a more abstract, geometric concern for space; a recent issue of the *Canadian Geographer* refers to "a generation of geographical treatment of the man-environment relationship as a measurable, objective, and mechanistic entity which may be examined through concepts and methods derived from the natural sciences." It goes on, however, to place the "high tide of [this] scientific geography in the last decade," the 1970s having shown signs of "a fundamental dissatisfaction with positivist philosophies of social science and the perceived implications of such study for our social and geographical world."[28] The geographers at my own university tell me the empiricist school must still be reckoned the dominant one, but in this field there seem to be signs of a "rise of soul against intellect," as Yeats would put the matter.[29]

I have mentioned only a handful of disciplines, and even in these have done little more than report some straws in the winds that have blown my way since I started to think about this essay. If they add up to no more than a straw man, there may be no problem. But if they are accurate in suggesting that the academic mind is leaning excessively toward the scientific model, what is to be done?

If it is true, as I have argued:

> first, that the exceptional power-to-control that modern science has made possible has made us reach out insistently, perhaps even desperately if we feel we are on a treadmill, for ever-increasing control;
>
> second, that this outreach has forged a new epistemology wherein knowledge that facilitates control and the devices for getting at such knowledge are honored to the neglect of their alternatives;
>
> and third, that this utilitarian epistemology has constricted our view of the way things are, including what it means to be fully human;

if, as I say, these contentions are essentially accurate, it behooves us to decide if we want to change our direction, and if so, what a better direction might be.

On the first question, it is obvious from the tenor of my entire essay that I think we can do better than continue down our present path. The main reason I would prefer an alternative is that I think that with respect to things that matter most, our present course is taking us away from truth more than toward it, but there is a supporting reason. There are reports that life in the cave we have entered does not feel very good. As I do not trust my own intuitions here—they could easily be self-serving—I shall let a colleague, who as a sociologist studies societies directly, make the point.

> It is by now a Sunday-supplement commonplace that the social, economic and technological modernization of the world is accompanied by a spiritual malaise that has come to be called alienation. At its most fundamental level, the diagnosis of alienation is based on the view that modernization forces upon us a world that, although baptized as real by science, is denuded of all humanly recognizable qualities; beauty and ugliness, love and hate, passion and fulfillment, salvation and damnation. It is not, of course, being claimed that such matters are not part of the existential realities of human life. It is rather that the scientific worldview makes it illegitimate to speak of them as being "objectively" part of the world, forcing us instead

> to define such evaluation and such emotional experience as "merely subjective" projections of people's inner lives.
> The world, once an "enchanted garden," to use Max Weber's memorable phrase, has now become disenchanted, deprived of purpose and direction, bereft—in these senses—of life itself. All that which is allegedly basic to the specifically human status in nature, comes to be forced back upon the precincts of the "subjective" which, in turn, is pushed by the modern scientific view ever more into the province of dreams and illusions.[30]

If we have trimmed our epistemological sails too close to the scientific desiderata of objectivity, prediction, number, and control (see diagram on p. 83), and it is this that has constricted our worldview and brought alienation, it seems only sensible to consider alternative guidelines—perhaps even opposite ones to get the matter in sharp relief. The alternatives to objectivity, prediction, control, and number are subjectivity, surprise, surrender, and words. With the exception of the last of these four terms, it sounds odd even to suggest that education might turn toward them. This shows how deeply committed we are to the scientific quartet. The question is, are we too deeply implicated with it even to imagine what an education that swung toward the neglected alternatives would look like?

Subjective education would recognize that it is as important to understand oneself as it is to understand one's world and its parts. It would distinguish between objective and subjective (or existential) truths, the latter being defined as truths we acknowledge not only with our minds but with our lives as well—we live as if we really do believe that they are true. And it would argue that "truth" deserves the prefix "subjective" as much as the prefix "objective."

Education for *surprise* would begin with, and keep always in full view, its indisputable premise: in comparison with what we do not know, what we do know is nothing. Balancing our present assumption that education's role is to transmit what we know, education for surprise would not reject that premise but would add that it is equally important to remember how much we do not know. Learning theory? Who knows, really, how we learn? Medicine? I go to visit my neighbor Robert Becker at New York's Upstate Medical Center because of interesting things I have heard about his research and he greets me with, "We know nothing!" "Welcome to the club," I reply, having studied the skeptical tradition in Western philosophy rather thoroughly. "That's not what I mean," he says. "It may be true generally, but it's especially true in medicine. Here I am, a director of medical research with thirty years behind me, and when I cut my face shaving I haven't any idea what makes it heal." Generalizing Becker's point, education for surprise would remind students that the more we know, the more we see how much we do not know. The larger the island of knowledge, the longer the shoreline of wonder. Noting that neither language nor science is rule-directed in the sense of proceeding by the application of rules we can discern and explicitly state, it would pay special attention to case studies where the long shot carried the day. It might even try to hone students' sensibilities to surprise by asking questions like, "Did anything surprise you yesterday?" On the flyleaves of the training manuals for such education we might paste this statement, titled "The Strangest Age," from *Newsweek*, 25 July 1977:

> Perhaps ours is the strangest age. It is an age without a sense of the strangeness of things. . . .
>
> The human race has grown up and lost its capacity for wonder. This is not because people understand their everyday world better than people did in earlier ages. Today people understand less and less of the social and scientific systems on which they depend more and more. Alas, growing up usually means growing immune to astonishment. As G. K. Chesterton wrote, very young children do not need fairy tales because "mere life is interesting enough. A child of 7 is excited by being told that Tommy opened the door and saw a dragon. But a child of 3 is excited by being

told that Tommy opened the door." The 3-year-old is the realist. No one really knows how Tommy does it.

Education for *surrender* sounds strangest of all, not only because of the military associations of that word but because it runs counter to the penchant that has created our modern world. Recognizing that it would be working against some of our strongest social instincts, such education would remind us that life proceeds by breathing out and in, giving and receiving, doing and being, left hemisphere and right, yang and yin. Moreover, too much imbalance between the poles can make life capsize. It would show that only in the realm of things—the realm I have called the terrestrial plane—are freedom (and the control to which it can be put) attractive even as ideals; the last thing a man in love wants to hear from his beloved is that he is free, while to enter a friendship or marriage with intent to control is to sully it from the start. In life's higher reaches, freedom and the will-to-power are symptoms of detachment in its pathological sense of inability to cathect. To be unable to give oneself—to a person, a cause, the call of conscience, God, something—is to lack a capacity that is integral to being fully human. It is to be incapable of commitment. Kurt Wolff says that "the seminal meaning of 'surrender' is 'cognitive love,'" and notes certain other meanings that "follow from it: total involvement, suspension of received notions, pertinence of everything, identification, and risk of being hurt."[31] Heidegger's continuing influence on our campuses in the face of his tortuous language and unpopular premises derives in part, at least, from the sense that there is something inherently right in the *Gelassenheit* toward which his philosophy points. Someone has translated *Gelassenheit* as "reverent, choiceless letting-be of what is in order that it may reveal itself in the essence of its being."

Reading, writing, and arithmetic: Education is always involved with words, but in opposing them to numbers I am focusing on a specific feature. Words are symbols, whereas numbers are only signs.[32] Because signs are univocal, they can lock together in logics that compel assent, but this cannot be said of symbols, which are multivalent in principle. Their inbuilt ambiguity makes logicians flee them for univocal signs,[k] but humanists prize their equivocality. A biologist has stated their case succinctly:

> Ambiguity seems to be an essential, indispensable element for the transfer of information from one place to another by words, where matters of real importance are concerned. It is often necessary, for meaning to come through, that there be an almost vague sense of strangeness and askewness. Speechless animals and cells cannot do this. . . . Only the human mind is designed to work in this way, programmed to drift away in the presence of locked-on information, straying from each point in a hunt for a better, different point.[33]

Language is biological in that we are programmed to learn it, Dr. Thomas concludes, but it is peculiar in being a "programming for ambiguity." An education-for-words that is alert to their symbolic virtues would teach that the need to be clear must not be allowed to sterilize language—rid it of the humus of adumbration and allusion that makes it fertile and capable of reaching into every crevice of the human soul. The point is crucial for dilating our sense of world. We cannot go back to very old civilizations where words virtually doubled for things by borrowing their full substance, but there is no reason why we cannot come again to see that at its best, symbolism is the "science" of the relationship between alternate levels of reality (al-Ghazali).

The foregoing has deduced the outlines of an alternative education by reversing the criteria of scientific knowing. I might have gotten to much the same place if I had asked what education would look like if it attended more

[k]Paul Ricoeur points out the irony in the phrase "symbolic logic" which, as the name for our ultimate, formal, abstract exactitude, exactly inverts symbolism's usual meaning (*The Symbolism of Evil*, trans. Emerson Buchanan [Boston: Beacon Press, 1969], p. 17).

to the things science is not skillful with: intrinsic and normative values, purposes, existential and inclusive meanings, and qualities. But I have said enough for today, save for a quick coda.

I hope what I have written has not contributed to the literature of indictment. I have tried, or hope I have tried, merely to ask myself where we are and where it might be good to go. The second half of this question, "Where might it be good to go," does not, I think, implicate me in the homilist's complaint of living in bad times, but it does bring my argument full circle in a way I had not anticipated. Going is a mode of doing, and doing includes an element of control. But the will-to-control, having caused our narrowed epistemology and ontology, is what we need to correct—this has been my argument.

The paradox—recommendations issuing from one side of a mouth that preaches *wu wei* (nonwillfullness, non-insistence) with its other side—could be embarrassing were it not in fact a virtue. For it shows that at least we have not been wrestling with a straw man. If motivations (intentions) do breed their respective epistemologies and worlds and it has been our historical destiny to push the problem-solving triumvirate to dangerous extremes, the question remains: What is the right balance between participation and control? I do not know the answer. If I were a university president forced to divide short funds between knowledge that furthers participation and knowledge that furthers control, I would agonize. Everything I have written is premised on the intuition that we are top-heavy on control, but those who disagree are powerful and worthy of the utmost respect and even fear. So much so that I shall ask Gregory Bateson to address to them my final rejoinder. His statement appears in an interview with Daniel Goleman in *Psychology Today*.

GOLEMAN: What's to be done?

BATESON: Funny question, "What's to be done?" Suppose I said that nothing's to be done. Way back in 1947, I was asked to address a group of physicists at Princeton.

They had all worked on the atom bomb, and then were terribly remorseful about what might be done with it. Robert Oppenheimer had organized a seminar for these nuclear physicists to examine the social sciences to see if there were any remedies. After my talk, I was Oppenheimer's house-guest. The next morning was a horrible, rainy winter day. The children had lost their rubbers and Mrs. Oppenheimer was going mad trying to get them off to school. The regular American breakfast scene.

And in the midst of all this hubbub, out of the blue, came the still, small voice of Oppenheimer, saying, unasked, "You know, if anyone asked me why I left teaching at Cal Tech and came to do research at Princeton, I suppose the answer was that at Cal Tech there were 500 students to face, who all wanted to know the answers."

I said, "I suppose the answers to these questions would have been rather bitter."

Oppenheimer said, "Well, as I see it, the world is moving in the direction of hell, with a high velocity, and perhaps a positive acceleration, and a positive rate of change of acceleration; and the only condition under which it might not reach its destination is that we and the Russians be willing to let it go there." Every move we make in fear of the next war in fact hastens it. The old deterrence theory. We arm up to control the Russians, they do the same. Anxiety, in fact, brings about the thing it fears, creates its own disaster.

GOLEMAN: So, just let it happen?

BATESON: Well, be bloody careful about the politics you play to control it. You don't know the total pattern; for all you know, you could create the next horror by trying to fix up a present one.

GOLEMAN: The patterns you talk about in which we are enmeshed seem much larger than we can grasp.

BATESON: There is a larger mind of which the individual mind is only a subsystem. This larger mind is perhaps what some people mean by "God." But it is immanent in the total interconnected social system and includes the planetary ecology.

GOLEMAN: It seems to be almost futile to try to perceive, let alone control, this larger web of patterns and connections.

BATESON: Trying to perceive them is, I'm sure, worthwhile. I've devoted my life to that proposition. Trying to tell other people about them is worthwhile. In a sense, we know it already. At the same time, we don't know. We are terribly full of screaming voices that talk administrative "common sense."

GOLEMAN: Rather than. . . .

BATESON: Wisdom. If there be such a thing.[34]

Notes

1. Huston Smith, "Teaching to a Camera," *Educational Record*, January 1956.

2. Expanded, it was published as Huston Smith, *Condemned to Meaning* (New York: Harper & Row, 1965).

3. Huston Smith, "The Humanities and Man's Condition," *Liberal Education* 50, no. 2 (May 1964).

4. Huston Smith, "Two Kinds of Teaching," in Thomas Buxton and Keith Prichard, *Excellence in University Teaching* (Columbia, S.C.: University of South Carolina Press, 1975); reprinted in *Key Reporter* 38, no. 4 (Summer 1973), and in *Journal of Humanistic Psychology* 15, no. 4 (Fall 1975).

5. Huston Smith, "Like It Is: The University Today," *Key Reporter* 34, no. 2 (Winter 1968-1969). Reprinted in *Wall Street Journal*, 20 March 1969.

6. Huston Smith, "Values: Academic and Human," in *The Larger Learning*, ed. Marjorie Carpenter (Dubuque, Iowa: William C. Brown, 1969); and Huston Smith, "Education beyond the Facts," (Charleston, W.V.: Morris Harvey College, 1962).

7. Jacques Monod, *Chance and Necessity* (New York: Random House, 1972), p. 21.

8. Sir Charles Sherrington, *Man on His Nature* (Cambridge: Cambridge University Press, 1963), p. 251.

9. E. F. Schumacher, *A Guide for the Perplexed* (New York: Harper & Row, 1977), p. 8.

10. Ernest Gellner, *The Legitimation of Belief* (Cambridge: Cambridge University Press, 1975), p. 206.

11. Ibid., pp. 206-7.

12. In Sartre's formulation when "real knowledge" is taken to be the kind Gellner is describing, human life becomes "absurd."

13. Ibid., p. 207.

14. Hannah Arendt, "Thinking and Moral Consideration," *Social Research* 38 (Autumn 1971): 240.

15. Ibid.

16. Taylor Branch, "New Frontiers in American Philosophy," *New York Times Magazine*, 14 August 1978.

17. Quine sees ontological positions—what is finally real—as relative precisely because they cannot be objectively grounded, and Kripke has written as follows: "Materialism, I think, must hold that a physical description of the world is a complete description of it, that any mental facts are 'ontologically dependent' on physical facts in the straightforward sense of following from them by necessity. No identity theorists [materialists] seem to me to have made a convincing argument against the intuitive view that this is not the case." (closing section of his "Naming and Necessity," in D. Davidson and G. Harmon [eds.], *Semantics of Natural Language* [Dordrecht: D. Reidel, 1972]).

18. For the reason why persons who are seeking "effective knowledge" (Gellner's phrase) are required to charge persons who work from alternative metaphysical premises with "begging the question," see my discussion of D. C. Dennett's work in *Forgotten Truth: The Primordial Tradition* (New York: Harper & Row, 1976), pp. 135ff.

19. Adam Smith, *New York Times Book Review*, 18 September 1977, p. 10.

20. Charles Taylor, "Interpretation and the Sciences of Man," in *Understanding and Social Inquiry*, ed. Fred Dallmayr and Thomas McCarthy (South Bend, Ind.: University of Notre Dame Press, 1977), p. 124.

21. Robert Ackerman, "J. G. Frazer Revisited," *American Scholar*, Spring 1978, p. 232.

22. Irving Yalom, *The Theory and Practice of Group Psychotherapy* (New York: Basic Books, 1975), p. 85.

23. Taylor, "Interpretation and the Sciences of Man," *op. cit.*, pp. 105-6.

24. May Brodbeck, ed., *Readings in the Philosophy of the Social Sciences* (New York: Macmillan, 1968), p. 2 of the "General Introduction."

25. Thomas Lawson, unpublished paper, 1974.

26. Alston Chase, "Skipping through College: Reflections on the Decline of Liberal Arts Education," *The Atlantic Monthly*, September 1978, p. 38.

27. Kathleen Raine, "Premises and Poetry," *Sophia Perennis* 3, no. 2 (Autumn 1977): 58-60.

28. *Canadian Geographer* 22, no. 1 (Spring 1978): 66-67.

29. As this article goes to press, something has come to my attention that suggests that philosophy, which in a sense is epistemology's custodian, may itself be starting to recover from the unautonomous way it has related to science thus far in this century. In *Reason, Truth and History* (Cambridge University Press, 1981), Hilary Putnam, chairman of the Philosophy Department at Harvard, argues: (1) that it is time for philosophy to lay aside the debunking posture that has characterized it for the last fifty years; (2) that the materialism that virtually *is* its current metaphysics and the empiricism that is its epistemology are both inadequate; (3) that its biggest present job is to develop a model of rationality more adequate than the three present contenders—inductive logic, relativism, and innate ideas à la Chomsky; and (4) this new model should be one that establishes philosophy as a cognitive domain situated between science on the one hand and art on the other.

And Richard Rorty, in what may be the most important philosophical work of the 1970s, *Philosophy and the Mirror of Nature* (Princeton University Press, 1979), asks philosophers to renounce their claim to being authorities on epistemology. Instead, they should turn to the hermeneutic task of facilitating conversation between different worlds of discourse.

30. Manfred Stanley, "Beyond Progress: Three Post-Political Futures," in *Images of the Future*, ed. Robert Bundy (Buffalo: Prometheus Books, 1976), pp. 115-16.

31. Kurt Wolff, "Surrender, and Autonomy and Community," *Humanitas* 1, no. 2 (Fall 1965): 77. See also his "Surrender as a Response to Our Crisis," *Journal of Humanistic Psychology* 2 (1962): 16-30; and *Surrender and Catch* (Netherlands: D. Reidel, 1976).

32. Numerology is a special case that need not concern us here. In 2 + 2 = 4 numbers function as signs, but in "God is one," one is a symbol.

33. Lewis Thomas, *Lives of a Cell* (Toronto: Bantam Books, 1974), p. 111.

34. Gregory Bateson, interviewed by Daniel Goleman, "Breaking Out of the Double Bind," *Psychology Today*, August 1978, p. 51.

5

FLAKES OF FIRE, HANDFULS OF LIGHT

The Humanities as Uncontrolled Experiment *

This essay continues the theme of the preceding one and relates it specifically to the humanities. It was originally delivered as an address that formed a part of the week-long festival, "In Celebration of the Humanities," that marked the move of Syracuse University's humanities division into new quarters in the autumn of 1979.

Those of us who saw "Einstein's Universe," that remarkable television program the British Broadcasting Company created for the centennial of Einstein's birth, remember the words that laced it like a theme: "Einstein would have wanted us to say it in the simplest possible way. Space tells matter how to move; matter tells space how to warp."

How, in the simplest possible way, can we describe the burden and promise of the humanities today?

I. The Humanities

First, by identifying their central concern. They have many facets, of course, but we will not be far from the mark if we think of them as custodians of the human image; one

---

*Reprinted from *Teachers College Record* 82, no. 2 (Winter 1980), and the British review *Temenos* 1, no. 2 (1982).

way or another, in cycles and epicycles, they circle the question of who we take ourselves to be—what it means to be a human being, to live a human life. We know that self-images are important, for endowed as we are with self-consciousness, we draw portraits of ourselves and then fashion our lives to their likenesses, coming to resemble the portraits we draw. Psychologists who are professionally concerned with behavior modification tell us that a revised self-image is the most important single factor in human change. It is when a person sees himself differently that new ways of behaving come to seem feasible and appropriate.

If then (in company with religion and the arts in our culture at large) the humanities are custodians of the human self-image, what is their burden and promise today?

II. Burdens: Social and Conceptual

Turning first to their burdens, they are of two kinds, social and conceptual. As the first of these stems from our culture's institutional forms I shall let a social scientist, a colleague, Manfred Stanley, tell the story. "It is by now a Sunday-supplement commonplace," he writes, "that the social, economic and technological modernization of the world is accompanied by a spiritual malaise that has come to be called alienation."[a] The social changes contributing to this alienation reduce most importantly, I suspect—I am not attributing this further point to Professor Stanley—to disruption of the primary communities in which life used to be lived. No longer rooted in such communities, our lives are seen less in their entirety, as wholes, by others; and in consequence (so fully are our perceptions of ourselves governed by others' perceptions

---

[a]There are two fairly extended quotations which, because they speak so precisely to the points they make, I use more than once in these essays which were written for different audiences. That by Ernest Gellner, which puts its finger on our current epistemology, is one of these; it appeared in the preceding essay and will reappear in this one. The other, which identifies the consequences of that epistemology, is this present statement by Manfred Stanley, which appeared previously on pp. 104-105, and in its present entry will resume on the next page.

of us) we have difficulty seeing *ourselves* as wholes. High mobility decrees that our associates know only limited time segments of our lives—childhood, college, mid-life career, retirement—while the compartmentalization of industrial life insures that at any given life stage our associates will know us in only one of our roles; worker, member of the family, civic associate, or friend. Once again, none knows us whole, and as our fellows do not so know us, we have trouble seeing ourselves as wholes as well.

This scattering of our lives in time and their splintering in space tends to fragment our self-image and in extreme cases to pulverize it. Engendering Robert Lifton's "protean man" and abetting the existentialist's conclusion that we have no essence, the disruption of the primary community is, as I say, the heaviest burden I see institutional changes laying on our efforts to see ourselves as complete persons.

The conceptual problem our age has wrought, however, is (if anything) even weightier. By this conceptual problem I mean the worldview the modern West has settled into: its notion of "the scheme of things entire" as it finally is. The statement by Professor Stanley that I began quoting two paragraphs above speaks to this conceptual side of our predicament too, so let me continue to let him speak for me. He was noting the alienation that modernization has occasioned, and after alluding to some of its social causes, he drives straight to the heart of the matter:

> At its most fundamental level, the diagnosis of alienation is based on the view that modernization forces upon us a world that, although baptized as real by science, is denuded of all humanly recognizable qualities; beauty and ugliness, love and hate, passion and fulfillment, salvation and damnation. It is not, of course, being claimed that such matters are not part of the existential realities of human life. It is rather that the scientific worldview makes it illegitimate to speak of them as being "objectively" part of the world, forcing us instead to define such evaluation and such emotional experience as "merely subjective" projections of people's inner lives.

> The world, once an "enchanted garden," to use Max Weber's memorable phrase, has now become disenchanted, deprived of purpose and direction, bereft—in these senses—of life itself. All that which is allegedly basic to the specifically human status in nature comes to be forced back upon the precincts of the "subjective" which, in turn, is pushed by the modern scientific view ever more into the province of dreams and illusions.

To say that it is difficult—burdensome—to maintain a respectable human image in a world like this is an understatement. The truth is, it is impossible.[b] If modern man feels alienated from this world he sees enveloping him, it shows that his wits are still intact. He should feel alienated. For no permanent standoff between self and world is possible; eventually there will be a showdown. And when it comes, there is no doubt about the outcome: the world will win—for a starter, it is bigger than we are. So a meaningful life is not finally possible in a meaningless world. It is provisionally possible—there can be a temporary standoff between self and world—but finally it is not possible.[c] Either the garden is indeed disenchanted, in which case the humanities deserve to be on the defensive, no noble image being possible in an a-noble—I do not say ignoble—world; or the garden remains enchanted and the humanities should help make this fact known.

---

[b]Christopher Lasch gives us one indication of this in *The Culture of Narcissism* which has as its subtitle, *American Life in an Age of Diminishing Expectations.* Saul Bellow's assessment was quoted on p. 96 above, and another Nobel Prize winner, the neuro-physiologist John Eccles, has this to say: Man is not just "a hastily made-over ape. . . . Science has gone too far in breaking down our belief in our spiritual greatness" (*Brain/Mind Bulletin*, 20 February 1978, p. 4).

[c]A certain metaphysical sensitivity is needed to see this—a talent for the long view—but the point must rest here with an analogy. From their beginning stars struggle against the force of their own gravity, which they can oppose only by generating tremendous amounts of energy to maintain high internal pressures. But the star can never win the battle, for when its fuel is exhausted, gravity wins and the star must die.

To set out to reverse the metaphysical momentum of the last four hundred years might seem a task so difficult as to be daunting, but there is another way to look at the matter. Here, surely, is something worth doing, a project to elicit the best that is within us, including resources we might not know we possess; so even if we fail in the attempt we shall do so knowing the joy that comes from noble doings. To get the project underway we must advance into enemy territory—we shall find it to be a contemporary form of what Plato called "upside down existence"—and to do this we must cross a no-man's-land of methodology, "no-man's" being precise here because if either side were to capture it the victory would be theirs. So, a short interlude on method to establish the ground rules for the "war of the worlds" (read "war of the worldviews") we are about to begin.

III. Methodological Interlude

In a university setting, any move to reinstate the enchanted garden can expect to be met by the question, "How do you know it is enchanted?" If we answer that we experience it so, that we find ourselves ravished by its mystery and washed by its beauty and presences—not always, of course, but enough to sustain conviction[d]—we shall be told that this is not to know, it is merely to feel. This crude response requires of us a choice. Either we blow the whistle at once on this cramped and positivistic definition of knowledge (as we shall soon see, its willingness to dignify as knowledge only such kinds as hold the promise of augmenting our power to control, rules out the very possibility of knowing things that might be superior to us, it being possible to control only subordinates or at most equals; in a word, it rules out the possibility of knowing transcendence) or we can let this restriction of knowledge to

[d]In his *God and Other Minds* (Ithaca, N.Y.: Cornell University Press, 1967), Alvin Plantinga says he does not know how to argue the existence of God, whose existence seems as obvious to him as anything he might try to argue it from.

what-can-be-proved stand, in which case knowledge becomes a foundation (one among several) for a higher epistemic yield—call it insight, wisdom, understanding, or even intelligence if we use that word to include, as it did for the Scholastics, Plato's "eye of the soul" that can discern spiritual objects. What we must never, never do is make proof our master. Fear that if we do not subject ourselves to it we may wander into error will always tempt us to this slavery,[e] but to yield to the temptation spells disaster for our discipline. Even physicists, if they be great ones, see (as Richard Feynman pointed out in his Nobel Lecture) that "a very great deal more truth can become known than can be proven." "Not to prove, but to discover"[f] must be the humanities' watchword.

To rise above the tyranny of proof and with pounding heart bid farewell to the world of the inadequate—the rope is cut, the bird is free—is in no wise to abandon thoughts for feelings, as if bogs could accommodate the human spirit better than cages. To relegate the health of our souls to the whims of our emotions would be absurd. To say that in outdistancing proof we take our minds with us is too weak; they empower our flight. At this higher altitude the mind is, if anything, more alive than before.[g] In supreme instances the muses take over and our minds go on "automatic pilot," that inspired, ecstatic state Plato called "the higher madness." We cannot here track our minds to those heights where myth and poetry conspire with revelation and remembrance, science joining them

[e]"I am so afraid of error that I keep hurling myself into the arms of doubt rather than into the arms of truth" (Petrarch).

[f]Epigraph of Carolly Erickson's *The Medieval Vision* (New York: Oxford University Press, 1976).

[g]Insight is an act, permeated by intense passion, that makes possible great clarity in the sense that it perceives and dissolves subtle but strong emotional, social, linguistic, and intellectual pressures tending to hold the mind in rigid grooves and fixed compartments, in which fundamental challenges are avoided. From this germ can unfold a further perception that includes new orders and forms of reason that are expressed in the medium of thought and language" (David Bohm, "On Insight and its Significance for Science, Education, and Values," *Teachers College Record* 80, no. 3 [1979]: 409).

at those times when hunches strike terror in the heart, so fine is the line between inspired madness and the kind that disintegrates. Such ozone atmosphere is not for this essay. Ours is the *to metaxy*, the intermediate realm between proofs that cannot tell us whether the garden is enchanted or not and inspiration that shows us, face to face, that it is. Proofs being unavailable in this "middle kingdom," there remains the possibility that reasons may have something to say—proofs, no; reasons, yes. Even here we should not expect too much, for the more we try to make our reasons resemble proofs—in justifications or arguments that compel, provided only that the hearer has rational faculties—the more they must take on proof's earthbound character; in grounding them in demonstrations that compel, we will "ground" them in the correlative sense of preventing them from getting off the ground.

This last point is worth dwelling on for a paragraph, for it points to a dilemma the university is caught in but does not clearly see. On the one hand, we take it for granted that an important part of our job is to train people to think critically; concurrently, we assume that the university is an important custodiam of civilization: we have the celebrated retort of the Oxford don who, asked what he was doing for the Battle of Britain, replied that he was what the fighting was *for*. What the university does not see is that the criteria for critical thinking it has adopted, work against the high image of man that keeps civilizations vital: the Aryans who fanned out in the second millenium B.C.E. to spread the Indo-European language base from India to Ireland—Aryurvedic medicine still flourishes in India, and Eyre is simply Aryur spelled differently—called themselves Aryan (noble), while the Muslims who entered history in the greatest political explosion the world has known were powered for that explosion by the Quranic assurance, "Surely We created man in the best stature" (XCV, 4). To cite but a single evidence of the contradiction the university is caught in here, "There is no doubt that in developed societies education has contributed to the decline of religious belief";[1] yet students of evolution tell us that "religious behaviors are . . . probably adaptive; [their] dialog with 'nature'... is an important integrator of [man's] whole self-view in relation to the world and to activity."[2] I suspect that the conjunction of these two facts—religion is adaptive and the canons of modernity erode it—contributed to Max Weber's pessimism about the future, a pessimism shared by the foremost contemporary British sociologist of religion, Bryan Wilson. Seeing current society as less legitimated than any previous social order, Wilson fears a breakdown of civilizing values in the face of an increasingly anonymous and rationalized culture.[3] I think we should ask ourselves very seriously whether the canons of critical thinking the university has drifted into may not be precipitating such a possible breakdown. It has been America's hope that these canons make for a better, more "rational" world. It seems to be her experience that they do not necessarily do so.

But to proceed. If our first methodological point noted that attempts to force the question of the world's worth into the arena of proof preclude a heartening answer by that move alone, the second point concerns an innuendo that must be anticipated and dismissed so discussion can proceed on a decent level. I refer to the charge, more frequently insinuated than openly expressed, that affirmative worldviews are products of wishful thinking. What are put forward as good reasons to support them are not the real reasons. The real reasons are psychological.

At risk of protesting too much, I propose to raise a small electrical storm here to clear the atmosphere. As barometer to show that the storm is needed, I shall refer to the British philosopher and sociologist Ernest Gellner. In his *Legitimation of Belief* he proposes that only such knowledge as lends itself to "public formulation and repeatability" be considered "real knowledge." He admits that the "moral, 'dehumanizing' price" of this move is high, for it leads to the conclusion that "our identities, freedom, norms, are no longer underwritten by our vision and comprehension of things, [so] we are doomed to suffer from a tension between cognition and identity"—note the enchantment departing the garden like helium from a punctured balloon. But we should pay this price manfully, Gellner contends, for its alternative is "styles of thought [that are] cheap, . . . cozy [and] meretricious." It is rhetoric like this that demands a storm to dispatch it. Gellner does not argue that the kind of knowledge he baptizes as "real" in fact is so; only that "we have become habituated to and dependent on" such knowledge and so "are constrained" to define knowledge this way. "It was Kant's merit," he acknowledges, "to see that this compulsion is in us, not in things. It was Weber's to see that it is historically a specific kind of mind, not mind as such, which is subject to this compulsion."[4] But if anyone questions the worth of this compulsion to which "we have become . . . bound" and proposes to try to loosen its hold on us, he must face, atop this already demanding task, Gellner's insults. For to take exception to his delimitation of "real knowledge" is, to repeat his charge, to engage in "styles of thought [that are] cheap and meretricious." That last word drove me to my dictionary; I wanted to discover with precision how my mind works. According to the *Oxford English Dictionary* it is "showily attractive . . . befitting a harlot."

I deplore this whole descent into name calling. Unworthy of discussions in a university setting, it leaves a bad taste in my mouth; part of me feels petty for allowing myself to have been drawn into it. But the phenomenon is real, so it must be dealt with. Volumes of so-called arguments of this kind could be assembled, wherein a psychologically angled vocabulary is used without apparently taking into account the effect this is likely to have on uncritical minds. Though this kind of language is doubtless not intended to degrade the humanities, it does nevertheless betray an artless style of thinking in its authors. For if "real knowledge" is restricted to what is public and repeatable, what is left for the humanities is mostly unreal knowledge or no knowledge at all.

I hope we are agreed that ad hominem arguments get

us nowhere. Naturally, I wonder from time to time if my high regard for life and the world is fathered by desire and mothered by need, but this is a shoe that fits either foot. Psychologists tell us that people give themselves on average more grief through too poor estimates of themselves than through ones that are inflated; it is with self-contempt, not pride, that we have basically to deal. So if we insist on playing this psychologizing game perhaps we should invite our champions of the human nadir to join us on the psychiatrist's couch—Beckett, who admits he was born depressed; Camus, Sartre, whoever your list includes—to see if Diane Keaton in *Manhattan* was right in seeing their gloomy worlds as personal neuroses inflated to cosmic proportions.[h] Wittgenstein once remarked that the world of a happy man is a happy world.

The storm is on its way out, but a last, receding clap of thunder as it makes its departure. When the question of whether we are saved by grace or self-effort became an issue in Japanese Buddhist thought, a militant advocate of self-power (Nichiren) made a statement that was counterdependent to a degree worthy of Fritz Perls. Personal responsibility being everything, he argued, a single supplication for help from the Buddhas was enough to send a man to hell. To which a member of the other-power school replied that as he was undoubtedly destined for hell anyway, being totally incapable of saving himself, he might as well take his supplications along with him as comforts. I confess that, taste for taste, I find this latter posture more appealing than that of existentialists who strut life's stage, hurling histrionically their Byronic defiance—"there's no meaning but my meaning; that which each of us personally creates"—at an unhearing universe; Ernest Becker is but one culture hero in this existentialist camp. And I can say *why* I find this latter group less appealing. (This switch, from the psychologizing

[h]"Despair is, theologically considered, not only a sin but the greatest of sins; and yet at the same time there is a sort of pride in it, a pleasure even, as in the only great thing left to us. It is also a kind of revenge on those whom we imagine have driven us to it" (Kathleen Raine).

and subjectivism I have allowed myself to be dragged into, to recourse to reason is sign that the storm is over.) The existentialists are more self-centered—so, at least, their writings come through to me. In countering the mechanistic image of man that science produced, existentialism arose precisely to recall us to ourselves, to remind us of our individuality and freedom—properties that science cannot deal with. In making this correlation it served an important function; we humanists stand greatly in its debt. But there was something it did not see—probably could not see at mid-century. In countering science's push for uniformities and determining forces. it uncritically accepted a third scientific premise, the man/world divide that Descartes and Newton first moved into place. This third premise no more describes the actual nature of things than do the first two; all three are science's working principles, no more, no less. This uncritical acceptance of the third working principle of science drove the existentialists into an alienated, embattled, egocentric depiction of the human condition. In mistaking the separate, self-contained part of us for our true part, existentialism made a fatal mistake that has confused and lowered our self-estimate. I use the past tense in speaking of it because increasingly it has a passé flavor. It lingers on because theology and humanistic psychology have not gathered the academic strength to replace it with a convincing alternative, and philosophy has not given them much help in their efforts.

So we come to our central question, asking not if an image of man loftier than either science or the existentialists have given us is possible in our times—that would again divert us to a psychological question, this time the question of whether Western civilization still has the vitality to believe great things.[i] Instead, we ask whether this loftier image is true. Even here, though, we have not reached the bottom line, for as we noted earlier, the final

---

[i]Cezlaw Milosz thinks we do not have the requisite vitality, living as we do in a time when great art is no longer possible.

question is not whether man is noble but whether reality is noble, it being impossible to answer the first question affirmatively unless the second is so answered.[j] If it be asked why I do not produce a moral culprit for our reduced self-image (evil men who have ground that image into the dust by exploiting us) or even a social culprit (what hope for man in an age of mechanization and technique?), the answer is that important as these tyrannies are, they are not our final problem. Our final adversary is the notion of a lifeless universe as the context in which life and thought are set, one which without our presence in it would have to be judged inferior to ourselves. Could we but shake off our anodynes for a moment we would see that nothing could be more terrible than the condition of spirits in a supposedly lifeless and indifferent universe—Newton's great mechanism of time, space, and inanimate forces operating automatically or by chance. Spirits in such a context are like saplings without water; their organs shrivel. Not that there has been ill intent in turning holyland into wasteland, garden into desert; just disastrous consequences unforeseen. So we must pick up anew Blake's Bow of Burning Gold to support "the rise of soul against intellect" (Yeats), as intellect has come to be narrowly perceived. To continue with Yeats, this time paraphrasing him, we must hammer loud upon the wall till truth at last obeys our call. We must produce some reasons.

IV. Leaving the Wasteland

Aimed not at individuals (scientists, say) or disciplines (science or the social sciences) but at habits of thought that encroach on us all in the modern West—"there never was a war that was not inward" (Marianne Moore)—the reasons are of two sorts, positive and negative. As the negative reasons mesh better with current styles of thought —what we currently take to be reasonable—I shall begin with them. They are negative because they say nothing

[j]"Plato understood that all attempts to form a nobler type of man—i.e., all *paideai* and all culture—merge into the problem of the nature of the divine" (Werner Jaeger).

about what reality is like; they merely show that the claim that it is a lifeless mechanism does not have a rational leg to stand on. My *Forgotten Truth* joins the preceding essay in this book to work out this exposé in some detail. Here I can only summarize their combined argument.

1. We begin with *motivations*. Nothing is more uncompromising about ourselves than that we are creatures that want.

2. These wants give rise to *epistemologies*. From the welter of impressions and surmises that course through our streams of consciousness we register, firm up, and take to be true, those that stay in place and support us like stepping stones in getting us to where we want to go. In the seventeenth century, Western man stumbled on a specialized way of knowing that we call the scientific method, a packet of directives counseling, first, what we should attend to, and then what we should do with the objects that come into focus through this attention. This new epistemological probe dramatically increased our understanding of how nature works and our control over it.[k] As we welcomed this increase, we "went with" this way of knowing, enshrining it as the supreme way of getting at truth, and what it discloses as truth itself.

3. Epistemologies in turn produce *ontologies*—they create world views. In the case in question, the epistemology we fashioned to enlarge our cognitive bite into the natural world produced an ontology that made nature central. It may not be accurate to call this new ontology materialism, but clearly it is naturalistic. Everything that exists must have a foothold in nature (space, time, and matter), and in the end it must be subject to that footing.

4. Finally, ontologies generate *anthropologies*. Man

---

[k]It was the corridors of power that yawned before Bacon and his cohorts in the seventeenth century that made science so heady. Forming their Invisible College, they divided power into three kinds. Power over themselves, science did not seem to offer. Power over others it did dangle, but in the imperialism and colonialism it foreshadowed there seemed to be moral ambiguities, so they scratched this topic from their agenda. It was power over nature that excited them as the unqualified good science was deeding to man.

being by definition a part of reality, his nature must obviously conform to what reality is. So a naturalistic worldview produces, perforce, a humanistic view of man, "humanistic" being used here as adjective not for the humanities but for a specific doctrine that makes embodied man, man's measure.

So far have we ventured down the road to this Promethean epistemology, naturalistic ontology, and humanistic anthropology that it is virtually impossible for us to see how arbitrary the entire outlook is—how like a barren moonscape it would have appeared to our ancestors and continues to appear to everyone but ourselves. My own birth and early experience in China may make it easier for me to see Weber's point, earlier referred to, that the way our Western minds work is not the way human minds must work; but nothing turns on this. I think we can say that the negative way of making our case for the humanities—our point that rationality in no way requires us to think that the garden is not enchanted—has objective standing. We can argue with those who dispute us here.

V. Entering the Holy Land

Not so with reasons we may adduce for thinking that the garden *is* enchanted. These positive reasons are not illogical, but whether we admit the fact grudgingly or glory in it, the fact itself remains: these positive reasons require, as their premises so to speak, sensibilities that are unevenly distributed and cultivated. So strictly rational clout cannot be expected of them.[1] But as the Buddha said to Mara the Tempter when the latter tried to persuade him not to bother to teach because there was no hope that others could fathom his culminating insight: "There will

[1]A scientist has written that whatever we consider ultimate reality to be, one of the reasons we find it to be mysterious and awe inspiring is precisely "its failure to present itself as the perfect and articulate consequence of rational thought" (Henry Margenau in Paul Schilpp, *Albert Einstein: Philosopher-Scientist* [New York: Harper Torchbooks, 1959], p. 250).

be some who will understand." So I shall continue. Over the entrance to the magic lantern show in Hermann Hesse's *Steppenwolf* was inscribed, "Not for Everybody." The following four arguments will seem like such only to those who at some level of their being have not been permitted to forget the immensity of what it means to be truly human.

1. *The argument from the human majority*. No culture save our own has disjoined man from his world, life from what is presumed to be nonlife, in the alienating way we have. As Gilbert Durand has pointed out,

> the traditional image of man does not distinguish, nor even want to distinguish, the I from the Not-I, the world from man; whereas the entire teaching of modern Western civilization . . . strives to cut the world off from man, to separate the "I think" from what is thought. Dualism is the great "schizomorphic" structure of Western intelligence.[5]

Laurens van der Post tells of the South African bushmen that wherever they go, they feel themselves known, hence at home. There is no threat, no horror of emptiness or strangeness, only familiarity in a friendly, living environment, hence also the absence of any feeling of loneliness.[6] One of my favorite possessions is a *kakimono* that was given to me by a Japanese friend. In four Chinese characters that are bold and beautiful it proclaims that heaven and earth are pervaded with sentience, infused with feeling. This "majority rule" argument that I am beginning with must naturally face the suspicion that attends all reasonings to the effect that "fifty million Frenchmen can't be wrong." But unless the minority (in this case ourselves) can show reasons for thinking the majority is mistaken (and in this case such reasons do not exist: that was the gist of my negative formulation of the case for the humanities), it seems wise to side with the majority. From within Western parochialism, the view that man is of a piece with his habitat may look like it belongs to "the childhood of the human race." Freed from that parochialism, it looks like man's central surmise when the full range of human experience is legitimated and pondered profoundly: the view that is normal to the human condition because consonant with the complete complement of human sensibilities.

2. *The argument from science.* We must be careful here, for science cannot take a single step toward proving transcendence. But because it does prove things in its own domain and that domain has turned out to be impressive in its own right, science has become the most powerful symbol for transcendence our age affords. I shall list three teachings of contemporary science that carry powerful overtones for those with ears to hear.

a. Fred Hoyle tells us that "no literary imagination could have invented a story one-hundredth part as fantastic as the sober facts that [science has] unearthed."[7] That reality has turned out to be quantitatively more extravagant than we had supposed suggests that its qualitative features may be equally beyond our usual suppositions. If the universe is spatially unbounded, perhaps it is limitless in worth as well.

b. Wholeness, integration, at-one-ment—the concept of unity is vital to the humanities; it is not going too far to cite radical disunity (the man/world split as a final disjunction) as the fiction that has reduced the humanities to their present low estate. Yet science has found nature to be unified to a degree that, again, we would not have surmised without its proofs. Matter and energy are one. Time and space are one, time being space's fourth dimension. Space and gravity are one: the latter is simply space's curvature. And in the end matter and its space-time field are one; what appears to us as a material body is nothing but a center of space-time's deformation. Once again: If we could be taken backstage into the spiritual recesses of reality in the way physics has taken us into its physical recesses, might we not find harmony hidden there as well—earth joined to heaven, man walking with God?

c. The Cartesian/Newtonian paradigm will not work for

quantum physics. It is going to be very difficult to fashion an alternative, for the new physics is so strange that we will never be able to visualize it or describe it consistently in ordinary language. But this is itself exciting. We do not know where we are headed, but at least the door of the prison that alienated us and produced the Age of Anxiety is now sprung. It is true that we do not know where we are going, but scientists themselves are beginning to suggest that our haven may be nowhere in the space-time manifold since that manifold is itself derivative and relative. Our final move may be into a different dimension of reality entirely. David Bohm calls this dimension "the implicate order," an order to which Bell's theorem, Chew's S-matrix bootstrap model as Fritjof Capra interprets it, and Karl Pribram's holographic model of mind all seem (in their various ways) to point.

3. *The argument from human health.* "Pascal's wager" and James' "will to believe" have made their place in philosophy by virtue of their sensible suggestions as to how to proceed in the face of uncertainty. I propose that we add to them what might be called "the argument from human health." I shall use something John Findlay has written about Hegel to make my point here, replacing his references to Hegel with phrases that describe life's final matrix—what in this essay I have been calling, with Weber, life's garden.

> In my not infrequent moods of exaltation I certainly sense my garden to be enchanted. When I do hard theoretical work and succeed in communicating its results to others, I feel that the whole sense of the world lies in endeavors such as mine, that this is the whole justification of its countless atrocious irritants. I feel clear that the world has sense, and that no philosophy that sees it as disenchanted can express this sense satisfactorily. But in my more frequent mood of mild depression I do not see the world thus. I see it as bereft of sense, and I submit masochistically to its senselessness, even taking more comfort in its cold credibility than in the rational desirability of an enchanted existence. I am not even convinced that there

> is one best or right perspective in which the world should be viewed: it seems a provocative staircase figure always idly altering its perspective.[8]

The point is this: "depression" and "masochism" are pathological terms. To cast our lot with them, assuming that we see most clearly when we are unwell rather than well, is itself a pathological move. The healthy move, it would seem, is to ground our outlooks in our noblest intuitions. This leads to my fourth and final consideration.

4. *The argument from special insights.* End meets beginning: I come at my close to my title. The title of William Golding's novel *Free Fall* has obvious affinities with my subtitle, "The Humanities as Uncontrolled Experiment," but it is an account its hero gives of something that happens to him in the course of that story that gives me my title proper. Samuel Mountjoy—his name itself elicits a small gasp in the context of the burden and promise of the humanities—is in a Nazi concentration camp awaiting questioning about plans for a prison break. Frenetically he rehearses the tortures that are sure to be inflicted on him to extract the scrap of information he possesses when suddenly, in his own words, "I was visited by a flake of fire, miraculous and pentecostal; and fire transmuted me, once and forever."[9]

Intimations like these come, and when they do we do not know whether the happiness they bring is the rarest or the commonest thing on earth, for in all earthly things we find it, give it, and receive it, but cannot hold onto it. When it comes, it seems in no way strange to be so happy, but in retrospect we wonder how such gold of Eden could have been ours. The human opportunity, always beckoning but never in this life reached, is to stabilize that gold; to let such flakes of fire turn us into "handfuls of light." This second image comes from a tradition in Islam that reads, "God took a handful of His light, and said to it 'Be Muhammad.' " In its esoteric, Sufic reading, the Muhammad here referred to is the Logos, the Universal Man, the Image of God that is in us all; our essence that awaits release.

Notes

1. Edward Norman, *Christianity and the World Order* (New York: Oxford University Press, 1979), p. 6.

2. Alex Comfort, *I and That* (New York: Crown Publishers, 1979), pp. 69-70. It is not likely that this estimate of religion's importance, coming as it does from the author of *The Joy of Sex*, is skewed by excess piety.

3. Bryan Wilson, *Contemporary Transformations of Religion* (Oxford: Clarendon Press, 1976), p. 100.

4. Ernest Gellner, *The Legitimation of Belief* (Cambridge: Cambridge University Press, 1975), pp. 206-7.

5. Gilbert Durand, "On the Disfiguration of the Image of Man in the West," monograph published by Golgonooza Press, Ipswich, 1977.

6. Laurens van der Post, *The Heart of the Hunter* (Baltimore, Penguin, 1965), p. 188.

7. Fred Hoyle, *The Nature of the Universe* (New York: New American Library, 1950), p. 120.

8. John Findlay, in Alasdair MacIntyre, ed., *Hegel* (South Bend, Ind.: University of Notre Dame Press, 1976), pp. 19-20.

9. New York: Harcourt, Brace, 1960, p. 188.

6

THE CRISIS IN PHILOSOPHY*

Walker Percy says today's novel is in a mess. He admits that it's always been in a mess, but he sees its current mess as singular. Always before there was a background of shared meanings against which authors could make their characters stand out, but today no such consensual backdrop exists.

Philosophy also seems to be in a singular mess, one evidence being the number of influential philosophers who see no future for the discipline, or at most a minimal one. Wittgenstein came to see its only real service as therapy—undoing the mental knots philosophy itself creates. Heidegger announced the end of metaphysics to which Rorty adds "the end of epistemology." And now James Edwards and Bernard Williams are turning down the lights on philosophical ethics with their *Ethics without Philosophy* and *Ethics and the Limits of Philosophy* respectively. What remains after these closures seems to be "conversation" and "play," to which neither Rorty nor Derrida sees philosophy as having anything distinctive to contribute. Hilary Putnam says "the tradition is in shambles,"[1] and Kai Nielsen concurs: "There is no defending the tradition. Systematic analytic philosophy and its Continental cousins along with their historical

*Emended version of a paper delivered at the meeting of the American Philosophical Association, Pacific Division, March, 1987. Reprinted from *Behaviorism*, Spring 1988, Volume 16, Number 1.

ancestors must be given up."[2] "Epitaph-writing," Alasdair MacIntyre reports, "has been added to the list of accepted philosophical activities."[3]

The object of this paper is to trace the steps that have led to this identity crisis for the discipline, and to ask what might be done in the face of it. I shall use the plenary address that Richard Rorty delivered at the Eleventh (1985) Inter-American Congress of Philosophy in Mexico City as my entrée to the project.

If nineteenth-century philosophy began with Romantic Idealism and ended by worshipping the positive sciences, Rorty points out, twentieth-century philosophy began by revolting against a narrowly empiricist positivism and is ending by returning

> to something reminiscent of Hegel's sense of humanity as an essentially historical being, one whose activities in all spheres are to be judged not by its relation to non-human reality but by comparison and contrast with its earlier achievements and with utopian futures. This return will be seen as having been brought about by philosophers as various as Heidegger, Wittgenstein, Quine, Gadamer, Derrida, Putnam and Davidson.[4]

That says a lot in small compass, so let me repeat it adding a few particulars. The nineteenth century began with a reaction against the scientism of the Enlightenment, protesting its claim that mathematical demonstration provides the model for inquiry and positive science the model for culture. It ended, though, by swinging back to Enlightenment predilections and shunting off into literature the counter-Enlightenment sentiments that had given rise to the Romantic Movement and German Idealism. So philosophy entered the twentieth century allied to science. Experimental science being outside its province, this meant following Husserl and Russell into mathematics and logic. Husserl soon deviated from that program to found a brand-new approach to philosophy—phenomenology—which would replicate science's apodicticity without using its logic. Heidegger's *Being and Time* subverted that move and thenceforth Continental philosophy renounced both apodicticity and deduction. In English-speaking countries, though, Russell's slogan that "logic is the essence of philosophy" persisted, and ability to follow completeness proofs for formal systems replaced foreign language as a professional requirement.

Even the Anglo-American attempt to "do philosophy" via logic eventually abandoned apodicticity, though, for non-Euclidean geometries showed logic to be flexible; since it works equally well with whatever primitives we begin with, it produces nothing that is unequivocal. In their *Principia Mathematica*, Whitehead and Russell spelled this out by developing a "logic of relations" to replace the reigning logic of things, and Cassirer and C. I. Lewis went on to relativize Kant whose *Critique* had dominated modern epistemology. The human mind is not programmed to see the world in a single way. It sees it in different ways as time and cultures decree.

This drive towards pluralism didn't stop with epistemology; it pressed on into ontology. Having satisfied themselves that *our minds* require nothing of us, philosophers proceeded to argue that *the world* doesn't require anything of us either. Their way of doing this was to go after Plato's essences and Aristotle's substance, for if these exist they could draw the mind up short and thinking would not be indefinitely malleable. Again, it is important to see this second rejection—the rejection of the fixity of things to accompany the rejection of the fixity of logic—as motivated by the same determination to stem the tide of the Enlightenment Project in its twentieth-century positivistic version, for if there is a way things *are* it was pretty clear that the twentieth century would take it to be the way the sciences collectively report; the Vienna Circle with its "unification of science movement" was championing just this dénouement. Rorty brings these two rejections together and shows how central they have been to our century's philosophy:

> I do not think it far-fetched to see such different books as Carnap's *Logische Aufbau der Welt*, Cassirer's

> *Philosophy of Symbolic Forms*, Whitehead's *Process and Reality*, Quine's *Word and Object*, Nelson Goodman's *Ways of Worldmaking*, Putnam's *Reason, Truth and History*, and Davidson's *Essays on Truth and Interpretation* as developments of the anti-Aristotelian and anti-substantialist, anti-essentialist implication common to *Principia Mathematica* and to the development of non-Euclidean geometries.

Again, we should not lose sight of the motivation in all this. Seeing no way in which (in the face of the scientific temper of our century) it could register a view of reality that could compete with the scientistic one that was gaining ground, philosophy took the next best step. It went after the notion of a single worldview *period*: the notion that there is one unequivocal, comprehensive way that things actually are, or if there is, that human minds can have any knowledge of what that way is. This meant renouncing what historically had been philosophy's central citadel, metaphysics. Better no metaphysics at all than the one that was threatening to take over.

But if the "post-Nietzschean deconstruction of metaphysics" excused philosophers from thinking about the world, what should they be thinking about? We saw that during the early, positivistic decades of our century when philosophers thought science was the royal road to truth, they latched onto logic as the slice of science that they could service: let the experimental scientists discover synthetic truths; philosophers would monitor the analytic truths that were also needed. In 1951, though, Quine demolished the analytic/synthetic, fact/meaning distinction with his *Two Dogmas of Empiricism*. With the analytic rug thus pulled out from under them, philosophers retreated to ordinary language for a preserve of meaning that didn't depend on logic, yet needed attention. Now, though, the wall around that refuge is being dismantled by Donald Davidson's critique of the distinction between the "formal" or "structural" features of discourse and its "material" ones. The correct theory of meaning, Davidson argues, is one that dispenses with entities called "meanings" altogether; instead of asking "What is the meaning of an expression?" it asks, "How does this expression function in this particular linguistic move?" With this total de-logicizing and naturalizing of language, the division between it and the rest of life disappears. Instead of a "structure" or body of rules that philosophers can discover and help others to see—or even the multiple structures and rules that Lewis and Cassier talked about—language now looks like simply another human way of coping with the world.

It really isn't surprising, therefore, to find philosophers closing shop, for if logic isn't philosophy's essence (Quine) and language isn't either (Davidson), the question "what essence remains?" cannot be avoided. We can argue over whether "essence" is the right word here, but let us come to the point. The deepest reason for the current crisis in philosophy is its realization that autonomous reason—reason without infusions that both power and vector it—is helpless. By itself, reason can deliver nothing apodictic. Working (as it necessarily must) with variables, variables are all it can come up with. The Enlightenment's "natural light of reason" turns out to have been a myth. Reason is not itself a light. It is more like a transformer that does useful things but on condition that it is hitched to a generator.

Clearly aware of reason's contingency, medieval philosophy attached itself to theology as its handmaiden. Earlier, Plato too had accepted reason's contingency and grounded his philosophy in intuitions that are discernible by the "eye of the soul" but not by reason without it. In the seventeenth century, though, responding to the advent of modern science with the controlled experiment as its new and powerful way of getting at truth, philosophy unplugged from theology. Bacon and Comte were ready to replug it at once, this time into science, but there were frequencies science still couldn't register, so philosophy took off on its own. Why suppose that reason requires support? If we liken reason to a lever, philosophy as deployed in the modern age has been philosophy as conceived in liberty and dedicated to the proposition that reason possesses its own Archimedian point. There are debates as to what that point is—Descartes' innate ideas? Kant's categories of reason? The positivists' sense data? But that reason *has* a fixed point of reference from which to proceed was not, for the three centuries during which modernity was in place, seriously doubted.

And because it was not doubted, philosophy could have a healthy self-image. For culture is an assemblage of components—science, history, morality, religion, and art, among others—all of which make knowledge claims. Because knowledge *per se* is philosophy's province—in the modern period epistemology became its central occupation—it seemed to "stand to reason," as we say, that philosophers were the ones who were qualified to monitor the conceptual foundations of culture's components, validating where appropriate, debunking where not. In a very real sense this made it, not just in its own eyes but in those of the general public, culture's arbiter—philosophy was foundational to culture. Kantians and positivists saw their talents as especially fitting them for this position, as have analytic philosophers who monitor the language we all must use.

It is to Rorty's and MacIntyre's great credit that they have had the courage and insight to see that these claims for philosophy are hollow. In a dramatic exchange during the December, 1980, meeting of the American Philosophical Association, Rorty pressed his critics to offer examples of cases "where some philosophical inquiry into the conceptual foundations of X provided any furtherance of X or anything else, or even any furtherance of our understanding of X or anything else." Kai Nielson tells us that the challenge has not been met.[5]

The collapse of a self-image that has powered a profession for almost four hundred years, giving it in that stretch both hope and a sense of high calling, is no small occurrence. It makes it impossible for the discipline to continue as usual. There seems to be a consensus that if philosophy is to continue as a profession it must take a new turn.

To see what that turn might be, we can go back to Rorty for a moment. We watched him point out that for most of this century Anglo-American philosophy was powered by science's problems and premises, whereas Continental philosophy turned to literature. He ends his address by noting that politics provides a third possible generator for philosophy, but he advises against it since "to assume that it is our task to be the avant-garde of political movements" would reduce philosophy to propaganda.

There is a fourth possible "primer" for philosophy though, which Rorty doesn't mention, perhaps because he is himself powered by it to the point where he simply takes it for granted. This fourth generator is social science, and the rising importance of names like Habermas and Gadamer suggest that the human sciences are bidding to displace the natural sciences in providing philosophers with their premises and problems. If science shouldn't monitor our thinking because it countenances only half of reality, and metaphysics (which tries to work from reality's whole) is pretense and delusion, let societies—"forms of life," or cultural-linguistic wholes—be the final arbitors of meaning, reality, and truth. George Will is right: "The magic word of modernity is 'society.' "[6]

The notion that points philosophy towards the social sciences is holism. Even while philosophy was powered by science, mounting evidence for the mind's propensity to gestalt its experiences led Hanson to argue that "all facts are theory-laden" and Thomas Kuhn to write *The Structure of Scientific Revolution*, which for a quarter of a century has been the most cited book on college campuses and has turned "paradigm" into a household word. Heidegger and Wittgenstein had already pushed matters beyond the philosophy of science, though, by grounding theoretical in practical holism, and their augmented version too is now all but accepted.[7] Because thinking invariably proceeds in social contexts and against a backdrop of social practices, meaning derives from—roots down into and draws its life from—those backgrounds and contexts. This means that in considering an idea, not only must we (if we are to be thorough) take into account the conceptual gestalts of which it is a part. We must also consider the social "forms of life" (Wittgenstein) whose "micro-practices" (Foucault) give gestalts their final meaning. "Agreement in judgments means agreement in what people *do* and *say*, not what they *believe*," Wittgenstein insists.[8]

This move to work in concert with the human sciences signals more vitality than the proposal to abandon ship, but it seems unlikely that philosophers will content themselves indefinitely with deadending their questions in forms of life. For social wholes are self-enclosed; unrelieved, a form-of-life is a kind of collective "egocentric predicament" if not solipsism. Those predicaments can seem invincible if one accepts their premises, but philosophy has never, on balance, knuckled under to them.

The two kinds of boundaries that social holism acquiesces to are, first, the kind that separates such wholes from one another, and second, the one that isolates configurations of phenomenal experiences as such from the noumenal world that transcends the human. Admittedly, both kinds of walls are difficult to breech. Two decades of trying to figure out how tribes that speak different languages could communicate have underscored the difficulty of transcending cultural-linguistic horizons, while phenomenology's *epoche* all but gives up on the prospect of breeching the noumenal/phenomenal barrier; David Pears calls Wittgenstein's conclusion that "there is no conceivable way of getting between language and the world and finding out whether there is a general fit between them," the central thesis of his later years.[9] When all is said and done, however—when we have made every concession we can think of to the difficulty (verging on impossibility) of climbing out of our skins, out of our languages, out of our times—the fact remains: Of all the life forms on earth, we and we only possess the ability to view the world detachedly, which is to say to some degree trans-perspectivally and objectively. This is the important point in Thomas Nagel's *The View From Nowhere*: that we can think about the world in terms that transcend our own experience and interest and, yes, times and culture, too, considering it from a vantage point which, being not entirely perspectival save as it is humanly so, is "nowhere in particular."

The first place where the limitations of cultural-linguistic holism are beginning to show up is in the difficulties it is having with the problem of relativism. If the issues of philosophy lead to (and dead-end in) a plurality of collective, phenomenal configurations of experience, leaving us no more than social functionaries, there appears to be no court of appeal for adjudicating between these collective experiences. If forms of life are the bottom line, what recourse is there for affirming that one such form is better than another? Is there any way we can take seriously the possibility that our own cultural-linguistic epoch, say, may have taken a wrong turn, and if it has, what criterion prompts that verdict? Pragmatic outcomes seem to be the only court of appeal, but though useful for provisional purposes, pragmatic criteria never tell the whole story, for if cockroaches are to inherit the earth, that would not induce us to consider them our superiors. Cultural-linguistic holism stammers answers to relativism; it can counter "vulgar relativism" by appealing to currents of consensus that underlie superficial differences. But this no more saves the day than the structural sturdiness of a house redeems it if it is about to slide off its mountain perch.

A second besetting problem for holism concerns truth, for which it can provide no basis other than consensus. It seems strained, for example, and in the end indefensible to argue (as Kripke contends Wittgenstein argues[10]) that even the rules of arithmetic have no validity beyond the social consensus that supports them.

These difficulties alone are enough to suggest that social holism is at best a way-station on philosophy's sojourn. If we try to anticipate where it might go next, the most I can suggest is that, riding its current realization that thinking is invariably "situated," it take another look at the possibility that its basic situation is a condition that is generically human. The roots of thinking do not stop with collectivities. They extend deeper into soil that human collectivities share in common.

But getting philosophy out of its present crisis was not the object of this paper.

Notes

1. Hilary Putnam, "After Empiricism," in John Rajchman & Cornel West (Eds.), *Post-Analytic Philosophy* (New York: Columbia University Press, 1985), p. 28.

2. "Scientism, Pragmatism, and the Fate of Philosophy," *Inquiry*, 29, p. 278. I have converted Nielsen's rhetorical questions into straightforward assertions.

3. From an address, "Philosophy: Past Conflict and Future Direction," delivered to the Pacific Division of the APA in March, 1987.

4. *Proceedings of the American Philosophical Association*, Vol. 59 (July 1986), p. 748.

5. Kai Nielsen, "The Withering Away of the Tradition," a paper delivered at the meeting of the APA mentioned in footnote 3.

6. *Statecraft as Soulcraft* (New York: Simon & Schuster, 1983), p. 34.

7. For the clearest statement of the difference between theoretical and practical holism, see Hubert Dreyfus, "Holism and Hermeneutics," in Robert Hollinger (Ed.), *Hermeneutics and Praxis* (Notre Dame: University of Notre Dame Press, 1985).

8. Hubert Dreyfus' paraphrase of Wittgenstein in ibid., p. 235.

9. *The New Republic*, May 19, 1986, p. 3.

10. See Saul A. Kripke, *Wittgenstein on Rules and Private Language* (Cambridge: Harvard University Press, 1983). For a critique of Wittgenstein's position on this point, see Ernest Gellner, "The Gospel According to Ludwig," *The American Scholar*, Spring 1984.

7

SCIENCE AND THEOLOGY
The Unstable Detente *

From higher education (our intellectual frontier), through its most value-laden regions (the humanities and philosophy in particular) to God the source of it all—the essays in this section ascend in the regions they examine. As loss of transcendence and the sense of the sacred is one of Postmodernism's defining features, sight naturally has to labor more as the eye ascends: one must look more intently, as in unfamiliar territory. As the two preceding essays emphasized, the central energies of the West have moved steadily into science and technology, a relentless spirit of rational inquiry aimed at control. One important consequence of this was already evident in the nineteenth century: not only religion but art were moving to the margins. Hegel spoke of both together when he said that, however splendid the gods look in modern works of art, whatever dignity and perfection we might find in the images of God the Father and the Virgin Mary, it is of no use: we no longer bend our knees. "It is a long time," Saul Bellow adds in his Nobel Laureate Lecture, "since the knees were bent in piety."

A. Thesis

Against the prevailing assumption that "the warfare between science and theology" (to resurrect W. E. H. Lecky's phrase) is a thing of the past, I propose to argue

*Reprinted with permission and negligible modifications from *The Anglican Theological Review* 63, no. 4 (October 1981).

that if this is true it can only be because science has won the war. Only an exhausted theology, one about to sink into the sands of science like a spent wave, could fail to sense the enormous tension between its claims and those of a scientific worldview.

There is, of course, a sense in which no tension exists or ever has existed. As truth is one and religion and science are both concerned with it, in principle they must be partners. But that is principle only—de jure, not de facto. For the partnership to work we would need to see clearly the inherent limitations of science and keep them in sharp focus. But we do not see these limitations, largely (I suspect) because we do not want to. Because science augments our power and possessions, we would like to think that it has no cutoff point; that its present limitations are provisional only, and that in time it will break out of them to service our complete selves in the way it now services our bodies. So we encourage it to expand, and count on its doing so. Mostly we want its technological fallout, but we want its theory too. For modern science derives from the controlled experiment, and as that is as close to proof as we can get, a scientific worldview would be one we could wholeheartedly believe. It would be true.

It happens, though, that a scientific worldview is impossible. I do not mean that we are a long way from having such a view; I mean that we never will have one—it is impossible in principle, a contradiction in terms. For "world" implies whole and science deals with part, an identifiable part of the whole that can be shown to be part only—most of this paper will be devoted to this showing. Again, it is crucial to see that this is not a temporary limitation but one that is built into science's very nature. To hope for a worldview from science is like hoping that increasingly detailed maps of Illinois will eventually produce the ultimate map of the United States.

Three times before in this book I have walked up to this point, approaching it from different directions to try to see precisely where the boundaries of science lie. Here I propose to pull these sallies together—that the *Oxford*

English Dictionary defines "sally" as "rush of besieged upon besiegers" makes the word poetically exact. But because I shall be riding this issue hard, devoting most of my space to it, I should say why I see the limits of science as at once the most important point we need to be straight on in relating science to theology, and concomitantly the one we have yet to see clearly.

It seems to be agreed that a defining feature of modernity is loss of transcendence. The sense of the sacred has declined; phrases like "the death of God" and "eclipse of God" would have been inconceivable in earlier days. I assume that readers will agree, in addition, that this is a real *loss*; fading of the belief that we live in an ordered universe which is related to other, unseen realms of order in a total harmony cannot but have serious consequences. That people now believe less in theologies generally is one thing,[a] but we must note too that the content of the theologies they are now offered has been diluted. It has been toned down to fit better with our prevailing, largely secular, mindset.

This last is the most controversial point I shall make, and it may be mistaken though I do not think so. As section three of this essay will be devoted to it, I hurry on here to ask: If our age *is* theologically on the defensive, what drove it into the corner? Many things, one can assume, but it seems clear to me—so clear that I will not even argue the point here—that its chief assailant has been modern science. Science has spawned an outlook whose chief features are *naturalism* (the view that nothing that lacks a material component exists, and that in what does exist it is its physical component that has the final say), *evolution* (generalized as the belief that the more derives exhaustively from the less, the higher from the lower), and *progress* (the centering of hope on a this-worldly, historical future). If we match these planks

[a]To repeat a quotation I used in an earlier essay, "there is no doubt that in developed societies education has contributed to the decline of religious belief" (Edward Norman, *Christianity and the World Order* (New York: Oxford University Press, 1979), p. 6.

against the platform that issues from revelation, we get the following lineup:

Epistemology:	Science ↓	vs.	Revelation ↓
Ontology:	naturalism ↓		supernaturalism ↓
Efficient cause:	Darwinian evolution ↓		creation ↓
Final cause:	progress		salvation

Were we mentally capable of keeping the science column in its place, there would be no problem, but the triumphs of science have been too impressive to allow this. Method has mushroomed into metaphysics, science into scientism, the latter defined as the drawing of conclusions from science that do not logically follow. I do not charge this against science, nor its votaries whom I regard with a blend of gratitude, affection, and awe. Scientism is a mark of our times, one we are all victims of and responsible for: in Descartes's fall, we sinned all. As there is no space here to trace its workings piecemeal, I propose to strike at the root. Through the three demonstrations of science's limitations I have alluded to, I hope to expose the delusion that our prevailing, predominantly secular outlook is scientific by showing that no inclusive outlook can be such. If my strategy succeeds, it will show that theology need cater to our prevailing styles of thought only if it wishes to. Nothing in the way of evidence requires that it do so.

II. The Limits of Science

A. First Demonstration

In *Forgotten Truth* I noted that though science is not monolithic, its distinctive way of getting at truth—the scientific method—gives it a defining thrust. No knowledge deserves to be called scientific unless it is objective in the sense of laying claim to intersubjective agreement, but we move closer to science proper when we discover truths that enable us to predict, and closer still when we reach truths that facilitate control. Each move we make along this line finds our knowing meshing increasingly with mathematics, number being (as we say) the language of science.[b]

The achievements of this probe for truth have been so dazzling that they have blinded us to the fact that they proceed from an extremely restricted kind of knowing. There are four things science cannot get its hands on.[c]

1. *Intrinsic and Normative Values*

Science can deal with instrumental values, but not intrinsic ones. It can tell us that smoking damages health, but whether health is better than somatic gratification it cannot adjudicate. Again, it can determine what people *do* like, but not what they should like. Opinion polls and market research are sciences, but there cannot be a science of the *summum bonum*.

2. *Purposes*

Teleonomy, yes; teleology, no. The biological sciences acknowledge that living organisms are goal directed, and therefore purposive in that sense. They must insist, though, that biological drives, homeostasis, and the like, be explained in terms of things that themselves derived nonpurposively, for to introduce intentions into explanations is anthropomorphic, and anthropomorphic explanations are the opposite of scientific ones. Francis Bacon said this early on. "Teleological explanations in science are the province of theology, not science," he wrote. "They are like virgins dedicated to God, and therefore barren of empirical fruit for the good of man."[1] His point has stayed in place. "The cornerstone of scientific method is . . . the *systematic* denial that 'true' knowledge can be got at by interpreting phenomena in terms of final causes—that is to say, of 'purposes.' "[2]

---

[b]This model is presented diagramatically on p. 83 above.

[c]They were noted in the essay "Excluded Knowledge," but are repeated here in slightly different form.

3. *Ultimate and Existential Meanings*
Science is meaningful throughout, but there are two kinds of meanings it cannot handle. One of these is ultimate meanings (what is the meaning of it all?), while the other type is existential (the kind we have in mind when we say something is meaningful). There is no way science can force the human mind to find its discoveries involving; the hearer always has the option to shrug his shoulders and walk away. Unable to deal with these two kinds of meanings, science "fails in the face of all ultimate questions" (Jaspers) and leaves "the problems of life . . . completely untouched" (Wittgenstein). "Only questions which cannot be answered with scientific precision have any real significance" (E. F. Schumacher).

4. *Quality*
This is fundamental, for it is their qualitative components that make values, meanings, and purposes important. But qualities, being subjective, barely lend themselves to even the minimum requirement of science—objectivity—let alone submit to quantification. Certain qualities (such as colors or sounds) have quantifiable substrates (electromagnetic waves of varying lengths), but quality itself is unmeasurable. Euphrometers have been attempted, but without success, for two pains do not add up to one that is twice as painful, and half a happiness makes no sense. Science's inability to deal with the qualitatively unmeasurable leaves it working with what Lewis Mumford called a "disqualified universe."

This account of what science cannot deal with can expect to encounter resistance, but not (as far as I have been able to discern) because it is untrue. Given the importance of normative values, final causes, existential and ultimate meanings, and intrinsic qualities, the fact that science is no closer now than it ever was to dealing with them would seem to be clear indication that it is not designed for their investigation.[d] Appeals to the

---

[d]The current (as I write these lines) issue of the *Scientific American* confirms this nonprogress with respect to qualities. Its article by

infancy of science only obscure the issue by postponing the question of whether its advances can possibly fill in the lacunae. The answer is no: the change from classical to relativity physics was momentous, but it did not move physics a whit closer to the untended areas. And we can see why it did not do so. For science to enter the domains it has thus far eschewed it would have to relax the demands for objectivity, prediction, control, and number from which its power in quantitative domains derives. We are free, of course, to turn science in this new direction if we want to, but we must realize that every step toward humanizing the enterprise will be a step away from the effectiveness it has thus far manifested. For to repeat, it is precisely from the narrowness of its approach that the power of science derives. An effective and restricted science or one that is ample but does not enable us to control the course of events much more than do art, religion, or psychotherapy—we can define the word as we wish. What is not possible is to have it both ways.

B. Second Demonstration

Whereas the preceding demonstration sought to show how barren a scientific worldview would have to be, disclosing perhaps as much of reality as an X-ray negative discloses of a human self, this second demonstration notes that it would also be stunted—or better truncated.

The reasoning behind that statement is as follows.[e]

Jerry Fodor on "The Mind-Body Problem" espouses functionalism as the most promising current approach to understanding mental states and operations, but concedes that "the functionalist account does not work for mental states that have qualitative content" (243, no. 7 [January 1981]: 122).

[e]This second demonstration appears three times in these essays, in "Excluded Knowledge," here, and in "Beyond the Modern Western Mindset." I have retained it in all three places because (as I noted in my Preface), quite apart from the holes that would result if it were removed, the repetitions serve a constructive purpose. The argument they condense is complex, and as it is crucial for perceiving the limitations of our current mindset, it is important that it sink in. I hope its force will mount each time the argument is repeated.

Worldviews arise from epistemologies which in turn are generated by the motivations that control them. In the seventeenth century Europe hit upon an epistemology (empiricism, the scientific method[f]) that augmented its control dramatically—over nature to start with, but who knew where such control might eventually reach? This increase in power pleased us to the point that we gave this way of knowing right of way. And with that move the die was cast respecting worldview. Empiricism proceeds through sense knowledge, and that which connects with our senses is matter. I do not say that the worldview this epistemology has generated is materialism (the view that nothing but matter exists), for our thoughts and feelings are, on the one hand, too conspicuous to be denied and, on the other, too different from what we experience matter to be to be reduced to it. It is safer to dub our worldview naturalism, defining this (as I did in section one) as the view (a) that nothing that lacks a material component exists, and (b) that in what does exist the physical component has the final say. That at the level of quantum mechanics this component seems to be "dematerializing" has not shaken our naturalism because matter (however we define it, however ghostly it may seem) remains what we can get our hands on and control. The problem lies deeper than willfullness—wanting to have our way with nature—for even our search for disinterested truth is drawn to naturalism and empiricism. Control includes, importantly, the controlled experiment, and this (more than any other form of validation) inspires confidence.

Now comes the point: the kind of world (view) the will to control generates. Again let me characterize it negatively. An epistemology that aims relentlessly at control rules out the possibility of transcendence in principle.[g]

---

[f]I am not overlooking the rational, mathematical component in science, but the crucial role of the controlled experiment gives empiricism the edge.

[g]That modern epistemology so aims was documented in "Excluded Knowledge." I shall not reproduce here the evidence I there

By transcendence I mean something superior to us by every measure of value we know and doubtless some that elude us. To expect a transcendental object to appear on a viewing screen wired by an epistemology that is set for control would be tantamount to expecting color to appear on a television screen that was built for black and white. We can "put nature to the rack," as Bacon advised, because it is our inferior; possessing (in the parts we can get at, at least) neither mind nor freedom, these parts can be pushed around. But if things superior to us exist—extraterrestrial intelligences superior to our own? angels? God?—these are not going to fit into our controlled experiments.[h] It is they who dance circles around us, not we them.

Naturalism's exclusion of things superior to nature combines with its discovery that within nature the superior comes after the inferior, and (to a yet undetermined extent) can be controlled via its inferior components, leaves it no option regarding etiology. Accounting must proceed from inferior to superior, from less to more. Chronologically and developmentally the more comes after the less; causally it comes out of the less, the only other determining principle allowed being chance.[i] In biology (with Darwin) higher forms come after and out of the lower; in sociology (with Marx) the classless society comes after and out of class struggle; in psychology (with Freud) the rational ego comes after and out of the irrational id. Even when the higher has appeared, the thrust is to understand and interpret its workings in terms of the

---

assembled; it will be enough to refer the reader to Ernest Gellner's summary verdict on pp. 97-98 above.

[h]Human beings must be kept in the dark if they are to be subjects for controlled experiments in regions where they are free. But transcendental subjects, if they exist, cannot be kept in the dark. By definition they know more than we do.

[i]On reading this, the physicist-theologian William Pollard wrote to me: "But science does not see the significance of chance and therein lies its Achilles Heel." He probes this point powerfully in his *Science and Transcendence*, his contribution to the Eric Rust *Festschrift, Creation through Alternative Histories*, and his *Chance and Providence.*

lower. The name for this mode of explanation is, of course, reductionism, and the growth of the scientific worldview can be correlated with its advance. For Newton, stars became machines. For Descartes, animals were machines. For Hobbes, society is a machine. For La Mettrie, the human body is a machine. For Pavlov and Skinner, human behavior is mechanical.

C. Third Demonstration

If the preceding demonstration showed that a scientific worldview cannot rise above ourselves in the sense of providing a place for anything that is superior to us, this final check on its limitations shows that it cannot even accommodate ourselves. For scientific knowledge is theoretical whereas the bulk of human understanding is practical.[j] Practical understanding cannot be accommodated to theoretical knowledge.

Scientific knowledge is theoretical in that it consists of identifiable elements that are systematically related, and this differentiates it sharply from practical knowing—knowing how to ride a bicycle, say, or how to swim. In these latter cases our knowledge proceeds in almost total oblivion of the components involved—muscles, nerves, cells, and the like—and their coordinations. It is a "knowing how," rather than a "knowing that."

Another way to put the difference is to say that theoretical knowledge is context-free whereas practical understanding is not. Once we consciously identify something, our minds can isolate it from its context. In looking at a vase I cannot separate my sensation of blue from the vase, but once my mind tells me that the vase *is* blue, though the copula purports to join blueness to vase, in a far more fateful way it disjoins the two. For I can now think blueness without vase and this frees me to move it around my conceptual world at will. In abstracting—extracting—

[j]Martin Heidegger appears to have been the first to work out this difference clearly. My account here is indebted to Hubert Dreyfus's treatment of the matter in his "Holism and Hermeneutics," *Review of Metaphysics* 34, no. 1 (September 1980).

blueness from vase. cognition makes it context free.

Science capitalizes on this freedom from context and tries to show us a contextless world, a view of things that is not affected by even the fact that it derives from our human angle of vision. And when it goes on to try to understand human beings (through the social sciences), this goal continues. It searches for behavior ingredients that are invariant—the same regardless of their context—and the lawful relations these exhibit. The theories that summarize these relations currently take the form of formal models in which the facts are context-free elements or attributes or features or information bits, and the model is a computer program or flow chart showing how such elements are combined to produce complex individual or social behavior.

That these models, be they in structural anthropology, cognitive psychology, or decision analysis, have succeeded no better than their predecessors in enabling their practitioners to predict, or in snowballing into a unified theory of human nature that compares in any way to the unified view of nature that undergirds the physical sciences, should not surprise us, for to return to the nub of this third demonstration, most human knowledge is not theoretical but practical, and even theoretical knowledge rides on a practical base. Practical knowing can no more be separated from its context (to become available to abstract theory) than knowing how to swim can be separated from water. Through cultivated body responses, the "tentacles" of our swimming skill grip the physical world like a root system; and in social skills it is the same, the difference being only that here the context is a background of shared beliefs and practices which we internalize through imitation. Social skills, such as how far to stand from a conversational partner depending on age, sex, status, and purpose, embody a whole cultural interpretation of what it means to be a human being, what a material object is, and (more generally) what counts as real. Heidegger, Merleau-Ponty, and Wittgenstein have shown convincingly, I believe, that this inherited background of practices can never be spelled out in a theory (to be fed into a computer), first, because it is so pervasive that we cannot stand outside it to make it an object of analysis, but even more because in the last resort it is not composed of cognitive features such as beliefs and assumptions at all, but rather of habits and customs, the sort of subtle skills which we exhibit in our everyday interaction with things and people—what Michel Foucault calls micropractices. No one has the slightest idea how to construct formal rules for the skills involved in swimming or speaking a language, let alone those embodying our understanding of what it means to be a human being and live a human life.

III. Theological Compromise?

That was a long section, so let me reiterate its point. Believing that the decline in our sense of transcendence is a loss, and that the chief reason for the decline has been the rise of a rival outlook presumed to be scientific, I think that it is important to show that that supposition is mistaken. Lacking space to show point by point where the error enters, I am going (in this essay) after the notion of a scientific worldview itself, presenting three lines of argument that converge in the conclusion that there can be no such thing. When we find someone writing that "science is the measure of all things, of what is that it is, and of what is not that it is not,"[3] we know automatically that scientism, not science, is speaking.

But now comes the touchy part. Of the five postures Richard Niebuhr showed the church to have assumed toward culture in the course of its history—against it, with it, above it, paradoxical toward it, and with design to transform it[4]—we are clearly in a "with culture" phase; Vatican II formalized this for Roman Catholicism and Bultmann's victory over Barth is a weather vane for Protestantism. But if our culture is riddled with scientism —the problem being, as Victor Frankl puts it, not that the scientists are specializing, but that the specialists are generalizing,—in being *with* culture, the church runs the danger of scientistic rub-off.

There is no way to insure against this danger, but the guidelines (at least) seem clear. It goes without saying that theologians should respect the proven findings of science, and can continue to affirm as they have (in the past two decades especially) that:

> Scientists are no less blessed with *human virtues* than the rest of us. Their work does not pull against their idealism, good will, and natural piety (Harold Schilling, William Pollard, Ian Barbour).
>
> Their *intellectual virtues* are not mechanical—limited to logic and linear thinking. Great science requires as much imagination, inspiration, and "art" as any other creative endeavor (Abraham Maslow, Michael Polanyi).
>
> Equally, as institution, science is as *fallible* as other social efforts. False starts, blind alleys, in-house vendettas and outright dishonesty plague it as much as they do the church (Thomas Kuhn, James Watson's *The Double Helix*, and again Polanyi).

These commonalities, though, should not be allowed to obscure (first) the distinctiveness of scientific knowing, and (second) the limited character of the conclusions that can issue from that distinctiveness.

The first of these two dividing, rather than reconciling, tasks is currently complicated by a move within the philosophy of science itself that slurs the difference between scientific and other ways of knowing. Because at advanced levels the components of science are not tested against experience one by one but only as a whole via theories, it is now generally accepted that scientific facts are theory laden. In verifying a theory we move in a circle from hypothesis to data, data to hypothesis, without ever encountering any bare facts which could call the whole theory into question. From this (now recognized) holistic character of science—from the point, to repeat it, that the facts of science, like most others, must be "interpreted" in the light of the systems in which they appear[5] —this new thrust concludes that science doesn't differ in kind from other self-contained systems of thought such as common sense, or even witchcraft. Paul Feyerabend's

Against Method pushes this claim to anarchist extremes, but its basic point, which can be traced back to Pierre Duhem in the last century, appears in varying degrees in the writings of N. R. Hanson, Willard Quine, and Richard Rorty.

We can agree that science is holistic, but the theoretical character of its holism, which gestalts explicitly identified, context-free components, still differentiates it from other kinds of holism; this was the burden of the third demonstration in the preceding section. The difference must be kept in mind. For if we lose sight of the distinctive, restricted way science goes after knowledge we will think that its findings harbor more implications for theology than they logically can.

As these implications slope toward naturalism, evolution,[k] and progress, if we insist on drawing them—or, what is more common, if we lower our guard, in which case they are sure to enter undetected—theology will suffer. I think I see this happening. I say this tentatively. Kennett Roshi of Mount Shasta Zen Abbey once remarked that she was working on a new *ko'an*, "I could be wrong," and I would like to have that apply to the balance of this section.

So numerous are the theological innovations of modernity that one wonders if, at some unconscious level, they may not be fed by the assumption that as scientific knowledge is cumulative, all knowledge should be.[l] Be

---

[k]I use this word to refer, not to the proven facts of biology and the fossil record, but to the theory (assumed to be established by those facts) which claims that natural selection working on chance mutations adequately accounts for how we got here. No major theologian I know is currently challenging this doctrine—"the most influential teaching of the modern age," as E. F. Schumacher calls it—leaving it to Billy Graham and fundamentalist creationists on the one hand, and concerned laymen like Schumacher himself and secularists like Arthur Koestler on the other, to expose this "crumbling citadel," as Koestler calls it. The next chapter of this book is devoted entirely to this issue.

[l]For my part, I find it more likely that our forefathers—less harried by life's accelerated pace, less deluged and distracted by avalanches of information, less insulated from illness, death, and nature generally—had the theological edge. I find what Origen said of St.

that as it may, when I scan the content of these innovations, what I mostly see is loss—loss that has been suffered, not from the proven facts of science, but from vapors that rise from them like steam, obscuring our sight. (1) Personalism concludes that we must relieve God of either his omnipotence or his goodness. (2) Bultmann's demythologizing rides the dismantling of a pre-Copernican picture of the physical universe to dismantle, in addition, the great chain of being. If only because of what Heidegger (from whom Bultmann draws) will not permit us to *say*, on pain of inauthentic objectivizing, I do not see his Being as a match for either the living God of the Bible or the *ens perfectissimum* of medieval theology. (3) The theology of hope historicizes Christian expectations and introduces development into God, who in ways is "not yet." (4) Teilhard de Chardin's notion of Christ as "the term of evolution" upsets his alpha-omega balance and makes meaning turn on the fate of nature.

(5) As I was myself weaned on process theology, I shall give it three paragraphs, beginning again with loss.[m] It deprives God of exclusive ultimacy, asking that he share that status with three other givens: creativity, eternal objects, and the structure of actual occasions.[n] It rules out the possibility of a concrete, timeless perfection; only abstract entities (eternal objects) are eternal. And it replaces subjective human immortality with an objective version in which we are remembered by God; the traditional teaching that we must all one day awaken from

---

Paul, that he understood Moses far better than we can, altogether plausible.

[m]Since writing this essay process theologian David Griffin and I have written a book-length debate on this point: *Perennial Truth and Process Philosophy* (Albany: SUNY Press, 1989). See also my Bellarmine Lecture, "Has Process Theology Dismantled Classical Theism?," *Theology Digest*, 34:4 (Winter 1988).

[n]In the following statement, John Cobb seems to withdraw ultimacy from God altogether: "The direction is to accept without hesitation or embarrassment the distinction between ultimate reality and God, and to recognize that the God of the Bible . . . is a manifestation of ultimate reality—not the name of that reality" ("Can a Christian Be a Buddhist, Too?" *Japanese Religions*, December 1978, p. 11).

life's dream into other dimensions in which the lie shrivels, the fiction is destroyed, and all deceptions are swept away, is discounted. On what authority, save the naturalism to which process theology is beholden? We can at least be clear, this essay has argued, that science doesn't force that naturalism on us.

Process theologians themselves, of course, do not see these revisions as losses, for to them classical theism is incoherent. Had their notion of coherence ruled at Nicea and Chalcedon, the creeds could not have come down to us as they have. Or to approach the point from a contemporary angle, is there any "incoherence" in classical theism—many are charged—that does not have its analogy in the paradoxes of quantum mechanics, and cannot, with deep discernment, be brought under Niels Bohr's claim that, whereas the opposite of a small truth is false, the opposite of a great truth is another great truth?

I was not myself conscious of the loss in this "updated"° Christianity until, seeking to expand my horizons through the study of world religions, I came (first) on the Vedanta, whereupon I found that my interest in process theology dropped markedly, and with it my interest in Christianity until I discovered that its classical expressions include everything of importance I had discovered in the Upanishads. Why, then, is this loss—process theology—being inflicted on Christians? (That is a strong charge. I keep repeating to myself, like the Jesus Prayer, "I could be wrong, I could be wrong!") Because—I answer from introspection, it being a part of my former self that I am trying to understand—theologians saw in Whitehead the prospect of reconciling religion with modern science. This is a chancy move. As Jeremy Bernstein observed in his review of Fritjof Capra's *The Tao of Physics*, "to hitch a religious philosophy to a contemporary science is a sure route to its obsolescence, [for] the science of the present will look as antiquated to our successors as much

°Schubert Ogden claims that process theology has achieved "something like a Heideggerian 'dismantling' (*Destruktion*) of the history of philosophical theology" (*The Reality of God* [New York: Harper and Row, 1977], p. 48).

of nineteenth-century science looks to us now."[6] Whitehead's philosophy of organism, focusing in its doctrine of prehensions, was modeled on (and thereby powered by) the most sophisticated science of its day; it followed carefully Einstein's prescription, required by his relativity theory, that as no coherent concept of an independently existent particle is possible, reality should be regarded as constituted of fields whose localized pulses do not end abruptly but spread to arbitrarily large distances with decreasing force. As this banished the spectre of clockwork mechanism, which for three hundred years had haunted theology with its view of the world as constituted of entities which are outside of each other in the sense that they exist independently in different regions of space (and time) and interact through forces that do not bring about any changes in their essential natures, it was a thrilling synthesis—I speak for myself; I felt it. But science keeps moving, and it now appears that the unified field theory Einstein had hoped for is not going to happen short of another paradigm change, which would carry us beyond Einstein and Bohr, and therefore beyond Whitehead. Relativity and quantum theory proceed from such opposite premises that it seems impossible for either to accommodate the other.[p] "What is probably needed," David Bohm writes,

> is a qualitatively new theory, from which both relativity and quantum theory are to be derived as abstractions.... The best place to begin is with what they have basically in common. This is undivided wholeness. Though each comes to such wholeness in a different way, it is clear that it is this to which they are both fundamentally pointing.[7]

Undivided wholeness sounds more like God's simplicity (in its technical medieval sense) than like the time-involved creativity and discrete eternal objects Whitehead took for ultimates.

---

[p]Relativity theory requires continuity, strict causality, and locality. Quantum theory requires noncontinuity, noncausality, and nonlocality.

IV. Science As Symbol

It is possible that the preceding section was squandered in what Freud called "the narcissism of small differences," though I do not think so. In any case, though I have exhausted the space allotted me I do not want to end without noting that there is another side to the science/theology question, one that is very different and filled with possibilities that counter the pitfalls I have dwelt on here. If, instead of rummaging through science for direct, literal clues to the nature of reality, we could outgrow this fundamentalism and read science allegorically, we would find sermons in cloud chambers. That the deeper science advances into nature the more integrated it finds it, lends resonance to (though it does not prove) the faith claim that the same holds for being as a whole: God, who is all in all, is likewise one. Or again, that science has found reality in its physical aspect to be incomparably more majestic and awesome than we had supposed suggests—it does not prove—that if we could see the full picture we would find its qualitative depths to be as much beyond what we normally suppose as science has shown its quantitative ones to be.[q]

And remember, we are speaking of light-years.

Notes

1. *Works*, ed. J. Spedding and R. L. Ellis (London, 1858), 4:365.
2. Jacques Monod, *Chance and Necessity* (New York: Random House, 1972), p. 21.
3. Wilfred Sellars, *Science, Perception, and Reality* (New York: Humanities Press, 1963), p. 173.
4. *Christ and Culture* (New York: Harper and Brothers, 1956).
5. It is interesting to find the word hermeneutics, and names like Heidegger and Hans-Georg Gadamer, now surfacing in the philosophy of science.
6. *American Scholar* 48 (Winter 1978-1979): 8.
7. *Wholeness and the Implicate Order* (London: Routledge & Kegan Paul, 1980), p. 176.

---

[q]Chapter five of my *Forgotten Truth* is devoted to the symbolic power latent in science today.

8

TWO EVOLUTIONS*

The preceding essay is not the only one in which science figures prominently; it would not be going too far to see all of the essays save the last in this third, "looking around," section of the book as an effort to understand how, appropriately and inappropriately, science has affected our view of things. This is the only essay, however, that zones in on a specific scientific claim.

The scientific view of how we got here was the obvious choice. When, under the Romans, the Jews faced dispersion, they often asked their rabbis to encapsulate the Torah for them; they needed a formula that could easily be kept in mind during those years of tribulation and disruption. Rabbi Akiba's "You shall love your neighbor as yourself" proved to be the favorite, but alternates were proposed. The strangest of these was the one Rabbi Ben-Azzai put forward, for he nominated as the most important verse in the Bible, "This is the book of the generations of Adam." That sounds flat by comparison, until we remember that "Adam" means "man," which makes the Bible the book of how we got here—an account that differs markedly from the one science puts forward.

This essay was written for the 1982 colloquium on the philosophy of nature which was sponsored by the Boston University Institute for Philosophy and Religion.

---

*Reprinted, with permission and minor emendations, from Leroy S. Rouner (ed.), *On Nature* (University of Notre Dame Press, 1984).

Walker Percy in his *Message in the Bottle* points out that we do not know who we are. There exists in the contemporary West no coherent theory of human nature, no consensus view such as prevailed in thirteenth-century Europe, in seventeenth-century New England, or in traditional societies still. Whether these views were true or false, they were viable beliefs. They animated their cultures and gave life its meaning. They were outlooks people tried to live by.

In contrast to such embracing theories, what we have today is a miscellany of *notions* as to who we are. These notions do not cohere, but they do fall into two rather clearly demarcated camps. On the one hand is the view, backed by modern science, that the human self can be understood as an organism in an environment, endowed genetically like other organisms with needs and drives, who through evolution—natural selection working on chance mutations—has developed strategies for learning and surviving by means of certain adaptive transactions with the environment. Over and against this is the Judeo-Christian view that the human being was created in the image of God with an immortal soul and occupies a place in nature somewhere between the beasts and the angels. At some point humankind suffered a catastrophic fall in consequence of which we have lost our way and, unlike the beasts, have become capable of sin and seekers after salvation. The clue to this second scenario derives not from science or philosophy, but from two historical events—the Exodus and the Incarnation—which produced respectively a people, the Jews; and an institution, the Christian Church.

Not only do these views not mesh; they are in head-on opposition, for according to science we are the more who have derived from the less, whereas our religions teach that we are the less who have derived from the more. In thus contradicting each other, our two views—one taught by our schools, the other by our churches and synagogues—cancel each other out, leaving us without a clear self-image or identity. It is impossible for both views to be true, yet simply by having been born into today's West, all of us believe parts of both of them. Even those who have abandoned the theological specifics of the religious view continue to affirm the afterglow that lingers from its light: the belief that human beings are endowed with certain unique properties—inherent dignity and inalienable rights—that other organisms do not possess, and that (as a consequence) the highest value a democratic society can set for itself is respect for the sacredness and worth of the individual.

How does one live one's life if one tries to take these two contradictory propositions seriously? The standard way is to see oneself as an organism that has evolved enough to have developed certain values. What is not noticed, Walker Percy concludes, is that the moment the sanctity of the individual is turned into a "value," an act of devaluation has already occurred.

An age comes to a close when people discover that they can no longer understand themselves by the theory their age professes. For a while, its denizens will continue to think that they believe it, but they feel otherwise and cannot understand their feelings. This has now happened to us. We continue to believe Darwinism, even though it no longer feels right to us. Darwinism is in fact dying, and its death signals the close of our age.

My rationale for a negative project—deflating Darwinism—is this: with respect to the problem at hand (our point of origin as it bears on who we are), our need is not just to relieve an inconsistency but to do so in the right way, with the better of the two hypotheses triumphing. By the better hypothesis I mean the one that is closer to the truth and more serviceable. Darwinism is obscuring what I believe to be this doubly better answer to the question at stake. If I could prove that we have derived from what exceeds us, I would naturally take that direct route, but metaphysical propositions do not admit of proof, so I resort to this *via negativa.* Rabbis say that if we cannot believe in God, we might at least try to stop believing in idols. Less faith in the Darwinian idol might help to clear a space in which the divine might appear more regularly than it now does.

We would be better off it we could believe that our origin is momentous, and Darwinism counters that belief. Peter Drucker, the industrial consultant, says he never tells managers anything they don't know. He gets them to see that what they have been discounting as incidental information is actually critical information. So it is here. Not being a scientist, I obviously have nothing to contribute to evolutionary theory in its technical aspects. My own thrust takes a different turn. I want to work on the way the entire Darwinian theory looks to us, and to change that look by *gestalting* it in a different way; specifically, by placing it in the context of the premises with which this paragraph began. When it is thus placed, my project can be visualized as a triangle to emphasize the interdependence of its three propositions. If any leg is weak, the triangle (argument as a whole) collapses.

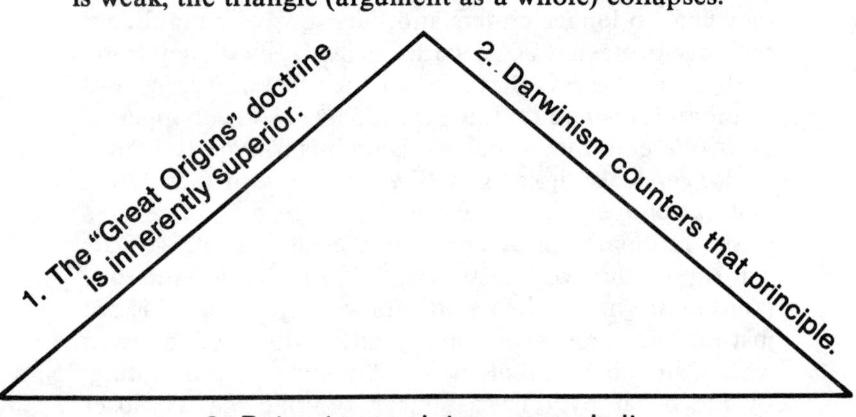

I derive the phrase "Great Origins" from Joseph Addison's "Ode" in *The Spectator*:

> *The spacious firmament on high,*
> *With all the blue ethereal sky,*
> *And spangled heavens, a shining frame,*
> *Their great Original proclaim.*

But the point is this: the force of my critique of Darwinism turns on its position in this triangle. There are some who conclude that the theory should be shelved for scientific reasons alone, but my argument is a different one: Even if it remains useful as a working hypothesis in science, that is not sufficient reason for us to believe that its basic delivery, the Small origins hypothesis, is true. For the game of evidence which Darwinism as a scientific theory plays is an idiosyncratic one that introduces both contraction and inflation. Contraction occurs when Darwinism sees itself as answerable only to empirical evidence; other considerations, such as metaphysical ones relating to first and final causes or the intuitive ones (with which this paper will close) are discounted from the start. This reduction of the field of evidence to which it is accountable already exaggerates its stature. An opposite, inflationary move follows hard on the heels of this contraction. To gain acceptance in science a working hypothesis does not need to show much in the way of proof; all it need do is stay ahead of its competitors. If its competitors are weak, the lead hypothesis can look strong without actually being so. And if it has no competitors? There was a period when the evidence turned against Darwinism conclusively; it didn't matter—its rating barely slipped. I refer to that pre-Mendelian moment—it extended for thirty-three years, actually—when an Edinburgh professor showed that by the mechanisms of heredity as they were then understood the emergence of new species from chance variations was logically impossible. For through admixture with the standard hereditary equipment of its mating partner, the strength of a promising evolutionary mutation would be reduced to one-half in its children, to one-quarter in its grandchildren, and so on until it vanished completely. Mendel rescinded this refutation with his discovery that genes do not blend and thus become diluted, but for a third of a century this conclusive disproof scarcely tarnished Darwin's star.

One is tempted to conclude with Julius Caesar that people believe what they want to believe, and there is much to this; the nineteenth and twentieth centuries wanted to believe Darwinism for its social implications and its prospect that progress would continue forever. But from the scientific standpoint there was something that was right about this tenacious clinging to a disproven theory. For Darwinism seemed (as it still seems) to be the only possible scientific explanation for life's origin and development, so it was appropriate to see how far it could succeed. That it has not succeeded enough to displace its Great Origins competitor is my contention, and it is time to proceed with the argument that leads up to it.

1. The Great Origins thesis is inherently superior.

Underlying this first proposition, naturally, is the supposition that notions regarding origins are important whatever their kind. Sociologically we see this in the search for roots that is cropping up in our highly mobile, transient society, while on a larger scale we find it in the cosmogonic myths that legitimize every known culture. The care with which these myths are transmitted from generation to generation and ritualistically rehearsed proves that more than curiosity is at stake in their origin. They came forward to meet a fundamental human need: the need to sense oneself as grounded in the cosmos and thereby oriented. Without orientation confusion sets in; if it persists, life loses its radar. Being ungrounded is part and parcel of this, for to be without grounding is to be adrift in ever shifting contexts that are unstable. The warning "not good if detached" applies not only to ticket stubs but to life as well. But is one surmise as good as another on this subject?

It seems unlikely. Self-image affects behavior, and to see oneself as descended from noble stock is to assume that one is made of noble stuff. This in turn disposes one to behave nobly, though of course it does not guarantee such behavior. Something like generational rub-off occurs, for where there is noble ancestry there are noble role models, and shoddy conduct cannot be blamed on shoddy genes. Traditional societies may have sensed such things, for Marshall Sahlins tells us that "we are the only people who think themselves risen from savages; everyone else believes they descended from gods."[1]

What is difficult is to pass from everyday considerations like these to ones that are metaphysical. Two difficulties are involved. First, in our empiricistic age the metaphysical imagination has to a large extent atrophied. The scientific account of origins, with its consistent theme of the qualitatively *more* deriving from the qualitatively *less*, so dominates our horizon that it is difficult to take seriously the opposite outlook which until five hundred years ago everyone took for granted. The second problem is of the opposite sort. The version of the Great Origins hypothesis that is most bandied about today puts that hypothesis in a bad light. I refer, of course, to Creationism, whose apostles have so muddied the waters with simplistic readings of the Scriptures and scientific claims that are sometimes bogus, that it is next to impossible for the Great Origins thesis to gain a fair hearing.[2]

Let me take this second obstacle to the Great Origins thesis first. As the precise way to characterize the opposite of the Darwinian thesis, I have chosen the phrase "the less from the more" for its generality and abstractness. As Adam and the animals were less than God, a literalist biblical account of how we got here fits the Great Origins hypothesis, but it is far from the only one that does so. All that the thesis requires is that we derive from Something that is superior to ourselves by every measure of worth we know. These transcendent objects include the ultimates of the great religious traditions—Allah, God, Brahman, Sunyata, the Tao, the Great Spirit—as well as philosophical ultimates, provided that they exceed human beings in intrinsic worth. Clearly included, for example, is the Neoplatonic One from which beings proceed by emanation rather than creation, and the Whiteheadian God whose primordial and consequent natures conspire to work upon the world their everlasting lure. I hope this latitude in the Great Origins thesis will keep it from being dismissed as Creationism.

The other bar to the Great Origins thesis, the poverty of the metaphysical imagination, is more difficult to deal with. Scientists who by virtue of their sensitivity are equally humanists are rhapsodic in hymning the grandeur of the universe. Einstein referred to its "radiant beauty which our dull faculties can comprehend only in their most primitive forms."[3] What is lacking is anything resembling Aristotle's Prime Mover, a first and final cause which in its very essence is luminously conscious and good. And if one does not sense the decisive difference these attributes make to a worldview, this is one evidence of the atrophy of which I speak.

How does one revive an ailing organ? Art might help if it were not itself at sea metaphysically; Walker Percy says that writers help us to understand the plight he cited, but have no remedy to offer.[4] The energy that enters life through the Great Origins hypothesis does not derive solely from the heightened self-image that results from the discovery of royal pedigree. It also derives from the fact that there is in the Great Origins thesis no answer to the question of human origins that does not include the answer to the origin of everything. Here humankind and world conspire. They issue from a single source, and as that source is good beyond all conceiving, it is impossible that its offspring not be kin. In a single stroke the self/world divide, laid wide by Descartes' mind/matter disjunction and the slash between primary and secondary qualities, is healed.

In favoring small origins, Darwinism challenges the Great Origins thesis. I shall argue that the evidence for Darwinism fails, but that demonstration is needed only if Darwinism and the Great Origins thesis are incompatible. Are they? They are.

2. Darwinism and the Great Origins hypothesis are incompatible.

Darwinism and the Great Origins doctrine cannot be squared. This needs to be argued, for it runs counter to the current drift of mainline theology which sees Darwin as assimilable. Vatican II instructs the faithful to combine modern scientific theories with Christian doctrine. It is widely held that evolutionary theory poses no contradiction to Catholic belief. Except for fundamentalists, Protestants concur, but scientists seem to feel that they are being co-opted. Darwin saw his discovery as strongly resistant to admixture with belief in God, while Jacques Monod goes further. "The mechanism of evolution as now understood," he tells us, "rules out any claim that there are final causes, or purposes being realized. [This] disposes of any philosophy or religion that believes in cosmic . . . purpose."[5] Realizing that this conclusion could be colored by Monod's personal philosophy, I turn to the entry on "Evolution" in *The New Encyclopaedia Britannica* for a statement that might reflect, as well as any, consensus in the field. It tells me that "Darwin showed that evolution's cause, natural selection, was automatic with no room for divine guidance or design."[6]

Which side is right? The question is complex, for a whole swarm of issues is involved, including the way two important intellectual currents and the institutions they represent are competing for the mind of our age. I spent fifteen years at the Massachusetts Institute of Technology without seeing what a few paragraphs in E. F. Schumacher's *Guide for the Perplexed* showed me clearly. There is not one science. There are two, which Schumacher dubs descriptive and instructional.[7]

Descriptive science is as old as the human race. Pivoting as it does on careful observation and the organization of data thus derived, no society could have survived without a touch of it, though the quantity can vary enormously. When in the seventeenth century John Ray took the first steps toward creating a suitable system of classifying species in the plant world, he provided a good example of this first kind of science, as did Carolus Linnaeus, whose naming of life forms in orderly classification established a context in which botanical studies could take place in a sustained fashion. Descriptive science is not confined to the study of nature; it is a part of every cognitive discipline. Even today in continental Europe, words for science tend to have this descriptive ring. *Wissenschaft* is an example. On the Continent, history is a science.

In the English-speaking world it is not, the reason being that here the word has come to denote *modern* science which turns on science in Schumacher's instructional mode. Instructional science takes the form: Do X, and Y will follow. In the formal, conceptual sphere we have geometry, mathematics, and logic, where we can issue instructions that work and thereby establish proof. Equally in the empirical, material world: our hands can manipulate objects, so again we can issue instructions as to what manipulations will achieve which ends and again establish proof. An important insight comes to view. Only through instructional science, which is to say, only in what we can ourselves do, can we truly explain and prove.

Applied to evolutionary theory, this distinction gives us descriptive evolution which tries to tell us *what* happened in life's ascent, and instructional evolution which takes up from there to explain *how* and *why* it happened. The ideal of descriptive evolution would be a complete cinematographic record of what has occurred in life's sojourn on this planet. We might think of it as a videotape which, accelerated enormously, PBS could run as a mind-boggling spectacular. It should be a silent film, in keeping with the eerie silence of the fossil record from which it would be primarily derived. Darwinism, on the other hand, is instructional evolution.

Descriptive evolution is essentially the fossil record. Fossils found in the earth's crust show that there have been changes in the constitution of plants and animals, and with the help of radioactive and potassium-argon dating these have been placed in historical sequence. Drawing primarily on this data, descriptive evolution weaves a story the chief features of which are: (a) that higher, more complex forms of life appeared later than simpler ones (much later); (b) that all organisms after the initial self-replicating protein molecule(s) issued from parents; and (c) that all species of life on earth can be traced back through their pedigrees to the simplest forms in which life initially appeared. Darwin contributed to descriptive evolution as just summarized, but his importance lies in his proposal for how it all happened: through natural selection working on chance mutations. It is this explanatory side of his work that I am calling Darwinism in this essay.

It is at once apparent that descriptive evolution is more compatible with the Great Origins hypothesis than is Darwinism, for, being silent on the question of causes, it leaves room for the possibility that God scripted and directs the entire production; if the heavens declare the glory of God, why not the fossil record? If we ponder the matter, though, we can see that psychologically, if not logically, descriptive evolution veils God's glory considerably.

Descriptive evolution works psychologically against the Great Origins concept. For on the one hand, though it brackets the question of *how* the more derives from the less, it nonetheless depicts it as so deriving. And it presents changes as occurring so gradually that nothing extraordinary seems to happen; miracle is reduced to microscopic, incremental accretions. Because these two features of descriptive evolution run psychologically counter to the Great Origins thesis, it is useful to remind ourselves that even descriptive evolution is not indubitable. Materially there are more anomalies, not to mention wide gaps, in the fossil record than the public recognizes, while formally the entire scenario rests on a postulate, uniformitarianism, which holds that the laws of nature do not change. Charles Lyell fixed this postulate into place in the 1830s with his three-volume *Principles of Geology*. As a geologist put it to me recently, "It's impossible to prove uniformitarianism; it's just that you can't be a geologist without it. We now know, as Lyell did not, that natural processes change—rates of erosion, for example. But natural laws must remain constant or geology isn't a science."

To his children's question, "Who made us, God or evolution?" a British theologian, Don Cupitt, found himself answering, "Both"; which answer, as we saw, is the one that most theologians are giving today. On reflection, though, Cupitt tells us, he concluded that his answer was "diplomatic, orthodox, and shallow."[8] For Darwinism does not purport to describe the instrumentalities through which God works. It is the scientific account for how we and other creatures got here, and as such it must, on pain of begging the question, proceed without recourse to anything remotely resembling divine intention or design. Monod has it exactly right when he writes: "The cornerstone of scientific method is . . . the *systematic* denial that 'true' knowledge can be got at by interpreting phenomena in terms of final causes—that is to say, of 'purpose.' "[9] It is important to see exactly what is being said here. As purposes and final causes entail realities that are greater than ourselves, Monod's dictum translates into saying that Small Origins accounts of how we got here are the only accounts that instructional science—on this point Darwinism—will allow. Darwinism qualifies as being scientific because its working principles are strictly nonteleological: natural selection is purely mechanical, and the mutations on which it works arrive solely by chance. But by the same token, if Darwinism is accepted as true, the Great Origins hypothesis is replaced by the Small Origins hypothesis.

3. In the face of its Great Origins rival, Darwinism fails.

I am not the first to call the claims for Darwinism into question, of course. A recent issue of *Environment* tells us that Darwin's ideas

> have long been under successful attack not just by religious fundamentalists or "scientific creationists" but by many biologists and such popularizers as the late Arthur Koestler . . . and Norman Macbeth. That this will be news to most educated laypersons and to many biologists is simply an example of cultural lag and the ability of dogmas to dominate not only religion but science as well.[10]

Macbeth's *Darwin Retried* (and in its author's eyes found wanting) has been out for over a decade now.[11] Asked on the November 1, 1981, PBS *Nova* program what his qualifications were for writing on a scientific subject, Macbeth answered that as a professional lawyer he considered himself an expert on evidence, and that it was in their handling of evidence that he faulted Darwin's defenders. More recently Jeremy Rifkin has published his *Algeny*, the central chapter of which is titled "The Darwinian Sunset." "Our children will not think of the world in a Darwinian way," he writes. "Darwin's theory of evolution will be remembered in centuries to come as a cosmological bridge between two world epochs."[12]

These are all lay verdicts, however, so we should go on to what the biologists themselves are saying. It came as a surprise to me to find that Darwinism has never gained much of a hearing in western Europe; *The New Encyclopaedia Britannica* notes that "natural selection is . . . not widely . . . recognized in western continental Europe" as evolution's cause.[13] Pierre Grassé occupied for thirty years the chair for evolution at the Sorbonne and edited the twenty-eight volume *Encyclopedia of Zoology*. In his *Evolution of Living Forms*, Grassé has this to say:

> The explanatory doctrines of biological evolution do not stand up to an objective, in-depth criticism. They prove to be either in conflict with reality or else incapable of solving the major problems involved. . . . Through use and abuse of hidden postulates, of bold, often ill-founded extrapolations, a pseudo-science has been created. It is taking root in the very heart of biology and is leading astray many biochemists and biologists, who sincerely believe that the accuracy of fundamental concepts has been demonstrated, which is not the case.[14]

Edwin Conklin, late professor of biology at Princeton, writes, "Religious devotion . . . is probably the reason why severe methodological criticism employed in other departments of biology has not yet been brought to bear on evolutionary speculation."[15] And in making the distinction between descriptive and explanatory evolution,

David Raup of the University of Chicago writes: "The record . . . pretty clearly demonstrates that evolution has occurred if we define evolution simply as change; but it does not tell us how this change took place, and that's really the question."[16]

A. The Fossil Record (diagrammed on page 176)

The only evidence that we have concerning the past history of life on our planet is found in fossils embedded in rock formations. Darwin admitted that in his day they did little to support his theory. "Geology . . . does not reveal . . . finely graded organic change," he wrote, "and this, perhaps, is the most obvious and gravest objection which can be urged against [my] theory."[17] He trusted, of course, that time would fill in the gaps, but how little it has done so Raup again attests. "We are now about 120 years after Darwin . . . and, ironically, we have even fewer examples of evolutionary transition than we had in Darwin's time," inasmuch as many that were thought to be valid are now known not to be.[18] Concerning links between species, an eerie silence prevails. "Evolution requires intermediate forms between species," says David Kitts, professor of geology at the University of Oklahoma, "and paleontology does not provide them."[19] The punctuated equilibrium theory—eons of invariance punctuated by quick (perhaps five- to fifty-thousand-year) spurts in isolated ecological niches—has emerged to account for the fact that, as Stephen Gould says, "phyletic gradualism [which would have left evidences of transitional links] is never seen in the rocks."[20] But does that theory amount to more than justification for continuing to believe in transitional forms when we have no traces of them?

B. Population Breeding

The breeding of domestic plants and animals which had begun in England in the 1760s had by Darwin's day produced famous breeds of Leicestershire sheep and Dishley cattle. Darwin was immensely impressed with this art and adopted it as a metaphor for his theory, not knowing that in the end it would work against him. For though mutations can effect changes within species (microevolution), with respect to species as wholes they insure stability rather than change. Species-continuity is insured by a constant barrage of subtle variations that allow the species to adapt if the environment should change; concomitantly, species-change (macroevolution) is blocked by the law of reversion to the mean. Beyond a certain point deviations become unstable and, instead of cresting into new species, die out. In a typical experiment that began with fruit flies that averaged thirty-six bristles, it was possible to raise the number to fifty-six or lower it to twenty-five, but beyond those numbers the lines became sterile and expired. As Luther Burbank noted early on, "there is a pull toward the mean which keeps all living things within some more or less fixed limitations."[21] Loren Eiseley is not the only one to have noted the unhappy consequences for Darwinian theory when he writes, "There is great irony in this situation, for more than almost any other single factor, domestic breeding has been used as an argument for evolution."[22]

C. Natural Selection

Darwin saw natural selection as his central discovery; he believed that he had found in it the engine of change that had brought higher forms of life into being. But problems have arisen.

If the fittest survive, why don't the less fit disappear, Gertrude Himmelfarb asks. If the hive bee's efficiency in containing a maximum of honey with a minimum of wax gives it a Darwinian edge, why are bumbling, inefficient bumblebees still around?[23]

Natural selection makes no room for long-range considerations; every new trait has to be immediately useful or it is discarded. How then are we to account for the emergence of complex organs or limbs which are made up of myriads of parts that would have developed independently of one another through thousands of generations during which they had no utility? Stephen

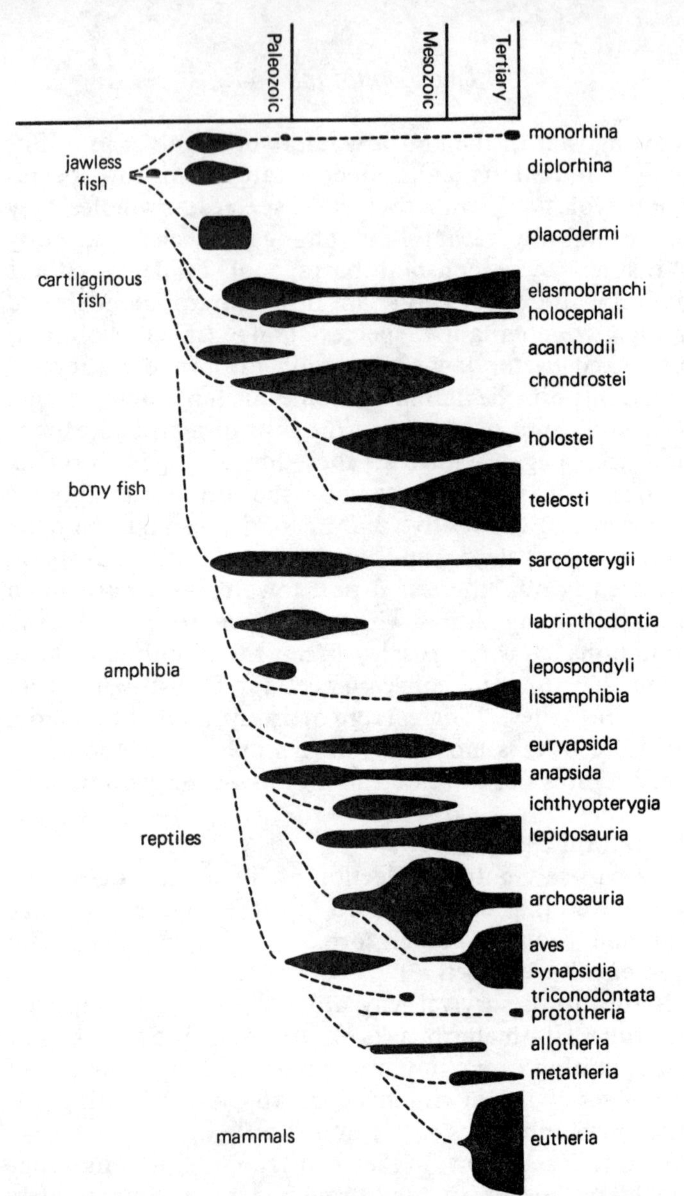

Adaptive Radiation of vertebrates showing stratigraphic abundance of the major vertebrate groups through time. The dotted lines represent hypothetical lineages required by evolution to link the various groups together. Reproduced from Michael Denton, Evolution: A Theory in Crisis *(Bethesda, MD: Adler & Adler, 1986), p. 173. A. S. Romer,* Vertebrate Paleontology, *Third Edition (University of Chicago Press, 1966), pp. 47 & 108, and G. S. Carter,* Structure and Habit in Vertebrate Evolution *(Seattle: University of Washington, 1971), p. 9 are credited for the information the diagram compacts.*

Gould reduces the problem to its simplest proportions when he asks, "What good is half a jaw or half a wing?"[24]

If novel faculties emerge because of their adaptive edge, why are some of them overqualified for that purpose, as Darwin and Wallace both conceded the human brain to be? Gould takes such points seriously, saying that it is time to free ourselves "from the need to interpret all our basic skills as adaptations for specific purposes."[25]

As no definition of fitness other than survival has been (or can be) proposed, the reasoning on this topic is circular. "Natural selection . . . amounts to the statement that the individuals which leave the most offspring are those which leave the most offspring. It is a tautology."[26] "The survivors, having survived, are thence judged to be the fittest."[27]

Finally, Darwin thought that natural selection accounts for the creativity in evolution—how life forms that are clearly higher emerged. Stephen Gould does not see that it does.[28]

D. Embryology and Vestigial Organs.

I was taught that the human embryo in the course of its development in the womb rehearses the entire evolutionary sequence—in Ernst Haeckel's catchy slogan, "ontogeny recapitulates phylogeny." Our useless tailbones were cited as vestigial remains of the tails our ancestors had swung from. When I mentioned this matter in presenting an early draft of this paper, a biologist expressed surprise at my bringing it up. "We haven't taught those things in years," he said. It turns out that what I had been taught were incipient gills in the embryo are not gills at all, and that the coccygeal vertebrae—tailbone is a clear misnomer—are in no wise vestigial. Without the muscles they support, our pelvic organs would drop out.

E. Biochemistry

It was expected that detailed knowledge of the chemical differences between biological forms would shed light on their lineages; descendants, it was thought, would be found to resemble their presumed progenitors in biochemical makeup. This has not proved to be the case. Similarities appear among forms that resemble one another taxonomically, i.e. structurally, but (with negligible exceptions) not between forms and their alleged ancestors; biochemically, "descendants" are just as likely to resemble creatures from which they could not possibly have derived. This finding has spawned a group of "transformed cladists" who have simply given up on Darwin's "tree of life" project of classifying life forms by lineal descent. Colin Patterson, senior paleontologist of the British Museum, is one of their number.[29]

F. Biogenesis

Darwin occupied himself only with the living world, but his followers extended his theory to explain how life originated from nonlife. In the early 1950s it was thought that experiments performed by Stanley Miller and Harold Urey had shown this to be possible, but it is now recognized, first, that the atmospheric conditions in which life arose were probably prohibitively different from those in the scientists' laboratory, and second, that the kind of amino acids that they produced—racemates—are not the kind that can support life.

G. Mathematical Improbability

It used to be thought that geological time was immense enough to allow almost anything to happen, and so it is if we are thinking of isolated events like the number nineteen turning up on a roulette wheel precisely when it is needed. Now, though, attention has turned to the extent to which innumerable precise components must converge, each making its appearance exactly on schedule. This is more like the number twenty-three coming up on all the tables at Monte Carlo simultaneously, followed by the numbers twenty-four, twenty-five, twenty-six, etc., all appearing simultaneously in sequence. For things like this to happen, even four billion years is insufficient.

Again a personal anecdote can make the point. At yet another presentation of this paper in progress, it happened that the president of the International Association for Mathematical Biology was in the audience. He did not enter into the discussion, but at its close he came forward and identified himself. Then, very quietly, he said, "There wasn't enough time." It is for this reason that Fred Hoyle, Francis Crick, and others are turning to outer space, deeming it more probable that our planet was "seeded" with life from elsewhere than that it developed here.

This completes my sketch of the major problems relating to Darwin's claim, but it should be noted that recent moves to recast Darwinism in cybernetic mode, as in Peter Corning's *The Synergistic Hypothesis*, do little to solve them. For though it is probably the case that a wide variety of factors relating to interactions between cells, organisms and their behaviors, populations, species, and multi-species ecosystems converged to effect the micro-evolutionary changes that have occurred, the claim that synergistic responses to selection pressures deriving from those interactions explain the appearance of new species remains a posit only. "What is not in doubt," says Stephen Gould, "is the fact of evolution," or what I have called descriptive evolution. "But as to its mechanism [here called Darwinism], there is observational evidence for natural selection [true, but outside of microevolution?], but it could be false that it [Darwinism in its distinctive claim] is as strong a determinant of evolution as we think."[30] More recent statements in which Gould associated adaptationism with Voltaire's joke—"Why do people have noses? To support their glasses!"—suggest that his own confidence in it is waning. *The New York Times Magazine* reported that "this forty-two-year-old paleontologist is putting himself more and more at odds with orthodox Darwinism,"[31] but the alternatives he is toying with—constraints imposed by developmental trends and anatomical architecture—are at this stage little more than conjectures.

The point of this critique of Darwinism has been to

show how little (in the way of hard evidence) has been allowed to eclipse so much (the Great Origins principle). This is the more so when to the paucity of firm empirical evidence we add intuitive considerations which can only be listed.

—Max Müller, according to Nirad Chaudhuri's book *Scholar Extraordinary*, wrote to Darwin saying that he found it quite possible to believe that the human physique has evolved from simpler bodies, but the idea that human language emerged from grunts and brays struck him as out of the question. Noam Chomsky supports him in this hunch. The module of the brain that governs linguistic ability has no counterpart among the other animals; it appeared in man suddenly and in its present form. This places the biological foundation of human language beyond the explanatory range of twentieth-century science, Chomsky concludes.

—Can something emerge from nothing? Can a stream rise higher than its source? When I ask my students these questions they almost inevitably answer no. Yet William Bartley, the biographer and foremost interpreter of Karl Popper, tells us that the foundation of Popper's philosophy is the claim that something can come from nothing. What are we to make of these opposite answers? My personal reading of the matter is that Popper, having steeped his life in the philosophy of science, saw clearly the fundamental point. Only if we grant science the counter-intuitive, something-from-nothing assumption can we look to it to explain anything above the material plane.

—The going word for that something-from-nothing legerdemain is *emergence*, and in countering reductionism by insisting that higher forms have ontological components that were not in their precursors, it looks in the right direction. But as an explanation for those novel components it is worthless; it recognizes their arrival while doing nothing to explain it. There would be nothing wrong with this if it did not presume to give an explanation, which it does by riding analogies that are spurious. The standard one is the liquidity of water which emerges from the convergence of two gases, hydrogen and oxygen.

This, though, overlooks the fact that apart from the way water looks and feels to us (which introduces an issue the analogy finesses, namely, the emergence of sentience and awareness) its liquidity is simply a different arrangement of molecules in motion, or primary qualities only. Nothing new in kind has appeared at all. The primary qualities have merely been reshuffled.

Conclusion

Is it impertinent for someone untrained in science to tamper with a theory as technical as evolution has become? Who owns this issue?

It has been my contention that more than technicalities are involved. My basic question has been whether we should believe that Darwinism explains how we got here, and my negative answer is predicated on the claim that beliefs take shape on an unrestricted horizon, which in this case includes considerations in addition to ones that are paleobiological.

It brings to mind the story of the ill-fated sky diver who, plummeting toward earth in a parachute that refuses to open, passes a hot-air balloonist whose blow torch won't shut off. "Know anything about parachutes?" he shouts, to which the balloonist counters, "No, but what about you? Know anything about gas stoves?" Whitehead predicted that, more than by any other factor, the future will be shaped by the way the two most powerful forces in history—science and religion—settle into relation with each other. That relationship has been my root concern. Though I have openly registered my perception that the Darwinian parachute has not opened very far, I know no more about such devices than the next person. I do know something about gas stoves, here representing convictions that can make the spirit soar. It is as Walker Percy says. Plummeting through sidereal time, we moderns under poor acoustical conditions shout across the expanses that divide our specialties, "Know anything about this? About that?"

The speaker who has the best grasp of both sides of this issue is the one who most merits our attention.

Notes

1. Marshall Sahlins, *Culture and Practical Reason* (Chicago: University of Chicago Press, 1976), p. 17.

2. I find myself in an awkward position here, for though I wish to extricate the Great Origins thesis from the Creationists' clutches, in ways they have my respect. Their deep commitment to one version of the Great Origins doctrine has made them more vigilant than other theologians in spotting places where Darwinism rides on faith rather than fact.

An important chapter in the sociology of knowledge is being written; one in which establishment forces as represented by the university, the American Civil Liberties Union, and mainline churches will not, in the eyes of history, emerge as heroes. I touch on these issues in Huston Smith, "Scientism in Sole Command," *Christianity and Crisis*, 21 January 1982; and in Huston Smith, "Evolution and Evolutionism," *The Christian Century*, 7-14 July 1982.

3. Albert Einstein, *Living Philosophies* (New York: Simon & Schuster, 1931), pp. 6-7.

4. I enter again Saul Bellow's verdict that was earlier registered: "The intelligent public is waiting to hear from art what it does not hear from theology, philosophy, and social theory, and what it cannot hear from pure science: a broader, fuller, more coherent, more comprehensive account of what we human beings are, who we are, and what this life is for. If writers do not come into the center it will not be because the center is preempted. It is not."

5. The conclusion of Jacques Monod, *Chance and Necessity* (New York: Vintage Books, 1972), as summarized in Don Cupitt, *Worlds of Science and Religion* (New York: Hawthorne Books, 1976), p. 12.

6. *The New Encyclopaedia Britannica*, s.v. "Evolution."

7. E. F. Schumacher, *Guide for the Perplexed* (New York: Harper & Row, 1976), pp. 100-10.

8. Cupitt, *Worlds of Science and Religion, op. cit.,* p. 1.

9. Monod, *Chance and Necessity, op. cit.,* p. 21, emphasis his.

10. Victor Ferkiss, review of *Algeny* by Jeremy Rifkin, *Environment* 25 (July-August 1983): 44.

11. Norman Macbeth, *Darwin Retried* (Boston: Gambit, 1971).

12. Jeremy Rifkin, *Algeny* (New York: Viking Press, 1983), p. 130.

13. *The New Encyclopaedia Britannica*, s.v. "Evolution."

14. Pierre Grassé, *Evolution of Living Forms* (New York: Academic Press, 1977), pp. 202, 206.

15. Edwin Conklin, *Man Real and Ideal* (New York: Scribner's, 1943), p. 52.

16. David Raup, "Conflicts between Darwin and Paleontology," *Field Museum of Natural History Bulletin* 50 (1979): 24.
17. Charles Darwin, *The Origin of Species* (London: J. M. Dent, 1971), p. 239.
18. Raup, "Conflicts between Darwin and Paleontology," p. 26.
19. David Kitts, "Paleontology and Evolutionary Theory," *Evolution* 28 (1974): 467. Darwinists must produce a family tree, a pedigree, Norman Macbeth observed on the *Nova* program earlier referred to, "and I regret to say that after 120 years they haven't produced a single solid phylogeny."
20. Stephan Jay Gould, with Niles Eldredge, "Punctuated Equilibria," *Paleobiology* 3 (1977): 115.
21. Luther Burbank, quoted in Macbeth, *Darwin Retried*, p. 35.
22. Loren Eiseley, quoted in Macbeth, *Darwin Retried*, p. 36.
23. Gertrude Himmelfarb, *Darwin and the Darwinian Revolution* (New York: W. W. Norton, 1959), pp. 341-42.
24. Stephen Jay Gould, "The Return of Hopeful Monsters," *Natural History* 86 (June-July 1977): 24.
25. Stephen Jay Gould, "The Evolutionary Biology of Constraint," *Daedalus* 29 (1980): 46.
26. C. H. Waddington, *The Strategy of Genes* (London: Allen & Unwin, 1957), pp. 64-65.
27. Himmelfarb, *Darwin and the Darwinian Revolution*, p. 316.
28. *Unitarian-Universalist World*, 2 February 1982.
29. Transcript of "Speech by Dr. Colin Patterson at the American Museum of Natural History" (New York City, Nov. 5, 1981).
30. *Unitarian-Universalist World, op. cit.*
31. James Gleick, "Stephen Jay Gould: Breaking Tradition with Darwin," *New York Times Magazine*, 20 November 1983, p. 50.

9

THE RELEVANCE OF THE GREAT RELIGIONS FOR THE MODERN WORLD*

With the collapse of confidence in what might transcend the human, attention has gravitated in recent centuries toward the human aggregate. "The magic word of modernity," George Will tells us, "is 'society.' " Even in the humanities, the Chair of the National Endowment for the Humanities, Lynne Cheney, reports that "faculty members have 'politicized' their research and teaching. . . . Viewing texts as though they were primarily political documents is the most noticeable trend in academic study of the humanities today. The key questions are thought to be about gender, race, and class" (*The New York Times*, Sept. 13 & Oct. 5, 1988).

To argue that the importance of politics is not diminished by recognizing that it is not all-important, I reach for an address I delivered at the closing session of the Spiritual Summit Conference that was convened in Calcutta in October, 1968. Though to that audience I thought it important to argue for the importance of social concern, in the act of placing that concern in perspective, the other side of the story comes through as well. Society is important, but not exhaustively important.

Religion can, of course, be irrelevant and often is. No human endeavor is immaculate, and one that traffics

*Abridged with permission from Findley P. Dunne, Jr. (ed.), *The World Religions Speak* (The Hague: W. Junk, 1970), where it was dedicated to Thomas Merton, who died in Bangkok a month after his participation in the Calcutta conference that is mentioned.

in millions is bound to emerge a mixed bag. In this respect religion is no different from other corporate enterprises—education which quickens and represses, government which orders and restricts. Religion has been revolutionary and conservative, prophetic and priestly, catalyst and incubus. It creates barriers and levels them, raises church budgets and raises the oppressed, makes peace with iniquity and redeems, to some extent, the world.

Such statements relate to the social relevance of religion, but it would be a mistake to assume that that is the only relevance religion possesses. I propose to distinguish three great ages through which humanity has passed, with an eye to what religious relevance has meant in each.

I

1. The first age, by far the longest, was the archaic. It lasted, roughly, up to the first millennium B.C. In this Archaic Period (Eliade's term) when humans were rousing out of animal innocence, their chief spiritual problem was time. Lower animals are oblivious of time for they possess neither foresight nor hindsight, neither anticipation nor memory. When human beings first acquired these time-binding faculties they found the implications terrifying: the future, they discovered, was contingent, and the past forever gone. Their recourse was to blink these terrors; insofar as possible simply to turn their backs on them and deny their existence by attending to their opposite. This opposite—Great Time—was in fact timeless. It consisted of momentous, originating acts which, their myths told them, had brought order out of chaos and established the patterns for meaningful activity: creation of the world itself, the first planting, the first mating, each act accomplished by the gods in epic proportions. For archaic peoples, being *was* these timeless, paradigmatic acts which were significant, secure, and impervious to time's decay. Their religion consisted of replicating these acts through rites that were myth-ordained and myth-prescribed. Through these rites they fused their lives with Being, merging them with the meaningful and the real.

Note how little ethics entered into this first, originating phase of religion. The reason is that at this stage ethics did not pose much of a problem, little more than it does for subhuman animals. People were living for the most part in small groups, in tribes or tiny villages wherein everyone knew everyone else and cooperated pretty much as do members of a normal family.

2. Following the terminology of Karl Jaspers, I shall call the second period the Axial Age, for during it human history took a marked turn, a giant swing on its axis so to speak. This is the period that witnessed the rise of the geniuses the world still honors: the great prophets of Israel, Zarathustra in Persia, Gautama Buddha and the Upanishadic seers in India, Lao Tzu and Confucius in China. This burst of religious creativity across the full arc of the civilized world—an extraordinary proliferation of prophetic genius diffused in space but condensed in time and amounting to nothing short of a mass religious mutation—this striking phenomenon has been often noted but never explained. I submit that it was at root the spirit's response to a marked change in the human condition, a crisis in history's development.

By the first millennium B.C.E. or shortly before, agricultural improvement had advanced population and settled existence to the point where people were dealing regularly with persons outside their primary group. As a consequence, familial feelings no longer sufficed to keep society intact. Perceptive souls—we call them prophets, seers, rishis, sages, magi—saw this and summoned religion to emerge from its Archaic phase to help meet the problem.

Rites and rituals are no longer enough, they said in effect.[1] You must watch how you behave toward your fellows, for human discord can reduce life to shambles. Interpersonal relations are not the sum of religion, but religion is stopped in its tracks if it skirts them. *Yogas* (spiritual techniques) must be prefaced by *yamas* (moral precepts), *dhyana* (meditation) and *prajna* (wisdom) by *sila* (ethical observances). "If you are offering your gift at the altar, and there remember that your brother has something against you, leave your gift there before the altar and go; first be reconciled to your brother, and then come and offer your gift" (Matthew 5:23-24). For "he who does not love his brother whom he has seen, cannot love God whom he has not seen" (I John 4:20).

Hence the Golden Rules of the great religions: Christianity's "Do unto others . . ."; Judaism's "What doth the Lord require of thee but to do justice, love mercy . . ."; Jainism's *ahimsa* and *aparigraha*; Buddhism's *metta* and *Karuna*, its "boundless heart toward all beings"; Hinduism's "highest [yogin] who judges pleasure or pain everywhere by the same standard as he applies to himself" (Gita, VI, 32); Islam's man who "gives his wealth . . . to kinsfolk and to orphans and to the needy and the wayfarer . . . who sets slaves free . . . and payeth the poor due"; Sikhism's "humility to serve"; Confucius' human-hearted *jen*. These counsels of concern for the well-being of others were one of the glories of religion during its Axial period.

3. The third great period in human history is the Modern Age which was inaugurated by the rise of modern science in the seventeenth century and the Enlightenment in the eighteenth. For purposes here, the Modern Age differs from its predecessors in seeing social structures as malleable. In previous ages, institutions—family systems, caste and class, feudalism, kingship, chief and emperor—were regarded in much the way we regard the laws of nature; as ingrained in the nature of things. Now they are recognized as contingent, and by the same token fallible! The corollary is immense. For if society *can* be changed, it often *should* be changed, in which case its members are responsible for seeing to it that it *is* changed.

Obviously this new perspective enlarges the scope of ethics enormously. Whereas religion's ethical dimension was minimal in the Archaic Period and personal in the Axial Period, today it has become both personal and social, both individual and collective. For to repeat: if social structures can be good or evil and are subject to human volition, people are responsible for their character.

II

Against the backdrop of these three stages of human history, the question of religious relevance becomes more manageable. What makes religion relevant depends on the age in question. Archaic religion was relevant without containing much in the way of ethics at all, for ethics was not then a pressing problem. But if religion had idled ethically in the Axial Period when ethics *became* a problem, it would have lost step with relevance and disappeared.

Similarly today, social ethics having emerged as a new human responsibility, if religion defaults on this responsibility it will lose the relevance it has thus far enjoyed. Personal kindness is no longer enough. Institutions affect human well-being no less than do interpersonal relations. This being so, enlightened compassion calls for social responsibility as much as for face-to-face good will.

In a way nothing is new here, for human well-being has always been affected by its social matrix. The novelty is that, brought to the realization that social institutions are to an appreciable extent humanly contrived, we now acknowledge our partial responsibility for them. We have reached the point in history where we see that to be indifferent to social institutions is to be indifferent to human life.

Not that religion should be converted into social action. Religion must be socially responsible without equating itself with such responsibility. Moreover, it should engage society in a specific way. These qualifications are subtle, but they are important—sufficiently so as to occupy us for the balance of this statement.

III

Let me recast in slightly different terms the three dimensions of religion which historically have appeared successively. Archic Religion did not focus on humanity, individually or collectively, at all. It looked beyond the human, to divine metaphysical realities from which humanity derived and in which it remained grounded. Religion anchored the current generation in those timeless realities through rituals which (as was noted) linked finite, ephemeral human acts to heroic paradigms that gave them enduring substance and meaning. It was as if its rituals and their attendant myths plugged human doings into timeless templates that charged them with significance and exempted them from time's decay. In subsequent ages, religion articulated this eternal tie explicitly; it spoke (and continues to speak) of immortality, and of anchoring life in the divine presence and the Eternal Now. The move, though, is the same. It counters time's vicissitudes by binding us to the eternal.

Axial Religion added interpersonal concerns to religion's original Archaic agenda, and nurtured conscience, compassion, self-knowledge, and forgiveness. In adding social responsibility to these two preceding agendas, Modern Religion effects a third extension. But it must be an extension, not a replacement—everything turns on this difference. If in the Axial Period religion had relinquished its eternal concerns when it picked up on love of neighbor, it would have cashed in religion for ethics. It did not, of course, do this; statements like "We love, because he first loved us" (I John 4:19) and "It is not for the love of creatures that creatures are dear, but for the love of the Soul in creatures that creatures are dear" (Bhidad-Aranyaka Upanishad, II, 4) make clear that the ethics of Axial Religion was in direct touch with its religious source. Whether the social thrust of Modern Religion is genuinely religious or only seemingly so, being in actuality indistinguishable from secular social action, depends on whether it represents an extension of religion's prior, transcendent-and-interpersonal concerns—love of God and love of neighbor, respectively—or has cut these lifelines.

Tracing our steps backwards through these three concerns, religion would no longer be religion if it attended only to society, for to do so would contradict its conception of the human self. A perfect society (if that notion makes sense) would not produce perfect selves, for the sufficient reason that human worth cannot be bestowed; it must be achieved, because our inner, self-creating, volitional pole is too much a part of our nature to allow us to be manipulated: we are not automata. Given our vulnerability, external circumstances can crush us, which is why organized religions must do what they can to prevent this from happening; but the opposite does not pertain. Circumstances, however well contrived, cannot fulfill us because (to repeat) fulfillment cannot be conferred. By providing food, controlling temperature, and introducing anodynes if need be, comfort can be bestowed, but not nobility, or even happiness; these must be won individually. Being aware of this fact, religion can never rest its case with doing things for other people. Working on oneself—the cleansing of the inward parts—is always part of its agenda. (We have the dictum that it is never possible to do as much for others as one can do for oneself, namely save one's own soul. The Zen version is earthier: everyone must perform his own toilet.) Neither the agents of social action nor its beneficiaries are exempt from this stricture.

This is the point of Whitehead's definition of religion as what a man does with his own solitariness, and why Kierkegaard gave such attention to human subjectivity. Because this inner, Archimedean point provides the springboard for both of religion's subsequent extensions—into Axial Religion's interpersonal *karuna* (compassion) and *caritas* as defined by St. Paul in First Corinthians 13, and into Modern Religion's further extension into social ethics—we can turn to it directly. Thus far I have described it as focused on time and eternity, but other issues get drawn in; they are elusive, but terribly real. In earlier times we could (in the West) have named the transcendent or eternal focus of religion which we encounter in the depths of our own inwardness "God," but in our century the contours of that word have blurred, beyond which stands the complicating fact that it has no exact equivalent in Afro-Asian faiths. Archaic, eternal religion is obsessed with "why" questions, beginning with why anything exists rather than nothing. It deals with the individual's stance toward his world, whether s/he feels at home in it or alienated from it—the ways s/he belongs to it and does not belong to it but is separate from and stands over against it, pointing thereby to an ultimate beyond it. Eternal religion grapples with the failure that in one form or another visits everyone—how we can live with ourselves and feel acceptable when in so many ways we know that we are not. Its root concern is (as I have said) in some way with time: how everything can matter, as we feel in some sense it does, when in the long run it would appear that nothing matters. Running throughout is the question of meaning; how life can be meaningful when so much of it reads like an idiot's tale. Eternal religion knows that there are no discursive answers to these questions. It ranges time and space for insight—*prajna*, vision, a revelation which, by-passing words, will disclose directly why we exist and why the world is the way it is, in much the same way that loving explains why we are male and female.

IV

Even Marxists now concede that "faith for the Christian [and by implication for Buddhists, Hindus, and the rest] can be a stimulus for social commitment,"[2] a marked qualification of their original perception of religion as the opiate of the people. It would be pleasant to think that religion's transcendent interpersonal dimensions protect it against the special dangers to which social programs are heir—fanaticism, projection, means-ends casuistry, and discouragement—but nothing turns on this. With such safeguards or without them, religion must now address the world.

Its social efforts differ from those of secularists primarily in their interpersonal, transcendent roots, but there is another difference: religion's guiding social goal must be general. Images of a new heaven and a new earth, of lions lying down with lambs, of messiahs and *maitreyas* and swords beaten into plowshares are vague, but in this case savingly vague. For sharpened much further they become ideologies. Ideologies have their uses, but sooner or later all are surprised by history. One or another may merit qualified support at a given moment, but to become tied to any would be to lose the freedom and flexibility religion needs if its social voice is to be timelessly contemporary. Probably no social goal more specific than that every human being—child of God in theistic idiom—have an equal change at life's opportunities deserves unqualified religious endorsement.

Though I have argued that religion must now include all three of the components enumerated, it would be foolish to contend that everyone should attend to them equally. People are irreducibly different; in religion this makes for priests and prophets, for hermits and householders. It is even appropriate that there be sects that highlight the components differently, as did Confucianism, Taoism, and Buddhism in traditional China. But in a tradition or culture as a whole the three should be reasonably balanced.

V

I have argued two theses: to remain relevant, religion must become socially involved; to remain religious, such involvement must retain ties with religion's earlier concerns. It happens that with respect to these theses, East and West have, today, complementing strengths and weaknesses. When in May, 1968, the "Ceylon Daily News" quoted the eminent Buddhist authority Dr. Walpola Rahula as asserting that development of a sustaining economy for all of the people is as much a religious duty as any other, and that "cultivating a farm properly is better than building many temples," it showed that Asian religions are not unmindful of the need to involve themselves deeply in their adherents' struggle to pull themselves out of the straightjacket of hunger, underemployment and indebtedness. Throughout Asia swamis, monks, and laymen are changing the image of Hinduism and Buddhism. Religious leaders of many stripes write tracts on problems of modernization, encouraging laymen and fellow leaders alike to participate in economic and social development. In much of Asia we seem to be witnessing something like a Protestant Reformation in its Weberian sense. If Max Weber were living today, he would have to revise his judgment of the Asian religions; he would find "worldly asceticism" beginning to operate in them too to break barriers to economic, social, and political modernization.

But the qualifying phrase "beginning to operate" is important. By virtue of their strong prophetic heritage and even more because industrialization has shown them how much society *can* be changed, Western religions can still help Afro-Asian faiths to see the necessity of social participation. Meanwhile Asian religions can alert those of the West to the danger that threatens them, the danger of focusing exclusively on society, neglecting religion's interpersonal, transcendent roots, and becoming in consequence unrelievedly secular. In "Up to Our Steeple in Politics," two ministers chide their fellow Christians for swallowing the prevailing American assumption that "the political order . . . is the *only* source and authority to which we can and ought to repair for relief from what ails us. . . . Politics has become *the* end. We have been gulled into believing that whatever ails us . . . can be cured exclusively by political and social nostrums."[3]

"If there be East and West/It is not wisdom," sang that delightful Tibetan saint Milarepa. In view of what East has to learn from West today about religious *relevance*, and West from East about *religious* relevance, his words acquire new meaning.

Historical Update

In the two decades since this essay was written, the fate of our planet has emerged as yet another human responsibility, its newest frontier. Consequently, the picture that was sketched above should now be emended to read as follows: Religion began in the individual's direct relationship with the transhistorical and ultimate—God by whatsoever name. From this inviolate starting point and continuing center, it has proceeded to shoulder, successively, concern for interpersonal relations and society's institutions and structures. To live up to its calling, it must now add to these agendas, concern for other species and life's sustaining environment.

Notes

1. "I hate, I despise your feasts, and I take no delight in your solemn assemblies" (Amos 5:21). "*Lower* . . . knowledge (is) of . . . ceremonials" (Mandaka Upanishad, italics added).

2. Heinz Kloppenburg, in: "The Civilization of the Dialogue," an Occasional Paper published by the Center for the Study of Democratic Institutions, Santa Barbara, California, p. 21.

3. Will D. Campbell & James Y. Holloway, *Christianity and Crisis*, XXIX, 3 (March 3, 1969), p. 36.

Part Four

THE WAY OUT

Sensibilities differ, and mine (clearly) are better tuned to the past than to the future. I see the optimism of our New Age Aquarians cancelled by the pessimism of our doomsday Cassandras and find myself hamstrung between them. If I could have my way I would redirect, unopened, to its opposite numbers the mail that reaches me from both camps. Let them fight it out while I hold their coats, for I cannot detect a futuristic gene in my makeup.

Obviously, then, the word "beyond" in this book's title does not portend prediction. This final section will not crystal-ball the future, trying to foresee what the ethos of the twenty-first century will look like. As for what it should look like, this has already been proposed; our hope lies in returning to an outlook which in its broad outlines is carried in the bloodstream of the human race.

The first two essays in this closing section begin by reviewing the strictures the Modern and Postmodern mindsets impose against such a return—stricture being defined (in the Oxford English Dictionary *as "a morbid contraction of some canal or duct in the body"—and proceed from there to suggest what an outlook released from those strictures might look like. "The Sacred Unconscious" asks how the human self might appear if seen in its full stature, while "The Incredible Assumption" capsules the thesis of the book as a whole and rounds it off with a flourish.*

10

BEYOND THE MODERN WESTERN MINDSET*

In "Excluded Knowledge," Chapter Four of this volume, I argued that worldviews arise from epistemologies, which in turn are generated by the motivations that control them. To summarize that argument, in the seventeenth century Europe hit on an epistemology (empiricism, the scientific method[1]) that augmented its control dramatically—over nature to start with, but who knew where such control might eventually reach? This increase in our power pleased us to the point that we gave this way of knowing right of way. And with that move the die was cast with respect to worldview. Empiricism proceeds through sense knowledge, and that which connects with our senses is matter. I do not say that the worldview this epistemology has generated is materialism (the view that nothing but matter exists), for our thoughts and feelings are, on the one hand, too conspicuous to be denied and, on the other, too different from what we experience matter to be, to be reduced to it. It is safer to dub our modern Western worldview naturalism, this being defined as the view that (a) nothing that lacks a material component exists, and (b) in what does exist the physical component has the final say.

It is ironic that the science that lured us into this worldview now seems to be abandoning it. With each successive

*Reprinted with permission from *Teachers College Record* 82, no. 3 (Spring 1981).

probe, matter had been growing more ethereal even before Einstein discovered that mass and energy are convertible. What this energy is, no one quite knows. If a thimbleful of vacuum contains more energy than all the atomic energy in the universe,[2] it cannot be less powerful than when it is impounded in mass; but as the reference to vacuum emphasizes, in its free state it seems less substantial. Priestly and Boscovich argued early on that Newton's acceptance of the Greek view that atoms are impenetrable was simple-minded; they are better conceived as mathematical points surrounded by fields of forces that repel up to a point, then attract with the inverse square of the distance. Now that we have split atoms we know that Priestly and Boscovich were wrong; atoms do have size. But their contention may still hold for electrons. Some current experiments suggest that they have a finite size, others that they do not. If something has no size, or no definite position as in the case of particles before they are subject to position measurements, are they still matter? The message that reaches us from frontier physics seems to be that the further we track matter toward its causal origins, the more it sheds the attributes it wears in the "middle region" of size that our senses and instruments register, until at some vanishing point on the horizon it seems to drop these attributes altogether to becoming something we can scarcely guess—disappearing, perhaps, into David Bohm's implicate order.[a]

This ghostly writing has been on the wall for the better part of our century, but it has not shaken our naturalism, which bids to exit this century more entrenched, if anything, than when it entered it. This is because matter remains what we can get at and control. The problem lies deeper than wilfulness—wanting to have our way over nature—for even our search for disinterested truth is drawn to naturalism and empiricism. Control includes,

---

[a] David Bohm, *Wholeness and the Implicate Order* (London: Routledge & Kegan Paul, 1980), Professor Bohm was in the audience when the initial draft of this paper was presented. When I came to this line I was gratified to see him nod in agreement.

importantly, the controlled experiment, and this, more than any other form of validation, inspires confidence. Bertrand Russell's mid-century BBC pronouncement that "what science cannot tell us, mankind cannot know" is absurd as it stands, but if we amend it to read "cannot collectively know for sure," it becomes less so. Propositionalized, this introductory point can be indicated as follows:

> Matter is that which (with whatever required amplification) registers on our senses.
>
> Our senses are where our worlds overlap.
>
> The parts of our worlds that overlap are the parts we trust most, for we are social creatures: down isolation's path lies madness.

It is all so plausible. To restate the point only slightly:

> Seeing is believing, touching is truth (an old American proverb).
>
> Science's extension of our seeing and touching has augmented our power and enabled us to solve certain problems spectacularly.
>
> With the collectivizing of society we look increasingly to government to solve our problems, while the government relies on science to help it do so.

Everywhere accent falls on the sense domain. It would be surprising if naturalism were not our worldview and empiricism our favored noetic probe.

But problems abound. "Our society is not working well and all signs indicate it will work less well in the future," sociologist Robert Bellah told the Woodstock symposium that this essay was initially written for. We need to look at our social problems, but first I should describe more systematically the outlook that contributes to them.

I. What the Modern Western Mindset Is

I think I see more clearly now than when I wrote either "Excluded Knowledge" or the book out of which that essay derived, *Forgotten Truth*, what the Modern Western

Mindset (hereafter MWM) is. The clue to it can be stated in a single sentence: *An epistemology that aims relentlessly at control rules out the possibility of transcendence in principle.*[b] By transcendence I mean something that is better than we are by every measure of value we know and some that elude us. To expect a transcendental object to appear on a viewing screen wired by an epistemology that aims at control would be tantamount to expecting the melody as well as the lyrics of a song to issue from a typewriter. We can "put nature to the rack," as Bacon advised, because it is inferior to us; possessing (in its elemental parts at least) neither mind nor freedom in the genuine sense, these parts can be pushed around. But if things that are superior to us exist, they are not going to fit into our controlled experiments, any more than self-consciousness or advanced forms of abstract thinking would fit into (and hence be brought to light by) experiments woodchucks hypothetically might devise. It being as impossible for us to acquire "effective knowledge" (see p. 97-98 above) over them as it is to nail a drop of mercury with our thumb, an epistemology that drives single-mindedly toward effective knowledge is not going to allow transcendent realities to exist.[c]

It follows that accounting can proceed only from the bottom up—from inferior to superior, from less to more. Chronologically and developmentally the more comes after the less; causally it comes out of the less, the only other determining principle allowed being chance, which of course is a nonprinciple, the absence of a principle. Even when the higher has appeared, the thrust is to understand and interpret its workings in terms of the lower.

---

[b]That current epistemology *is* geared to control has been argued in earlier essays, so I shall not remarshall the evidence here. See especially pp. 96-98 above.

[c]Signs of this are everywhere, but I shall confine myself to a single example, drawn from a participant at the Woodstock symposium. Owen Barfield points out that "the eighteenth century essay was allowed . . . to 'bring in' religion [i.e., transcendence], which is exactly what the twentieth century was not allowed to do. Not on any account" (*Journal of the American Academy of Religion* 47/2, Supplement (June 1979): 221-22).

The name for this mode of explanation is reductionism,[d] and the growth of the MWM can be correlated with its advance. For Newton, stars became machines. For Descartes animals were machines. For Hobbes society is a machine. For La Mettrie the human body is a machine. For Pavlov and Skinner, human behavior is mechanical.

How many boxes,
How many stars;
How long, O Lord,
Till they open the bars.[3]

This reductionistic momentum has not abated. Beginning with consciousness, we find Daniel Dennett telling us that "materialism in one form or another is the reigning orthodoxy among philosophers of mind"[4] and Carl Sagan saying in his *The Dragons of Eden* that his "fundamental premise about the brain is that its workings—what we sometimes call 'mind'—are a consequence of its anatomy and physiology and nothing more."[5] On our way from psychology to biology we cross sociology, where attempts to explain human behavior in terms of continuities with lower forms of life have spawned a vigorous subdiscipline, sociobiology. As this is currently one of the liveliest crossdisciplinary subjects on university campuses, I shall reserve it for separate treatment and pass on to biology. "Biologists," Harold Morowitz, professor of molecular biophysics and biochemistry at Yale tells us, "have been moving relentlessly toward . . . hard-core materialism."[6] Francis Crick, codiscoverer of DNA, agrees: "The ultimate aim of the modern movement in biology is to explain all biology in terms of physics and chemistry."[7] Going back to Morowitz: As "physiologists study the activity of living cells in terms of processes carried out by organelles and other subcellular entities, the study of life at all levels, from social to molecular

[d]The belief that human activities can be "reduced" to and explained by the behavior of lower animals, and that these in turn can be reduced to the physical laws that govern inanimate matter. For a full-scale critique of this belief, see Arthur Koestler and James Smythies, *Beyond Reductionism* (New York: Macmillan, 1970).

behavior, has in modern times relied on reductionism as the chief explanatory concept."[8] In nonlife, too, we may add; in geology, for example, the formations and properties of minerals are described using the features of the constituent crystals. To close the loop by returning to the top of the ladder, we find that not just mind in general but its finest achievements are approached from below. Ethnocriticism has emerged as the attempt to understand works of art in terms of animal behavior. A sample on my desk proposes to shed light on three literary classics —Moliere's *The Would-be Gentleman,* Diderot's *Rameau's Nephew,* and Zola's *Germinal*—by showing that "play" serves the same function in these works as it does in the animal kingdom. "Culture has to do the same job that instinct had been doing."[9]

This spot-check shows how widely the reductionistic approach is invoked, but I promised to say something about sociobiology. So let me conclude this section on what the MWM is with a quick look at the way reductionism proceeds in its province.

The Naked Ape and *The Territorial Imperative* are discounted for the glib way they transposed raw, isolated data from one species to another, but their search for biological roots of human behavior continues to be pushed to the hilt. Whether through Pavlov's dogs, Skinner's pigeons and rats, or Lorenz's greylag geese, the hope everywhere is to discover continuities, for only in lower registers are explanations for our basic propensities available. Piaget details continuities in play[10] and speech, seeing the latter as deriving from structures of thought that have their roots in sensorimotor mechanisms that are deeper than linguistics.[11] John Bowlby's fifteen-year, three-volume study *Attachment and Loss* is a detailed effort to bridge the gap between innate patterns of attachment in mammals and the attachment/loss complex in the human baby. Let me be clear: insofar as such studies simply indicate traits we share with other life forms, they do no harm and indeed some good, for until recently the modern world has made too much of the human/

subhuman divide. And there are practical lessons to be learned from the similarities. Bowlby's findings on the crucial role of early emotional attachments in the development of life forms generally, for example, might induce us to pay more attention to this area as we relate to our own children. If his study had concluded simply that "the basic structure of man's behavioral equipment resembles that of infrahuman species," there could be no objection. What must be watched is the sentence that follows, where he moves from the observation that "the early form is not superseded" to the inference that "it [the infrahuman form] shall *determine* the overall pattern."[12] Here the inferior-causes-superior assumption emerges in broad daylight.

It is Harvard's Edward O. Wilson, though, who (more than any other single scientist) moved sociobiology onto the pages of *The New York Review of Books* and made it a lively public topic, so his views deserve a paragraph or two in their own right. Like other sociobiologists, he draws on data from life forms generally to reason that human behavior, including actions and choices traditionally explained in terms of idealism and disinterested love of others, is ultimately to be understood as genetically determined. Even when we behave "nobly" we are in fact responding to genetic conditioning that moves us to seek our own interests or those of our kinship group.[13]

Wilson divides altruism into two kinds. Soft-core altruism looks like it is directed toward the welfare of others but actually redounds circuitously to its agent's benefit. Hardcore altruism is likewise disguised self-interest, but here the interested agent is not the individual organism, who may even sacrifice his life; it is the species whose will prevails. From the species' point of view individuals exist merely to produce genes and serve as their temporary carriers: "The organism is only DNA's way of making more DNA."[14] As mutual aid between its members helps a species to survive, genes that induce the hypothalamus and limbic systems of the brain to entertain warm feelings for one's fellows have a "Darwinian edge" and turn out to be winners. This is why we lay down our lives for our friends;[e] our genes prompt us to do so.

While the West's "brain," which for present purposes we can equate with the modern university, rolls ever further down the reductionistic path, other centers of society—our emotions, for example, as they find expression through our artists; and our wills, as evidenced in part by rise in crime and senseless vandalism—protest. These other centers of our selves feel that they are being dragged, kicking and screaming, down an ever-darkening tunnel. We need to listen to their protests, for they force us to ask if it is possible to move toward a worldview which, without compromising reason or evidence in the slightest, would allow more room to the sides of our selves that our current worldview constricts.

II. The Need for a Different Outlook

When individuals suffer the loss of something that implicates their sense of self—a spouse, a child, whatever it is that gives their life its focus and meaning—they

---

[e]These friends cannot be four-footed, feathered, or furry though—much less leafy and flowery. To be kind to the point of sacrificing human interests for these—restraining our predatory impulses towards the whales, say—is irrational, for in genetic ethics (the opening section of *Sociobiology* is titled "The Morality of the Gene") "rational" is what favors species survival.

It is irrational to defer to other species unless there is a gene that has caught on to the fact that species need environments to sustain them—I enter this suggestion on my own to caricature the lengths to which sociobiology has already stretched evidence in the interests of theory (see Marvin Harris, *Cultural Materialism;* Richard Dawkins, *The Selfish Gene;* and Stuart Hampshire, "The Illusion of Sociobiology," *The New York Review of Books*, 12 October 1978). Wilson is now quoted as saying that by "gene" he does not mean the actual physical entities we can see with electron microscopes. Officially he claims only that biological findings might plausibly be used to explain human behavior. But his suggestion meshes so neatly with current styles of explanation that a dropped hint is enough to place its author in vast demand. Sociologists and psychologists are already working with sociobiological hypotheses as if they were tested theories —Pierre van den Berghe and David Barash are examples.

grow ill; not invariably, but in greater proportion. They become more prone to cancer, for one thing. Here is a clear and direct causal flow from mind to matter. In dynamics it parallels exactly the way hypnosis can remove warts, and placebos cause the brain to secrete more pain-relieving endorphins. In all these cases a mental change effects a bodily one. But the MWM does not know what to do with mind; Barbara Brown tells of a symposium in which a scientist reacted to the suggestion that the mind is emerging as a new tool for medicine by roaring to the audience, "Talking about mind will set medicine back fifty years!"[15] We understand something of how the brain works, and, yes, through depth psychology something of how the mind works too. But when it comes to infusing the mind with motivation and meaning, the MWM is helpless.

In itself this can be excused, since anyone who claimed to have techniques for such infusion would be a charlatan. What is not attractive is the way the MWM works to erode the meaning lives already have. D. and C. Johnson report a pattern of disorder among Sioux Indians called *tawatl ye sni*, "totally discouraged." The syndrome involves feelings of helplessness and thoughts of death: "There is no way out . . . there's nothing he can do."[16] Conditions on the Dakota reservations doubtless go a long way toward accounting for this syndrome, but it would be naive to think that the near collapse of the Native American worldview is not also a factor. The six-volume *Handbook of Cross-Cultural Psychology*, which includes the Johnsons' study, illustrates how the MWM facilitates this collapse.[f] If the Sioux feels himself to be in touch with higher forces (it tells us), this is because his "reality bounds are not as firmly established as is the case in

[f]Or the collapse of any worldview with a religious component, for that matter. Edward Wilson says sociobiology is forced to conclude that "the predisposition to religious belief is the most complex and powerful force in the human mind"; but whereas elsewhere complexity is a biological virtue, here it shows only that the religious impulse is "in all probability ineradicable" (Edward O. Wilson, *On Human Nature* [New York: Bantam Books, 1978], p. 176).

certain Western societies."[17] If he senses his life to be in the hands of a higher power—well, this "actually serves a useful function in alleviating the stress of life."[18] The clinical, patronizing term for this function is, of course, compensation.

The maladies in our personal lives have become psychological and so have moved into an area we have abandoned. That psychology courses remain the most popular college electives and *Psychology Today* is a booming success does not counter this observation. As the passage on reductionism in the preceding section indicates, we have abandoned the mind by converting to efforts to understand it in terms of things other than itself and lower than itself.[g]

The consequences of this abandonment for our civilization as a whole are difficult to assess. Who is to tell us? Let me opt this time around for Alexander Solzhenitsyn, focusing on his 1978 commencement address at Harvard University.[19] As an exile, he is not likely to downgrade us in favor of Soviet Russia; he sees socialism of any type and shade as leading to a total destruction of the human spirit and to a leveling of mankind into death. But as an outside observer he may be able to see us more objectively than we see ourselves. And what he sees in the West today is "spiritual exhaustion."[20]

> How short a time ago . . . the small world of modern Europe was easily seizing colonies all over the globe. . . . It all seemed an overwhelming success. . . . Western society expanded in a triumph of human independence and power. And all of a sudden the twentieth century brought the clear realization of this society's fragility.[21]

If Solzhenitsyn saw only political factors as responsible for this twentieth-century reversal I would not be quoting

---

[g]"Psychology, or at least American psychology, is a second rate discipline. The main reason is that it does not *stand in awe* of its subject matter. Psychologists have too little respect for psychology" (James Gibson, as quoted in *The New York Review of Books* [Jan. 19, 1989], p. 15).

him here. As it is, his diagnosis points directly to the concern of this essay.

> How did the West decline from its triumphal march to its present debility? Have there been fatal turns and losses of direction in its development? It does not seem so. The West kept advancing steadily in accordance with its proclaimed social intentions, hand in hand with a dazzling progress in technology. And all of a sudden it found itself in its present state of weakness.
>
> This means that the mistake must be at the root, at the very foundations of thought in modern times. I refer to *the prevailing Western view of the world* which was born in the Renaissance and has found political expression since the Age of Enlightenment.[22]

Clearly, Solzhenitsyn is referring to what I am calling the Modern Western Mindset. He identifies this mindset as "rationalistic humanism or humanistic autonomy: the proclaimed and practiced *autonomy of man from any higher force* above him."[h] If superior forces are not allowed —current epistemology has no way to register them, I have argued—then human life has no alternative but to appear autonomous. If we are surprised to find Solzhenitsyn blaming this presumed autonomy for the fact that the Western world has lost its civic courage—"a fact which cannot be disputed is the weakening of human personality in the West," he tells us[23]—it is because, mechanists that

[h]Ibid., pp. 47-49; emphasis added. "It could also be called anthropocentricity," he adds, "with man seen as the center of it all" (p. 49).

On the day that I found myself writing these lines a letter reached me from a former student relating an anecdote from his freshman philosophy course at Harvard University. It seems that when Emerson Hall (where the class met) was built, the Philosophy Department selected for the motto to be inscribed on its main wall, "Man is the measure of all things." President Eliot, however, was of a different mind, and what actually appeared was, "What is man that Thou art mindful of him?"

The occasion for the student's note to me was a return visit to his alma mater. He found that vines had obscured the inscription, leaving only three words visible, those words being "that Thou art," the claim (in its Vedantic formulation) that man is indissolubly joined to the Absolute. I shall return to that in section V, 4 below.

we have largely and unconsciously become,[24] we assume that if superior forces exist they would tyrannize; we take their absence to be liberating. It seems not to occur to us that such forces might empower us. Submission (in Arabic, *Islam*) was the very name of the religion that surfaced through the Koran, yet its entry into history occasioned the greatest political explosion the world has known. If mention of this fact automatically triggers our fears of fanaticism, this simply shows us another defense our agnostic reflex has erected against the possibility of there being something that, better than we are in every respect, could infuse us with goodness as well as power were we open to the transfusion. It is usually said that the Copernican revolution humbled man by displacing him from the center of the universe, but this spatial dislodgment was nothing compared with the arrogance that followed in its wake, the arrogance of assuming that nothing exists that quite equals ourselves. For is it not we who ride the crest of evolution's advance? And what source of worth is there save evolution? For the MWM the question is rhetorical.

Mention of the individual and collective problems that the MWM abets has its place, but to seek a different outlook for the purpose of allaying them will not work. For this understandable (but in the end poorly conceived) motivation reinforces three assumptions of the very mindset it seeks to replace.

The first of these is the assumption that history can be controlled. (That preoccupation with control again.) Do X, and Y will follow; adopt a different worldview and a better world will result. Realistically there seems to be little evidence that history can be constructively controlled, though our destructive power might increase to the point where a madman could end it summarily.

Working hand in glove with this assumption that history can be controlled is a second: the assumption that happiness can be bestowed. Heirs to any better world we might create would be happier than we are—this is what "better world" means—so in creating such a world we would hand happiness to those who are born into it. But this is not how life works. Comfort can be handed to us inasmuch as physical discomforts, at least, can be alleviated from without; if we are hungry food can be given us, if we are in pain, anodynes can be provided. Happiness, though, is different. Happiness cannot be bestowed from the outside or passively received from within. It must be won. It follows that it is impossible to do as much for another as one can do for oneself—save one's soul, for example, however one wishes to parse that phrase. If the phrase sounds sanctimonious, we can substitute the Zen variant: "No one can go to the bathroom for you."

The third dubious assumption underlying the "better world" rationale for a new outlook is the notion that truth is instrumental.[25] Here again the Prometheanism of modernity comes squarely to view: truth is seen as what will take us where we want to go. In the punchy formula of its distinctively modern, pragmatic definition, truth is what works. As a partial truth this is unexceptionable; the pragmatic attitude is an appropriate part of life, the yang part of its yin/yang whole—we were not born for idleness. But to make it the whole of life, and the version of truth it sponsors the whole of truth, is a trap so obvious that it took the bait of science's success to lure us into it. Truths in the plural are indeed instrumental; they can and should be chosen for ends we have in mind. But with truth in the singular—a person's or a people's final surmise as to the way things are—it is otherwise. Truth in this final, last-ditch sense is like love. If one loves for any reason save the beloved's intrinsic lovableness, it is not love. Comparably, to hold X to be true for any reason save that in fact it is so, is a contradiction in terms. Suppose that to the observation that "all men must die" the response were to be, "But surely that can't be true, for it makes people sad and fatalistic." To suspect that one is holding a belief for any reason save that it is true is to undermine it immediately.

"There is no right higher than that of the Truth," a maxim from India reminds us. It follows that we owe it to the truth to accept it; metaphysics may not be moralized. Truth has no obligation to accommodate itself to us; it is we who must fashion ourselves to it. The appropriate reason for changing our outlook is not to create a better world or save the one we have. It is to see more clearly things as they are. All other considerations are secondary.

III. The Approach to a Revised Outlook Through Logic

Kilimanjaro is the highest mountain in Africa. A number of years ago, as Hemingway noted in the epigraph to "The Snows of Kilimanjaro," the frozen carcass of a mountain leopard was found near its 19,565 foot snow-clad summit. No one seems to know what it was doing at that altitude.

Perhaps it was curious. We have seen that no prudential reason for changing our mindset will do; in the end we must want a better one solely for the more accurate view it affords. But how can an improved outlook be acquired? To move from captivity toward a freedom we have yet to understand may be the most difficult task the mind can set for itself.

Let us begin with purely logical possibilities. Being no more than possibilities these will not persuade—that they are possible does not mean that they are true. But even to entertain alternatives to the MWM is a step toward loosening its hold on us, and if we can show that they are not inherently unreasonable, this will be an even longer step. It is as if, faced with a stake that has been driven deep into the ground, we begin in this section to rock it back and forth to loosen the hard earth around it. Not until the next section will we try to pull it up.

In section one we saw that exercise of newly discovered ways of controlling nature established an epistemology that produced the MWM. It follows that if we were to approach the world with intent other than to control it, it would show us a different guise. The opposite of the will-to-control is the wish-to-participate—a genuine desire to accent embracing yin over abrasive yang so that domination will not preclude partnership or assertiveness stymie cooperation. Such an alternative starting point would generate a whole new sequence, which (generalizing the diagram that was introduced in connection with theology on p. 146) contrasts with that of the MWM as follows:

	The MWM	*Logical Alternative*
anthropology:	alienation	fulfillment
↑	↖	↗
ontology (worldview):	naturalism	transcendence
↑	↖	↗
epistemology:	empiricism	intuitive discernment
↑	↖	↗
motivation:	control	participation

The payoff of the revised starting point would be an ampler view of reality, and as it turns out to include things that are superior to us, "transcendence" is a fitting name for it. Its greater inclusiveness gives it a starting edge over the MWM, for the fact that every advance in science's understanding of nature has shown it to contain more than we had suspected suggests that a generous ontological vision, too, stands a better chance of being right than does a paltry one. But I leave that as no more than a passing observation. The trickiest link in the right-hand chain is its epistemology. Refusing to accept as truth's final arbiter the controlled experiment (or even objectivity, the consensus requirements of which push it relentlessly, as we have seen, toward sense-verificational empiricism), this alternate epistemology is faced with the problem of distinguishing between veridical discernments and ones that are deceptive. It is not within the scope of this essay to develop this alternative model systematically. I shall refer to it occasionally in what follows, but I introduce it mainly to limber up our imaginations—to keep them supple against an ossifying shell that threatens to become so strong that only the crowbar of historical events could break it.

There is another way to show that the MWM is not the only way to look at the world. Even if we accept the modern world's penchant for control, we face a choice, for that road quickly forks. Control over what—the world or ourselves? More than once before I have referred to Ernest Gellner's report that for the MWM knowledge must be "effective" if it is to qualify as "genuine" (see again p. 97 above). But effective for what? For changing the objective, external world, or things within ourselves—the dispositions and predilections that constitute our characters and make us the persons we are? As self-transformation was not what interested the founding fathers of the MWM —Bacon's "knowledge is power" was not aimed at power for self-improvement—this mindset has not proved to be sophisticated in handling this side of the question. It does not have a great deal to say on how we might break out of our self-centeredness and relate lovingly to the world at large. Secretly, it may wonder if there is much to say on this topic; as evidence, note the inverse ratio between prestige and attention to self-change in academic departments of psychology as we pass from experimental and cognitive psychology to clinical psychology, then humanistic psychology, and then transpersonal psychology. When the MWM has its way completely, as in the deterministic behaviorism of B. F. Skinner, self-change is not even admitted as a possibility.

This has produced a paradox. Out of the practical side of our mouths we continue to urge people to exercise their freedom and take responsibility, fearing that if they do not our society may come apart at the seams; Solzhenitsyn is not alone in warning of "spiritual exhaustion." Meanwhile, out of the theoretical side of our mouths we serve notice on these attributes and place them in jeopardy. In the natural sciences where Skinner's model of man obviously falls and where Freud hoped his would eventually find its place, human beings are not free at all;[i] Heisenberg's indeterminacy principle

[i]"The deeply rooted belief in psychic freedom and choice is quite

has not made the slightest difference here. As for the social sciences, they remain dedicated to explaining human behavior in terms of stimuli that provoke it. (Is the victim the murdered man or the man who murdered him, the latter having been victimized by society?) Even in the humanities, according to the latest avant-garde literary movement, it is not man who speaks; rather, it is language and, beneath it, matter that speak through him—I am referring to Deconstructionism as headed by Derrida, Foucault, and the late Roland Barthes. Everywhere the individual subject is devalorized in favor of contexts that call the tunes and pull the strings. It is what comes our way that is accented, not what we do with it.

Living as we do in a civilization that prides itself on using everything at its disposal—its resources, its invention, every scrap of information its computers can deposit in their data banks—it is not idle to ask if our most valuable unused resource may not be the capacity of persons to recognize themselves as responsible agents; selves who ask not that the world deliver things into their laps, but that it provide a matrix for their moral and spiritual development—structures on which character can climb if it resolves to do so. There is a knowledge that is effective for this kind of climbing, but like poetry in the MWM, it is an outcast knowledge. For as Allan Wheelis has written:

> Among the sophisticated, the use of the term "will power" has become the most unambiguous badge of naivete. . . . The unconscious is heir to the prestige of will. As one's fate formerly was determined by the will, now it is determined by the repressed mental life. Knowledgeable moderns put their backs to the couch and in so doing may fail to put their shoulders to the wheel. As will has been devalued, so has courage; for courage can exist only in the service of the will. . . . In our understanding of human nature we have gained determinism: lost determination.[26]

---

unscientific and must give ground before the claims of a determinism which governs mental life" (Sigmund Freud, *General Introduction to Psychoanalysis* [New York: Liveright, 1935], p. 95).

IV. From Logic to Imagery

Logic can show us that if we were to approach the world with an eye to embracing rather than controlling it, or asking how it might school us rather than serve us, it would reveal a different guise. But what that guise would be it cannot say. For this latter report, insight is required. And insight, as David Bohm has noted,

> announces itself in mental images. Newton's conception of gravity and Einstein's notion of the constant speed of light came to them as perceptions, as images, not as hypotheses or conclusions drawn from logical deduction. Formal logic is secondary to insight [via images] and is never the source of new knowledge.[27]

To add a third example to the two Bohm mentions, the image of a randomly branching tree not only crystallized Darwin's theory of natural selection but guided him through his successive formulations of it. His notebooks show him drawing it repeatedly, lavishing on it a care for representation and detail that shows clearly his need to steep his mind in the image if he were to wring from it everything it had to offer.[28]

So I, too, reach for an image that picks up with our realization that there is a different world that awaits discovery and moves us toward picturing what that world might be like. The one I choose appears in a wise and beautiful book by Gai Eaton, *The King of the Castle*, (from which the opening sentence of my preface was also drawn) and I quote it in full.

> Let us imagine a summer landscape, bounded only by our limited vision but in truth unbounded; a landscape of hills and valleys, forests and rivers, but containing also every feature that an inventive mind might bring to thought. Let us suppose that somewhere in this measureless extension a child has been blowing bubbles for the sheer joy of seeing them carried on the breeze, catching the sunlight, drifting between earth and sky. And then let us compare all that we know of our world, the earth and what it contains, the sun, the moon and the stars, to one such bubble, a single

> one. It is there in our imagined landscape. It exists. But it is a very small thing, and in a few moments it is gone.
>
> This, at least, is one way of indicating the traditional or—taking the word in its widest sense—the religious view of our world and of how it is related to all that lies beyond it. Perhaps the image may be pursued a step further. The bubble's skin reflects what lies outside and is, at the same time, transparent. Those who live within may be aware of the landscape in quite different ways. Those whose sight is weak or untrained may still surmise its existence and, believing what they are told by others who see more clearly, have faith in it. Secondly, there are some who will perceive within the bubble itself reflections of what lies outside and begin to realize that everything within is neither more nor less than a reflection and has no existence in its own right. Thirdly, as by a miracle of sight, there will be a few for whom transparency is real and actual. Their vision pierces the thin membrane which to others seems opaque and, beyond faith, they see what is to be seen.[29]

The balance of this essay touches on several points this image raises, but before I proceed to them let me enter a covering observation. It is not possible to adjudicate between contending outlooks objectively, but it is possible to say which is the more interesting. And on this count Eaton's image wins over the MWM hands down, for it allows for everything in the latter and vastly more besides. Specifically, it directs us toward a reality whose qualitative reaches outstrip what the MWM discerns in the way that the latter's quantitative features—the size of the universe it sees, and its other countable features—exceed what Ptolemy had in mind.

V. The Image Explored

Remembering that we are tracking truth not for its practical consequences but for its intrinsic worth while expecting that each turn in the road will open onto vistas more interesting than the ones before, I proceed now to touch on five points latent in the image I have chosen as guide. The first relates to our ability to see beyond the obvious.

1. The Possibility of Certitude

Last spring I received a letter from a young man who had been reading the book in which the image I am working with appeared. "When at one point the author spoke of 'the inrush of the Real,' " he wrote, "I felt that happening to me."

This is an important experience. The word "inrush" implies confidence, while the capitalization of the word "Real" indicates that it pertains here to matters that are important.

There is no way that the MWM can validate both those points.[30] Karl Popper spoke for that mindset when he opened a colloquium at M.I.T. several years ago by saying, "Were it not for science, the skeptics would win hands down." Humanists tend to concur. In science we can verify hypotheses; elsewhere we must remain in doubt.

Meanwhile we must live, and this calls for choices and guidelines for making them, ones we consider dependable. It is no use to play games with oneself here, pretending that something is true while knowing that in all likelihood it is not,[j] but as I am trying to steer clear of prudential considerations I shall not dwell on this impasse. Time is better spent on why we think rationality drives toward skepticism, to see if we have that point straight.

There are times that visit us all when we feel at sea about everything. T. S. Eliot described them well when he wrote:

> *The circle of our understanding*
> *Is a very restricted area.*

[j] Sociobiology provides an instance of such game playing. On the one hand we are told that as human beings have been programmed by their evolutionary history to be incorrigible mythmakers, we require conceptual systems that engage our loyalties; while on the other, that these systems must "satisfy our urge for knowledge" (paraphrase of Edward O. Wilson, in *Religious Studies Review* 5, no. 2 [April 1980]: 102). Whether a conceptual system our knowledge tells us is a myth can engage our loyalties is never squarely faced.

Except for a limited number
Of strictly practical purposes
We do not know what we are doing;
And even, when you think of it,
We do not know much about thinking.
What is happening outside of the circle?
And what is the meaning of happening?
What ambush lies beyond the heather
And behind the Standing Stones?
Beyond the Heaviside Layer
And behind the smiling Moon?
And what is being done to us?
And what are we, and what are we doing?
To each and all of these questions
There is no conceivable answer.[31]

When these states come over us they must be respected: faced honestly and stayed with, to learn from them what we can. What is not required is the use of intelligence to glorify (and in certain versions of existentialism, romanticize) these states as if they constitute the acme of human authenticity rather than the mental counterpart of the common cold, or in severe instances the flu, to which we periodically succumb. To level the sharpest charge possible, the relentless championing of relativism, which in its cultural, historical, psychological, social, or existential form underlies all contemporary skepticism, is in the end naive.

Relativism sets out to reduce every kind of absoluteness to a relativity while making an illogical exception for its own case.[32] In effect, it declares it to be true that there is no such thing as truth; that it is absolutely true that only the relatively true exists. This is like saying that language does not exist, or writing that there is no such thing as script. Total relativism is an incoherent position. Its absurdity lies in its claim to be unique in escaping, as if by enchantment, from a relativity that is declared alone to be possible.

Relativism holds that one can never escape human subjectivity. If that were true, the statement itself would have no objective value; it would fall by its own verdict. It happens, however, that human beings are quite capable of breaking out of subjectivity; were we unable to do so we would not know what subjectivity is. As was noted in Chapter Two, a dog *is* enclosed in its subjectivity, the proof being that it is unaware of its condition, for, unlike a man or a woman, it does not possess the gift of objectivity.

If Freudian psychology declares that rationality is but a hypocritical cloak for repressed, unconscious drives, this statement falls under the same reproach; were Freudianism right on this point it would itself be no more than a front for id-inspired impulses. There is no need to run through the variations of relativism that arise from other versions of psychologizing, historicizing, sociologizing, or evolutionizing. Suffice it to say that few things are more absurd than to use the mind to accuse the mind, not just of some specific mistake but in its entirety. If we are able to doubt, this is because we know its opposite; the very notion of illusion proves our access to reality in some degree.

Our minds were made to know, and they "flourish"—no one has said this better than Aristotle—when they work meaningfully at that function. They need not be overweening nor claim omniscience; indeed, one of the important things they can know is their place. But that place exists, and it is not confined to the laboratory. To see, as E. F. Schumacher reminded us shortly before his death, that "only those questions which cannot be answered with [laboratory] 'precision' have any real significance"[33] is the first step toward knowledge about those questions themselves.

The most unnoticed reason for current skepticism is our assumption that earlier ages were mistaken. If their outlooks were erroneous, it stands to reason that ensuing eras will show ours to be mistaken too; so runs this argument, which is so taken for granted that it is seldom even voiced. But if we could see that our forebears were not mistaken—they erred in details, but not in their basic surmises, which were so much alike that in *Forgotten Truth*

I referred to them as "the human unanimity"—a major impediment to confidence in our global understandings would be removed. The next step would be to separate the reliability of our knowledge from questions of omniscience, to counter the suspicion that if we cannot know everything, what we do know must be tainted. I need not know the position of San Francisco relative to everything in the universe, much less what space and position finally mean, to be certain that, given the present position of our planet's poles, it lies predominantly west of Syracuse. From such simple beginnings we should be able to go on to separate the relativities that *should* give us pause, from ones that are irrelevant—or (at worst) are thrown like sand in the face of desert pilgrims.

2. A True Infinite

I have spent the time I did on certitude because there is not a great deal of point in asking how we might understand things differently if we have little confidence in understanding generally. On what a revalidated understanding might encompass, I shall be brief. There is space to do little more than point out several possibilities the future might explore.

An over-the-shoulder glance at the road we have come gives the lay of the land. That the region of reality the MWM has mapped with virtual certainty—its physical domain—has proved to be incomparably more interesting than we had suspected gives us reason to think that comparable extravagance awaits our astonished discovery in its other regions as well. And as I see no better star to steer by—better either in what it promises or in reasons for adopting it—I proceed to sketch the contours of the most interesting world I can image.[k]

---

[k]I suspect that the approach I am following—my methodology if you will—is clear by now, but let me state it explicitly. In place of our usual tendency to begin with the accepted world and add to it only what collective evidence requires, I am asking if it would harm us to conjure the most interesting world we can, and then drop from it what reason advises us to erase. There is some resemblance to

Eaton's soap bubbles floating in a stupendous landscape are again our guide. The entire universc the MWM knows —eight billion galaxies with over eight billion stars in each—is contained in one of those bubbles, so we pass now to the landscape that envelops them. It would be a mistake to approach that landscape quantitatively, as if its size were what mattered. Size is not irrelevant—vastness has a majesty of its own—but it is the qualitative features of the surround that the image dwells on: its hills and valleys, its forests and rivers, its sunlight and breezes, as these would show themselves not to a civil engineer or surveyer, but to an artist, a naturalist, or an awe-struck mountaineer.

The MWM has awesome instruments to register the quantitative marvels of reality, but its qualitative spectrum it cannot track—not beyond the cutoff point of human experience. So it acknowledges no field or center of awareness—no intelligence, "heart," sensibility, whatever term one prefers—that exceeds ours in the way human consciousness exceeds that of minnows or zebras. Eaton's image challenges this myopia; those who are confined by this anthropocentrism, "this bubble's skin," are persons "whose sight is weak or untrained." Gazing on the landscape as a whole, an observer would doubtless delight in our bubble were he to notice it, but "it is a very small thing," besides which most of its beauty derives from the way it "reflects what is outside" and enhances the majesty of the latter by its contrasting smallness.

The environment in question, we are told, is "in truth unbounded," which is to say infinite. The word is important in the MWM, but only in the sense in which it is used in physics and mathematics. And as these disciplines are interested only in the way the concept applies to sets and numbers, it is not a true infinite they are occupied with. From a metaphysical standpoint a

---

Anselm's *credo ut intelligam*, "I believe in order to understand." Or as Wilfred Smith, using current idiom to get at what *credo* meant in the Middle Ages, paraphrases Anselm, "I get involved in order to understand."

mathematical infinite is blatantly finite, for it disregards everything in the world save several of its most abstract features. Solzhenitsyn is right: "The concept of a *supreme complete entity*," one whose presence would "restrain our passions and irresponsibility," does not figure in the postmodern outlook.[34]

3. Downward Causation

In the image we are working with, everything in the bubble of our universe is the consequence of things superior to it. The bubble comes into being because a child wants it to, and its properties—the colors that glisten on its irridescent surface—are occasioned by the brighter colors in the world around it. Causation throughout is downward—from superior to inferior, from what is more to what is less.

The West has, of course, known a philosophy of this sort; Aristotle was the first to state it explicitly. "If anyone wishes to think philosophically, Aristotle is the teacher to begin with," a book at hand advises,[35] and it is especially appropriate to invoke him here because he was not overly other-worldly; it was nature that engrossed him, even as it does us. Yet attraction seemed to him a better model for causation than propulsion; things are lured more than they are driven.

Note to begin with how pleasing this sense of causation is, this notion that things move by being drawn toward what exceeds them, and will fulfill them to the degree that they refashion themselves to its likeness. For Aristotle, the entire universe was thus animated. Everything reaches toward its better in the effort to acquire for itself its virtues, as tennis players seek out opponents who play better than they do, children are drawn to slightly older playmates, and dogs prefer human company to their own kind—everywhere the compelling lure of that which we instinctively admire because of its manifest superiority. Aristotle's universe is like a pyramid of magnets. Those on each tier are attracted to the tier above while being empowered by that tier to attract the magnets below them. At the apex stands the only completely actual reality there is, the divine Prime and Unmoved Mover.

Grounded (or stuck, as one is sometimes tempted to say) in the MWM, we cannot today endorse this vision as true, but if our blinders have not grown grotesque we can at least respect its grandeur. In the terms of our image, the thought of bubbles blown for a child's delight has far more charm than the explanation (accurate, of course, but sufficient?) that credits them to the viscous properties of molecules. Extended to the cosmos, the child's delight translates into *lila*, the Indian notion of all creation as God's play, but here the human domain is enough. It may not be diversionary simply to pause for a moment to experience how good the notion of "downward causation" (as I am calling this principle of persuasion from above) might feel. To have a model that inspires, that shows us what we would like to become, while at the same time infusing us with the strength needed to approximate it, is as important a condition as life affords.

It is also one that, ontologically speaking, the MWM precludes. There is no way that mindset can allow the possibility that the universe might be ordered teleologically, in the fashion just described. For to announce again the leitmotif of this essay, the MWM is a conceptual balloon inflated by knowledge of the sort that facilitates control, and such knowledge is necessarily limited (as we have seen) to things that are inferior to us. Jacques Monod is so pertinent here that I shall quote him again, as I did in Chapters Four and Six: "The cornerstone of the scientific method is . . . the *systematic* denial . . . of final causes."[36] It should not escape us that such causes are not denied because they have been found *not* to exist; only because they have not been found *to* exist. But how could they have been so found when search for them is excluded on principle—"*systematic* denial" is Monod's term; even the emphasis is his. The unspoken, but in no wise obscure, reason for rejecting final causes out of hand is that every glance in their direction would divert us from the efficient causes the MWM is bent on getting its hand on.

It is all very clear, and also ironical. For if the only way we are permitted to account for ontological novelty—new things coming into being—is through antecedent inferiors, what is the logical terminus of this downspout that evolution converts into an upspout? We do not have to guess at the answer, for the leading philosopher of science of our generation has told us, having made it the cornerstone of his life's work. "The basic theme of Karl Popper's philosophy," his biographer and foremost expositor writes, "is that something can come from nothing."[37]

Quite apart from whether this notion has a shred of explanatory power, is it intuitively believable?

4. The Self/World Divide

In the mid-1970s a graduate student in psychology at New York University ran an experiment involving college undergraduates who were taking a six-week summer course in business law. Dividing them into two groups, he had both groups gaze at what looked like a blank screen for a minute or so before each class session. Four times in the course of that minute a momentary, tachistoscopic message appeared on the screen, but as its four microseconds duration was too brief for it to be recognized, all that the students consciously saw was a flicker of light. The messages that were flashed to the two groups differed; for the control group it was "People Are Walking," whereas the experimental group was treated to "Mommie and I Are One." The groups had been matched for grade-point average, but when the scores of the blindly marked final examination were tabulated, the "Mommie and I" group was found to have scored almost a full letter grade higher in the course than did the control group, the numerical averages being 90.4 percent and 82.7 percent respectively.[38]

Such is the increase in power and effectiveness that can accrue when one feels tuned to one's world, for the tachistoscopic message is presumed to activate an early and powerful level of consciousness where "Mommie" represented (and in that layer of consciousness still represents) the world at large. Some psychologists dispute this interpretation, insisting that the only way information can enter the nervous system is through the conscious mind, but if they are right, from whence come the improved performances? As of this writing eight studies along the lines of the one described have been conducted, and whether the subjects were trying to lose weight, stop smoking, get good grades, or improve their mental health, the results have been positive.[39] A book that summarizes the entire field of research speaks so directly to this section of my paper that its title, *The Search for Oneness*,[40] could have served for my heading.

It hardly seems necessary to say more on this point. So much is self-evident that I feel I need only arrange the pieces.

a. No other culture in history has tried to live by an outlook that isolates the human species from its matrix to the degree that ours does. Whereas formerly men and women sensed themselves to be distinguished from the rest of reality by no more than a bubble's skin, a film so thin as to be transparent (to call again on Eaton's image), we now face the impermeable wall of Descartes's disjunction. Once he categorically isolated matter from mind, science was able to seize that matter like a fumbled football and run with it. The tracks it has left inscribe a cosmos which, as earlier essays noted, is

> denuded of all humanly recognizable qualities; beauty and ugliness, love and hate, passion and fulfillment, salvation and damnation. . . . Such matters [have of course] remained existential realities of human life, [but] the scientific worldview makes it illegitimate to speak of them as being "objectively" part of the world, forcing us instead to define such emotional experiences as "merely subjective" projections of people's inner lives. . . . All that which is basic to the specifically human [is] forced back upon the precincts of the "subjective" which, in turn, is pushed by the

> modern scientific view ever more into the province of dreams and illusions.[1]

b. The consequence of this fateful divorce, so obvious that Professor Stanley refers to it as now "a Sunday-supplement commonplace," is

> a spiritual malaise that has come to be called alienation. . . . The world, once an "enchanted garden," to use Max Weber's memorable phrase, has now become disenchanted, deprived of purpose and direction, bereft —in these senses—of life itself.[41]
>
> The dehumanizing price [of this outlook] is that our identities, freedom, norms, are no longer underwritten by our vision and comprehension of things. On the contrary we are doomed to suffer from a tension between cognition [what we believe to be true] and identity [who we sense ourselves to be].[42]

c. We have been drawn into this alienating outlook, not because it is true, but by historical choice or accident; specifically, this essay has argued, by the way Western civilization has responded to its invention of modern science.

> It was Kant's merit to see that this compulsion [to see things this way] is in us, not in things. It was Weber's to see that it is historically a specific kind of mind, not mind as such, which is subject to this compulsion.[43]

Here, more than on any other point considered in this chapter, we may be beginning to see light at the end of the tunnel, for our ecological crisis is all but forcing us to reexamine the Cartesian premise we have built on for four hundred years. I bypass here the radical proposal, ventured by countercultural scientists like Fritjof Capra, that Mahayana Buddhism, which includes an important

[1]Manfred Stanley, "Beyond Progress: Three Post-Political Futures," in *Images of the Future*, ed. Robert Bundy (Buffalo: Prometheus Books, 1976), pp. 115-16. I have used this and the three quotations that follow in other essays, but enter them again because I have encountered no others, penned from within the MWM itself, that bring out the issues quite as crisply.

idealist component, provides the best philosophical model for quantum physics that is currently available, in favor of more modest suggestions that emanate from scientists who are more established. Gregory Bateson subtitled *Mind and Nature*, his last book, "A Necessary Unity"; and biologist Alex Comfort argues in his *I and That* that though the self-world (I/That) divide is to some extent inevitable, it can hypertrophy, and in our minds has done so. Finally, there is this suggestive statement by Lewis Thomas:

> It may turn out that consciousness is a much more generalized mechanism, shared round not only among ourselves but with all the other conjoined things of the biosphere. Thus, since we are not, perhaps, so absolutely central, we may be able to get a look at it, but we will need a new technology for this kind of neurobiology; in which case we will find that we have a whole eternity of astonishment stretching out ahead of us. Always assuming, of course, that we're still here.[44]

5. We Have What We Need

Once, when it had become clear that the days of Suzuki Roshi, founder of the San Francisco Zen Center, were numbered, his dharma heir, Richard Baker, asked him in distress, "How will we manage without you?" The Roshi answered, "Never forget: everything you need you already have." There is an echo of this in *The Autobiography of Malcolm X*. Describing his prison conversion to Islam and the difficulty he had in getting knees to bend in prayer that till then had bent only to jimmy locks, Malcolm remarks: "I was going through the hardest thing, also the greatest thing, for any human being to do; to accept that which is already within you, and around you."[45]

It is difficult to think of a presumption more foreign to the MWM than this one. In Eaton's image nothing turns on time, for the limitless landscape is there from the start, waiting to be seen by anyone who looks outside his bubble and adjusts his vision to the reaches that extend beyond it. In the MWM, however, the case is the opposite. There time is decisive. Buckminster Fuller refers to "our failed yesterday and our half-successful today." All eyes are on tomorrow.

Partisans of the MWM are quick to object that if the Roshi's claim were taken seriously it would cut the nerve of social concern. The objcction leaves the Roshi's own energetic life an anomaly, but let that pass. Once in the course of a television interview on progress I asked Reinhold Niebuhr if relinquishing the dream of historical progress would de-fuse social action. He answered with a question of his own: "To take his work seriously, need a doctor believe that he is eradicating disease?" We are back at the point that was made in section two. All myths are tied to the Golden Age of their origin, and in the case of the MWM it was an age when technology seemed to be effecting historical progress. So the MWM continues this mystique, focusing on society rather than the individual (specifically, on what society might give the individual), and on the future rather than the present (on what society might provide individuals with tomorrow that it cannot provide today).

This is why in the context of the MWM the heading of this section sounds bizarre. If we think of what we need as a happiness that is handed to us by society, then to say that "we have what we need" is cruelly false, for our society obviously hands us no such thing. But that society can hand people happiness is an illusion that was earlier exposed. Whether it can provide individuals on average with more opportunity than it now does to work out their own salvation, I leave as an open question.

VI. Conclusion

Do I expect our outlook to change in the directions I have tried to imagine? Not soon, and never for everyone.

The first half of that answer needs no elaboration. It is obvious that the MWM is not about to collapse in the way an avalanche of snow periodically slides off a roof. Section one of this essay was given to showing how firmly entrenched it still is.

The second half of my answer, though, may seem enigmatic, so let me conclude by making it less so. To revert for a last time to Gai Eaton's image, let us recall that those who live within its child-blown bubble can be aware of its surrounding landscape in different ways. Some merely surmise its existence. Others recognize its reflections on their bubble's surface, while still others, having a talent for the long look, pierce with their vision the bubble's membrane (which to others is opaque) and see what is to be seen.

This is not an egalitarian picture, ranking persons as it does by their respective powers of sight. But then, who claims that at face value our world is egalitarian? Only in its hidden harmony, in the respect in which we can all work on our power to see, is there the prospect that we are alike.

If the wisdom of the ages is indeed wisdom and teaches us anything, it is that the outlook I have been reaching for is, details aside, the most advanced to which mind can aspire; it represents, we might say, the higher mathematics of the human spirit. Civilizations and cultures can encourage their peoples to advance in its direction, but to dream of an age wherein everyone would enter it lockstep would be to perpetuate one of the errors of the MWM itself, its excessively temporal view of historical progress.

> *Because I do not hope to turn again*
> *Because I do not hope*
> *Because I do not hope to turn.*[46]

If it is too much to hope that our Western outlook will turn concertedly in the directions I have noted, it is not too much to hope that it will encourage, more than it has in this century, those who may choose to do so.

Notes

1. I am not overlooking the rational, mathematical component in science, but the crucial role of the controlled experiment gives empiricism the edge. One thinks of the opposition that

as fine a mind as Chomsky's has faced because his "Cartesian" linguistics leans toward rationalism.

2. See John Wheeler's address to the American Physical Society as summarized in Walter Sullivan, "Smallest of the Small," *New York Times*, 5 February 1967.

3. I do not know the author of this quatrain. It was chalked on the blackboard at a meeting of graduate students I recently attended.

4. Daniel Dennett, "Review of *The Self and Its Brain* by Karl Popper and John Eccles," *Journal of Philosophy* 76, no. 2 (February 1979): 97.

5. New York: Ballantine Books, 1978, p. 7.

6. Harold Morowitz, "Rediscovering the Mind," *Psychology Today* 14, no. 2 (August 1980): 14.

7. Francis Crick, *Of Molecules and Men* (Seattle: University of Washington Press, 1966).

8. Morowitz, *op. cit.*, p. 12.

9. Annette J. Smith, "Playing with Play: A Test Case of 'Ethocriticism,' " *Journal of Biological Structures* 1, no. 11 (1978): 199.

10. Jean Piaget, *Play, Dreams and Imitation in Childhood* (London: Routledge & Kegan Paul, 1951).

11. D. Elkins, ed., *Six Psychological Studies* (New York: Random House, 1967).

12. John Bowlby, *Attachment and Loss*, vol. 1 (New York: Basic Books, 1969), emphasis added.

13. "The emotions we feel, which in exceptional individuals may climax in total self-sacrifice, stem ultimately from hereditary units that were implanted by the favoring of relatives during a period of thousands of generations" (Edward O. Wilson, "Altruism," *Harvard Magazine*, November-December 1978).

14. Edward O. Wilson, *Sociobiology*, abr. ed. (Cambridge: Harvard University Press, 1980), p. 3.

15. Barbara Brown, *Supermind* (New York: Harper & Row, 1980), p. 199.

16. D. and C. Johnson, "Totally Discouraged: A Depressive Syndrome of the Dakota Sioux," *Transcultural Psychiatric Research Review*, no. 2 (1965): 141-43.

17. Anthony Marsella, "Depressive Experience and Disorder across Cultures," in *Handbook of Cross-Cultural Psychology*, ed. Harry Triandis and Jurgis Draguns, vol. 6 (Boston: Allyn & Bacon, 1980), p. 254. I am indebted to Kendra Smith for pointing me to the references in this section.

18. Ibid., p. 255.

19. Alexander Solzhenitsyn, published as *A World Split Apart* (New York: Harper & Row, 1978).

20. Ibid., p. 35.
21. Ibid., p. 5.
22. Ibid., p. 47; emphasis added.
23. Ibid., p. 35.
24. I refer the reader to what Gellner calls the "mechanistic insistence" of an epistemology that aims at power; see p. 97 above.
25. In *Computer Power and Human Reason: From Judgment to Calculation* (San Francisco: W. H. Freeman, 1976), Joseph Weisenbaum, another participant in the Woodstock Symposium, warns of "the imperialism of instrumental reason" in our time.
26. "Will and Psychoanalysis," *Journal of the American Psychoanalytic Association* 4, no. 2 (April 1956): 256.
27. Statement by David Bohm at the Woodstock Symposium, "Knowledge, Education, and Human Values," 1980.
28. See Howard E. Gruber, "Darwin's 'Tree of Nature' and Other Images of Wide Scope," in *On Aesthetics in Science*, ed. Judith Wechsler (Cambridge: M.I.T. Press, 1978).

Images figures prominently in the Woodstock Symposium. Peter Abbs followed David Bohm to argue the need for education "to restore the power of the living image, to confer on it a high epistemological status, to put it alongside concept as one of the key ways in which we symbolize and then come to know our world."

29. London: Bodley Head, 1977, pp. 11-12.
30. To Edward Norman's observation, quoted on p. 120-1 above, that "there is no doubt that in developed societies education has contributed to the decline of religious belief," Robert Bellah adds that the decline is not in religious belief only. "The deepest indictment of the university," he told the Woodstock Symposium, "is that it erodes belief" generally.
31. T. S. Eliot, "The Family Reunion," in his *Complete Poems and Plays* (New York: Harcourt, Brace & World, 1971), p. 291.
32. Frithjof Schuon's essay "The Contradiction of Relativism" in his *Logic and Transcendence* (New York: Harper & Row, 1975) has helped me crystallize the thoughts I set down in the next several paragraphs.
33. E. F. Schumacher, *A Guide for the Perplexed* (New York: Harper & Row, 1977), p. 5.
34. Solzhenitsyn, *op. cit.*, p. 57; emphasis added.
35. Mortimer Adler, *Aristotle for Everybody* (New York: Bantam Books, 1980), p. 174.
36. See note 7, p. 111.
37. W. W. Bartley, III, in *The Philosophy of Karl Popper*, ed. Paul Schilpp (La Salle, Ill.: Open Court, 1974), 2:675.

38. K. Parker, "The Effects of Subliminal Merging Stimuli on the Academic Performance of College Students," Ph.D. dissertation, New York University, 1977; reported in Lloyd Silverman, "Two Unconscious Fantasies and Mediators of Successful Psychotherapy," *Psychotherapy: Theory, Research and Practice* 16, no. 2 (Summer 1979): 220.

39. Lloyd Silverman, "A Comprehensive Report of Studies Using the Subliminal Psychodynamic Activation Method," issued by the New York Veterans Administration Regional Office and Research Center for Mental Health, New York University, 1980, p. 14.

40. L. H. Silverman, F. Lachman, and R. Milich, *The Search for Oneness* (New York: International Universities Press, 1982). I am indebted to a former student, Robert Ebert, for calling my attention to the whole matter.

41. Manfred Stanley. Reference is on p. 113.

42. Ernest Gellner. The reference is on p. 111.

43. Ibid., pp. 206-7.

44. Lewis Thomas, *The Medusa and the Snail* (New York: Viking Press, 1979), p. 87.

45. Malcolm X, *The Autobiography of Malcolm X* (New York: Grove Press, 1964), p. 164.

46. T. S. Eliot, "Ash Wednesday," in his *Complete Poems and Plays*, p. 60.

11

BEYOND POSTMODERNISM*

Historical epochs do not disappear overnight, and lingering Modern assumptions continue to jostle Postmodern ones in almost even array. For this reason, though this book points beyond the latest, Postmodern wave in Western thought, it has had to contend throughout with the Modern as much as with the Postmodern Mind. This and the preceding essay, though, address them separately.

The Modern Mind was flat because it took its directives from science which cannot get its hands on the component of experience that verticality tokens, namely values.[a] By contrast, the Postmodern Mind (as the Preface to this book indicated) is blurred and amorphous. Not only does it lack an embracing outlook; it doubts that it is any longer possible (or even desirable) to have one. It thereby signals the new chapter in intellectual history that this book pointed to in its opening essay.

It would be difficult to overestimate the size and importance of this conceptual shift. Whereas in the past

*Adapted from an address delivered at the Revisioning Philosophy Conference in Cambridge, England, in August 1989.

[a]For the qualifications that are needed to make this statement strictly accurate but which do not affect the central point, see pages 84-85.

people argued and battled over which view of reality was true, the Postmodern position is that none are true. Postmodernists even wonder if truth has any meaning in this context. As their perspective has gained ground, the former battles *between* beliefs—this one against that one: science against religion, capitalism against communism—have turned into battles over the status of belief itself.[1] At stake is the question of the mind's match with reality. Because the earlier view assumed that a match existed (an imperfect match, perhaps, but a match all the same) its view of the mind can be considered "perceptivist"—an awkward word, but one that points up the difference between it and the Postmodern view of the mind which is "constructivist." Postmodernism considers the assumption that we perceive reality to be naive. We construct reality, or rather realities, for our constructs are multiple. Realities are artifacts, and they abound.

The agent that effected this change was cultural pluralism. When people lived in isolated tribes, or even while their own civilization was virtually the only one they knew, they were not aware of *having* views of reality; there was, for them, simply the way the world was. It took confrontations between cultures to bring home the fact that people see the world in different ways. Once that realization was in place, the distinction between world and worldview could not be denied. Between the human mind and the way the world actually *is* lies the mind's *view* of the way it is.

In contending that minds construct their realities, it is not individual minds that Postmodernists point to. It is minds working together—in a word, societies—that are the agents. The title of an influential book, *The Social Construction of Reality*,[2] catches the point precisely, but the view itself is essentially the one that essays in this book (Chapters 2, 6, and 7) have noted under the name of "holism." Theoretical holism argues for the organic character of thought: concepts cannot be understood in isolation; their meaning derives from the theoretical systems in which they are embedded.[b] Practical holism goes on from there to argue that, because thinking invariably proceeds in social contexts and against a backdrop of social practices, meaning derives from—roots down into and draws its life from—those backgrounds and contexts. In considering an idea, not only must we take into account the conceptual gestalt of which it is a part; we must also consider the "forms of life" (Wittgenstein) whose "micro-practices" (Foucault) give those gestalts their final meaning.

And that is where things end, as far as Postmodernism is concerned. If we want to know where realities come from, the answer is: from societies, seen as cultural-linguistic wholes.

There are merits in seeing things this way, the obvious one being the tolerance which, on the surface at least, it seems to augur. If there is no reality in the singular but only realities, each sponsored by its respective society, these multiple realities would seem to be on an equal footing and therefore deserving of equal respect. Beneath this genial view, though, lurk problems which can be gathered under an inclusive head: the pendulum has swung too far in the direction of multiplicity.

I

Multiple views, yes; multiple realities, no. Constructivists who speak of "many realities" or "many worlds" speak either figuratively or misleadingly.[c] Perspectives on the world differ, and it is good that we have grown wise to that fact; if snapshots of a room were taken from the

[b]In the philosophy of science, "all facts are theory laden" (Norwood Hansen), and "the meaning of every term we use depends upon the theoretical context in which it occurs" (Paul Feyerabend).

[c]The same can be said of the name for the position. Ground or tinted, glasses affect our vision, but no one thinks they create what we see. As construction is equivalent to creation here, unrelieved constructivism turns out to be a brand of creationism —one that is as implausible as the version that capitalizes its name.

view of each of the persons who occupy it, no two would be identical. But they would be photographs of the same room. The same would hold for floor plans if the occupants were given yardsticks and asked to draw them, and it accounts as well for why—different snapshots (or VCR reels) notwithstanding—occupants rarely collide with one another. Even if reality were no more than the sum of all of the multiple realities the constructivist speaks of, that sum would stand as the inclusive reality which would not itself be multiple. William James did everything he could to break up the idealists' "block universe," but he could not get away from the idea of universe itself, as the title of his book, *A Pluralistic Universe*, attests.

These considerations should guard us against thinking of cultural-linguistic wholes as self-contained, totally dissimilar compartments that are hermetically sealed from one another. (This holds whether we are thinking of the Sapir-Whorf hypothesis of linguistic relativity, the anthropologists' cultural relativity, Wittgenstein's forms-of-life, Nietzsche and Heidegger's historical horizons, or epistemic *Ways of Worldmaking* a la Nelson Goodman; but I shall not consider these cases individually.) No society is totally different from other societies, so instead of thus  they should be visualized thus: Likewise, no society is completely isolated from its transhuman setting, so it should be visualized thus  rather than thus  . As the Postmodern, constructivist pendulum has swung too far in the direction of both of the misleading images, a few words should be said about each.

In support of cross-cultural overlap I shall be personal and brief. I once found myself in a stalled car on the Serengeti Plain where roads had long since petered out. In time, two shadowy figures appeared on the horizon. Initially they retreated with every step I took in their direction, but eventually they allowed me to catch up with them. Near-naked, spear-carrying Masai warriors that they turned out to be, human beings more different from myself could hardly have been conjured. Even so, after a bit of wary give-and-take, they let me drag them physically by their wrists to my car, and an hour later, additional bodies having been commandeered, I found myself "driving" in state across scrubby wastelands as a dozen good Samaritans, laughing and chatting throughout, pushed my car six miles to where the team of Louis and Mary Leakey was excavating Olduvai Gorge.

This was [a] substantial communication (sufficient to extricate me from a predicament that could have proven serious), [b] across a sizable cultural gap, [c] in short order (a single afternoon). Since that afternoon I have not been able to take seriously the thought that societies have nothing in common. (Someone has said that we are all card-carrying members of the human race. Each carries an individual signature, but otherwise the cards are alike.) But if there is overlap, these beachheads of commonality can be expanded. I shall come directly to the question of whether we want to expand them, but before that there is the second, transhuman divide to consider.

II

If in ways we belong to the human race, there is the larger question of whether we likewise belong to the cosmos. The Postmodern Mind sees no reason to think that we do. Walker Percy titled one of his books *Lost in the Cosmos*, and this essay opened with the constructivists' suspicion that the word "cosmos" itself—implying as it does reality-in-the-singular—has become a misnomer; multiple realities suggest something more like chaos. Twentieth-century philosophers have created an entire subdiscipline—phenomenology—to persuade the academic community that they have put the embarrassing subject of metaphysics behind them. Richard Rorty sums up the matter by noting (as quoted in Chapter 6) that the twentieth century is ending by returning "to something reminiscent of Hegel's sense of humanity as an essentially historical being, one whose activities in all spheres are to be judged *not by its relation to non-human reality* but by comparison and contrast with its earlier achievements." Wittgenstein provides a good chunk of the evidence for Rorty's assertion. David Pears calls Wittgenstein's conclusion that "there is no conceivable way of getting between language and the world and finding out whether there is a general fit between them" the central thesis of his later years.[d]

We know why (by Postmodern lights) the fit cannot be discovered, and why in consequence we cannot know where we stand in the world. To pick up again with Chapter 6, when modern science replaced revelation as the road to truth, reason struck out on its own. (By "struck out" I here mean only that it took off, but the baseball meaning also applies and could stand as modernity's epitaph.) Every journey has its point of departure, and Descartes chose to set off from the adamantine self. As he set that self off from the rest of the world, dualism was built into modern epistemology's foundation. It has remained in place. The entire story of Western philosophy in its modern phase could be told as the search for a bridge between mind and its matrix, between subject and object, that Descartes drove apart. It would be the story of failure.

The reason for the failure—Hume's skepticism, Kant's inaccessible noumena, right down to Wittgenstein's "cage" (his word) of language—is that once you set things up as Descartes did, there can *be* no solution. Garbage

---

[d]*The New Republic*, May 19, 1986, p. 39. Mention of Wittgenstein (the most influential philosopher of the twentieth century) elicits a comment on the role he played in getting us into our Postmodern, holistic predicament—not because of what holism asserts, but because of what it obscures by leaving unasked. Wittgenstein moved to his forms-of-life after concluding that science could not be grounded in the Vienna Circle's indubitable certainties of logic and sense data because such certainties do not exist. The move marked a major gain; the question concerns its stopping point. If science requires foundations—the forms-of-life Wittgenstein plausibly proposed—why should we suppost that forms-of-life (cultural-linguistic wholes) do not?

in, garbage out, as computer programmers say. Make disjunction your starting point and you live with it thereafter.

This leads naturally to the question of whether it might not be good to consider a starting point that would open onto wholeness and belonging. Postmodernism is disinclined to do so, and as this is a serious block to moving beyond its way of seeing things, the question deserves a section to itself.

III

Postmodernism arose as a coalition of reactions-against, two of which have been predominant. As an academic movement, it reacted (most emphatically through Deconstructionism) against the rigidities of structuralism, which for the preceding decade or two had insisted in anthropology, linguistics, and literary criticism that observed phenomena are best understood in terms of certain invariant structures which they exhibit and are controlled by. In this respect, "deconstruction is avowedly 'post-structuralist' in its refusal to accept the idea of structure as in any sense given or objectively 'there' in a text," a language, or a society.[3]

This reaction continues, but as partner to a second, political strain. Postmodernism was all but created by the French, and France was occupied in both world wars. This has sensitized her to the tyrannical tendencies that are latent, not only in academic fashions such as structuralism, but in political ideologies and regimes as well. As a word, Derrida's "Deconstruction" pulls against Postmodern "constructivism," but the tension lodges in cultural-linguistic wholes themselves: they unite, and at the same time divide by ostracizing—to some extent inevitably ostracizing—those who fall outside their pale. Deconstructionists are the volunteer brigade within Postmodernism that patrols this dark side of constructivism's socializing agent, society; they are pledged to seeing that pariahs—outcast ideas as well as outcast people—are redressed. It is in this light that their crusade against universalistic and tyrannizing claims generally, their celebration of difference over identity, and their obsession with variety, heterogeneity, plurality, and otherness in almost every guise is to be understood. Marginalizing, for them, is the unforgivable sin, and in their efforts to atone for it, the Other is raised to an object for holy concern.

The vocation is so noble and needed that it seems not only profane but radical (in Noam Chomsky's definition of a radical idea as one that lies outside the realm of acceptable discourse) to point out that it is not the whole story. Idealism is so exclusively directed toward power relationships today that discourse has come to sound almost ungrammatical if it does not contain at least a few passing allusions to injustice and the plight of the oppressed. This, though, is like dismissing pure research as irrelevant if it does not refer continually to practical applications that might accrue. Postmodern rhetoric is heavily political. The goals it espouses are mainly the right ones, but the question is whether the climate of opinion it is building is conducive to their realization.[4] That cause is not served by suggesting, as Deconstructionists come close to suggesting, that there is a one-to-one correlation between unity/diversity, on the one hand, and injustice/justice, on the other; unity producing oppression, multiplicity liberation. Discord and anarchy are not happy conditions; but we can be more direct. We would not honor the otherness of the Other if we did not also recognize her identity with us. However different she may be, she is identical with us in having idiosyncratic needs that are as entitled as are our own. Where is the place for Piaget's "decentration" to balance Postmodernism's incessant (and usually appropriate) plea for differences? Decentration is the process of gradually becoming able to take a more and more universal standpoint, giving up a particular egocentric or sociocentric way of understanding, and acting and moving towards the "universal communications community." Postmodern sensibilities are admirably honed to singularities, but they are flat toward the merits of bondings, even beneficent bondings. They regularly discount the energy, exhilaration, and compassion—let's not forget compassion—that can enter a life through the discovery of its connectedness with the Real; typically they dismiss such discoveries as delusions and preludes to fanaticism—perversions that can occur, but are not inevitable. Nowhere among Postmodern writers do I find an ear for the primacy of the whole over the part, which—if we can forgive him for using the word "man" generically—I shall let G. K. Chesterton register for me:

> The things peculiar to all men are more important than the things peculiar to any men. Ordinary things are more valuable than extraordinary things; nay, they are more extraordinary. Man is something more awful than men; something more strange. The sense of the miracle of humanity itself should be always more vivid to us than any marvels of power, intellect, art, or civilization. The mere man on two legs, as such, should be felt as something more heartbreaking than any music and more startling than any caricature. Death is more tragic even than death by starvation. Having a nose is more comic even than having a Norman nose.[5]

IV

If we could see Deconstruction as an eternally important office of culture, the office of ombudsman whose job is to prevent the oppression of minorities by majorities without opposing majorities in principle,[e] this would distinguish it from Postmodernism's lack of an overview, which lack could then be addressed. To begin to address

---

[e]Another analogy suggests itself: Deconstructionists are the Gödels among us. While mathematicians were trying to establish completeness, Godel established incompleteness. Since there can be no system that is complete and consistent, it is impossible that any one system has all the truth. Other voices should be listened to.

it is the object of this fourth part of this book. Believing that the sense of ultimate belonging is not only a psychological resource but a metaphysical birthright that has been obscured from view, I shall suggest where we might begin to look for it.

If our disinheritance derives (more than from any other single factor) from the dualism with which Descartes saddled his future, it seems appropriate to consider the possibility of removing that dualism. Science is on our side here, for twentieth-century science has found the world to be far more interconnected than we had supposed, with Bell's (validated) Theorem providing the outstanding example. In a two-particle spin, if one particle spin is up, the other is down. If researchers separate the two particles and give one particle a spin up, the other particle—however far it has been removed—instantly spins down at a speed faster than light. A recent discussion of this finding points up the conclusion: "in the most pervasive sense there can be no such thing as independent, real situations." Physicist Henry Stapp has called this "*the* most profound discovery of science."[6] If it be objected that this is all on the matter side of Descartes' dichotomy, we can add that the human mind, too, is proving to be fantastic. When a boy savant can read Edward Gibbon's *History of the Decline and Fall of the Roman Empire* and then recite it, albeit uncomprehendingly, word for word,[7] we are in the presence of mental connections we could not have suspected. Of course we do not understand the mechanisms involved, but neither do we understand the mechanism of gravity, nature's universal uniter.[f]

The point of these scraps of scientific trivia is to open us to the prospect that, as nature is wondrously connected and the mind likewise versatile beyond anything common sense supposes, that mind may possess connecting

[f]"That one body may act upon another at a distance through a vacuum without the mediation of anything else is to me so great an absurdity that . . . no man who has in philosophic matters a competent faculty of thinking could ever fall into it" (Isaac Newton, as quoted in Gary Zukav, *The Dancing Wu Li Masters* (New York: William Morrow, 1979), p. 49.

faculties that dropped from sight with Descartes' rearrangements. Prior to Descartes, philosophers started with unity and went on to diversity, not vice versa. The quickest way to indicate this is to say that thinking was regarded as the activity of beings (ourselves) who were theomorphic; human nature was, *au fond*, the *imago dei*, or Buddha-nature, or Atman. As "Divinity" is but another word for "Reality," to say that we are born of its likeness is to affirm our affinity with it from the start.

For amplification of this idea of primordial connectedness, I refer the reader back to Chapter 3. Here, for the balance of this section, I shall focus on places in the current intellectual landscape where the notion might escape being rejected out of hand. I shall use the word "Intellect" for the faculty or endowment in us that does the connecting, capitalizing the word to indicate the distinctive way I shall be using it.

We can ease toward the concept by noting that there is something in our mental workings that proceeds differently from reason while supporting reason and backing it up. Reason performs logical operations on information that is in full view and can therefore be described or defined. Through and through, though, we find that our understanding is floated and furthered by operations that are mysterious because all that we seem able to know about them is that we have no idea as to how they work. We have hunches that pay off. Or we find that we know what to do in complicated situations without being able to explain exactly how we know. This ability is unconscious, yet it enables us to perform enormously complicated tasks, from reading and writing to farming and composing music. Expertise is coming to be recognized as more intuitive than was supposed by cognitive psychologists; these students of learning and behavior are finding that, when faced with exceptionally subtle tasks, people who "feel" or intuit their ways through them are more creative than those who consciously try to think their way through. This explains why computer programmers no less than psychologists have had trouble getting the expert to articulate the rules they follow. The expert is not following rules. Workers in artificial intelligence are coming to see that "human intelligence can never be replaced with machine intelligence because we are not ourselves 'thinking machines.' Each of us has, and uses every day, a power of intuitive intelligence that enables us to understand, to speak, and to cope skillfully with our everyday environment."[8] This intelligence enables us to summarize unconsciously our entire past—all that we have experienced and done—and let that summary affect our future decisions and moves.[g] Programmers cannot instruct their machines to do this because no one has the slightest idea how we ourselves do it.

The above was the computer scientist speaking, but the mysterious cognitive faculty described seems to be ubiquitous. Michael Polanyi called in tacit knowing to emphasize its subliminal locus, and cognitive psychologists nod in its direction when they tell us that knowing, feeling, and action cannot be separated. We "perfink," Jerome Bruner reports; which is to say that we perceive, feel, and think simultaneously. "To separate the three is like studying the planes of a crystal separately, losing sight of the crystal that gives them being."[9]

If psychologists now recognize something besides reason at work in our knowing, epistemologists, even Modern ones, have granted this for some time. Hume saw this most clearly, and the realization drove him to skepticism, for, blind to the Intellect, he saw nothing to vector reason save the passions.[10] His successors resisted that conclusion. Rallying behind Kant, they found ways to prolong their faith in reason, but the point here is that

---

[g]A striking example: Japanese chicken sexers are able to decide with 99% accuracy the sex of a chick, even though the female and male genitalia of young chicks are ostensibly indistinguishable. No analytic approach to learning the art could ever approach such accuracy. Aspiring chicken sexers learn only by looking over the shoulders of experienced workers, who themselves cannot explain how they do it. The most thorough discussion of this matter appears in Hubert and Stuart Dreyfus, *Mind over Machine* (New York: The Free Press/Macmillan, 1986).

in doing so they too had to recognize extrarational cognitive capacities. The Germans distinguished *verstehen* and *verstand* from *vernunft.* Romantic philosophers and poets followed Blake in proposing an active imagination that in important respects resembles the Intellect proper, and Heidegger came to extoll "thinking" over reasoning of the calculative sort.

Thus even modernity, with all its efforts to do so, was unable to fit the mind's full repertoire into reason's mold. Prior to Modernity, this overplus was not only countenanced but accorded pride of place. The Vedanta grounds *manas* in *buddhi*, while Buddhists point to *prajna* as knowing's supreme capacity. Both of these serve as the Intellect's rough counterparts, but it is the Western tradition that identified the faculty most precisely. Released by Socrates from the tyranny of the obvious, Plato discovered an organ of knowledge which, because it "outshines ten thousand eyes," he called the Eye of the Soul. Aligning it with Aristotle's notion of the Active Intellect as the supraindividual component of the mind which knows (though in individuals only potentially) everything, the Medieval Schoolmen worked the concept of the *intellectus* into its mature form. It is the mind's foundational faculty, clearly distinguishable from *ratio* which is its emissary.

More intuitive than discursive and lodged at a level that is largely out of sight, the Intellect is something like the tropism of plants that orients them toward light. If we try to connect an animal in the wilds to its environment via what textbooks say about the physiology of perception, we encounter so many inexplicable gaps that rationally we would have to conclude that the animal does not perceive its world at all. (This is the psychological counterpart of philosophy's inability to bridge with reason the subject/object divide that Descartes fixed in place.) Yet all the while the animal behaves as if it perceives the world; it proceeds toward food and shelter almost unerringly. With J. J. Gibson's *The Ecological Approach to Visual Perception* pointing the way, animal psychologists are coming to see that they have lost sight of this incontrovertible fact.[11] Trying to account for knowledge as inference from noetic bits does not work. We must begin the other way around, Gibson insists, with the recognition that there is a world out there (realism), and that animals are oriented to it.

V

Whether the time is ripe to consider the possibility of an innate faculty in the human self that extends *through* cultural-linguistic wholes to the heart of Reality itself, fulfilling thereby our deepest wish to ultimately belong, I do not know; I present it simply as the most promising prospect I see. Four centuries of trying to put Humpty Dumpty back together having failed, it does not seem unreasonable to ask whether, analogous to the DNA that is identical in an organism's every cell, there might be something in Humpty Dumpty's parts that was not affected by his fall.

Writing this concluding paragraph on the day that I learn of the death of a great Tibetan teacher, Kalu Rimpoche, I think of something he once said. "Reason tells me I am nothing. Love tells me I am everything. Between these poles, my life unfolds."

So, too, do our lives unfold between the poles of the Postmodern world and its sequel that is struggling to be born.

Notes

1. For the way controversies throughout the world are increasingly being fought across this battle line, see Walt Anderson, *The Future of Belief* (New York: Harper and Row, 1990).

2. Peter Berger and Thomas Luckmann, *The Social Construction of Reality* (Garden City, NY: Doubleday, 1966).

3. Christopher Norris, *Deconstruction: Theory and Practice* (London & New York: Methuen, 1982), p. 3.

4. Feminists, whose cause Deconstructions think they are supporting, are beginning themselves to ask this question.

> Rape, domestic violence, and sexual harassment . . . are not fictions or figurations that admit of the free play of signification [a favorite Deconstructionist phrase]. The victim's account of these experiences is not simply an arbitrary imposition of a purely fictive meaning on an otherwise meaningless reality. A victim's knowledge of the event may not be

exhaustive, . . . but it would be premature to conclude from the incompleteness of the victim's account that all other accounts . . . are equally valid or that there are no objective grounds on which to distinguish between truth and falsity in divergent interpretations (Mary Hawkesworth, "Knowers, Knowing, Known: Feminist Theory and Claims of Truth," *Signs* 12:555).

Nominalism threatens to wipe out feminism itself (Linda Alcoff, "Cultural Feminism versus Poststructuralism," *Signs* 13:419).

Should postmodernism's seductive text gain ascendancy, it will not be an accident that power remains in the hands of the white males who currently possess it. In a world of radical inequality, relativist resignation reinforces the status quo (Evelyn Fox Keller, in a course on feminist theory, University of California, Berkeley, Spring 1989).

S. P. Mohanty generalizes this point to show that it does not apply to feminism only:

To believe that you have your space and I mine; to believe, further, that there can be no responsible way in which I can adjudicate between your space—cultural and historical—and mine . . . is to assert that *all spaces are equivalent*; that they have equal value. . . . I end by denying that I need to take you seriously (*Yale Journal of Criticism* 2:14).

I am indebted to Priscilla Stuckey-Kaufmann for directing me to the statements I have here quoted.

5. Gilbert K. Chesterton, *Orthodoxy* (Garden City, NY: Doubleday Image Books, 1959), pp. 46-47.

6. H. Stapp, "Bell's Theorem and World Process," Il Nuovo Cimento, 29B (1975), p. 271.

7. *The Sciences*, January/February 1989, p. 31.

8. Hubert and Stuart Dreyfus, *Mind over Machine* (New York: The Free Press, 1986), p. xiv.

9. Jerome Bruner, *Actual Minds, Possible Worlds* (Cambridge: Harvard University Press, 1986).

10. "Reason is . . . the slave of the passions, and can never pretend to any other office than to serve and obey them" (*Treatise of Human Nature*, II, iii, 3). Before Hume, Hobbes had proposed that "the Thoughts are to the Desires, as Scouts, and Spies, to range abroad, and find the way to the Things Desired" (*Leviathan* [Oxford 1960] Ch. 8, p. 46).

11. See Marjorie Grene, "Perception, Interpretation, and the Sciences," in D. Depaw & B. Weber, *Evolution at a Crossroads* (Cambridge: M.I.T. Press, 1985).

12

THE SACRED UNCONSCIOUS*

More than once I have foresworn prophecy; the preceding essays point to places where breathroughs *may* occur, not necessarily *will* occur. There are times, though, when to act as if something *has* happened helps to make it happen, and this next statement adopts this approach. Taking the human self as its object, it describes that self "from the further shore," as Buddhists would say.

There is need to see it in that light, for the view from this shore does not do us justice; as Saul Bellow points out in the Nobel Lecture I have already quoted, "we do not think well of ourselves." The complete edition of the works of Sigmund Freud contains over four hundred entries for neurosis and none for health, and even if we bracket pathology, what account of ourselves is given by psychologists, sociologists, historians, journalists, and writers? "In a kind of contractual daylight," Bellow continues,

> they see [us] in the ways with which we are so desperately familiar. These images of contractual daylight, so boring to us all, originate in the contemporary worldview. We put into our books the consumer, civil servant, football fan, lover, television viewer. And in the contractual daylight version their life is a kind of death.

---

*Reprinted with negligible changes from Roger Walsh and Dean Shapiro (eds.), *Beyond Health and Normality: The Exploration of Extreme Psychological Well-Being* (New York: Van Nostrand Reinhold, 1982).

> There is another life, coming from an insistent sense of what we are, that denies these daylight formulations and the false life—the death in life—they make for us. For it is false, and we know it, and our secret and incoherent resistance to it cannot stop, for that resistance arises from persistent intuitions. Perhaps humankind cannot bear too much reality, but neither can it bear too much unreality, too much abuse of truth.

Two psychiatrists, dissatisfied with the current model of the self, have brought together a book that challenges its "desperately familiar . . . boring . . . false" self-estimate. It includes this essay as my contribution to their venture.

In *The Next Million Years*, a book published around the time of Darwin's centennial, his grandson, Charles Galton Darwin, considered the prospects for genetic engineering. Writing as a geneticist, he concluded that the difficulties were formidable but solvable. What was not solvable, he thought, was the goal of such engineering —agreement as to the kind of person we would like to produce. Nietzsche and Van Gogh were geniuses but went mad—would we want their genes in our gene pool? It's a good question. It makes us see the nerve of a book that tries to define the highest good for man.

Writing as a philosopher and historian of religions, let me venture my perception of this "human best" as follows. If Marx unmasked our social unconscious and Freud our personal unconscious, both piercing through superstructures, or rather substructures, that hide true causes and motives, the supreme human opportunity is to strike deeper still and become aware of the "sacred unconscious" that forms the bottom line of our selfhood.

I shall not go into reasons for assuming that this final unconscious exists; I have discussed some of them in my *Forgotten Truth* where I use the word "spirit" for what I am here calling the sacred unconscious. Nor will I map here our human consciousness to show the relation of this deepest level to ones that are more proximate; that I attempted in the chapter on "The Levels of Selfhood" in the book just mentioned. Instead I shall try to surmise what our lives would be like if our deepest unconscious were directly available to us. What would a supremely realized human being, here conceived as one that is consciously aware of his or her sacred unconscious, be like? How would such a person look to others and feel to him/herself?

It is easier to say what s/he would not be like than to picture him or her positively, as the "tragic flaw" theory of art reminds us. No writer would dream of trying to create a perfect hero; he would sense instinctively that such a figure would seem completely fictitious—a cardboard cutout. But let the author endow an otherwise strong character with a tragic weakness—Hamlet's indecision is the standard example—and our imaginations will correct that weakness on their own; convincingly, moreover, for we graft the missing virtue onto a character whose imperfection makes him believable. The same principles apply when we try (as here) to describe human wholeness not concretely as the artist does, but abstractly: we are on firmest ground when we state the case negatively. To cite an historical instance, the Buddha's characterization of enlightenment as the absence of hatred, greed, and ignorance draws its force from being solidly anchored in real life: its key terms refer to traits we live with all the time. But if we try to restate his formula in positive terms and say that to be enlightened is to be filled with love, wisdom, and an impartial acceptance of everything, our description becomes abstract. Obviously we have some acquaintance with these virtues, but acquaintance is not what is at stake. The goal is to be suffused with these virtues; to be filled by them completely. That we have only the faintest notion of what these positive terms mean when they are raised to their maximum, goes without saying.

Definition of a Jivanmukta

So now we have two wise caveats before us: Darwin's, that we do not know what the *summum bonum* is; and Buddha's, that we do best to approach it negatively. I propose to throw these warnings to the wind and attempt a positive depiction of a *jivanmukta*, as the Indians would refer to a fully realized person: a *jiva* (soul) that is *mukta* (liberated, enlightened) in this very life. The project must fail, of course, but that does not keep it from being interesting. Perhaps, in keeping with the tragic flaw theory I just alluded to, its very failure may induce the reader to round out in his own imaging the picture which words can never adequately portray.

An enlightened being, I am proposing, is one who is in touch with his deepest unconscious, an unconscious which (for reasons I shall be introducing) deserves to be considered sacred. Our century has acquainted us with regions of our minds that are hidden from us and the powerful ways they control our perceptions. My thesis is that underlying these proximate layers of our unconscious minds is a final substrate that opens mysteriously onto the world as it actually is. To have access to this final substrate is to be objective in the best sense of the word and to possess the virtues and benefits that go with this objectivity.

Normally we are not in touch with this objective component of ourselves—which paradoxically is also our deepest subjective component—because intermediate layers of our unconscious screen it from us while at the same time screening the bulk of the world from us. Our interests, drives, and concerns, their roots largely hidden from our gaze, cause us to see what we want to see and need to see; most of the rest of reality simply passes us by. The Tibetans make this point by saying that when a pickpocket meets a saint, what he sees are his pockets. Moreover, the things we do see we see through lenses that are "prescription ground," so to speak; our interests and conditionings distort the way they appear to us. When poor children are asked to draw a penny they draw it larger than do children for whom pennies are commonplace; it looms larger in their minds' eye. In many such ways, what we take to be objective facts are largely psychological constructs, as the Latin *factum*, "that which is made," reminds us.

This much is now psychological truism. We enter more interesting terrain when we note that at a deeper level the thoughts and feelings that control what we see are themselves shaped by what the Buddha called *the three poisons*: desire (lust, greed, grasping), aversion (fear, hatred, anger), and ignorance.[a] And the greatest of these is ignorance. For it is ignorance—most pointedly ignorance concerning our true identity, who we really are—that causes us to divide the world into what we like and dislike. Thinking that we are separate selves,[b] we seek what augments these selves and shun what threatens them. What we call our "self" is the amalgam of desires and aversions that we have wrapped tightly, like the elastic of a golf ball, around the core of separate identity that is its center.

This tight, constricted, golf-ball self is inevitably in for hard knocks, but what concerns us here is that on average it does not feel very good. Anxiety hovers 'round its edges. It can feel victimized and grow embittered. It is easily disappointed and can become unstrung. To others it often seems no prettier than it feels to itself: petty, self-centered, drab, and bored.

I am deliberately putting down this golf-ball self—hurling it to the ground, as it were, to see how high our total self can bounce; how far toward heaven it can rise. To rise, it must break out of the hard rubber strings that are normally stretched so tightly around it, encasing it in what Alan Watts called "the skin-encapsulated ego." If we change our image from rubber to glass and picture the three poisons as a lens that refracts light waves in keeping with our private, importunate demands, then release from such egocentric distortions will come through

[a]I could get where I want to go through any of the great traditions, but having started with Buddhism, I shall continue with it where historical pointers seem helpful.

[b]One of the most interesting and original recent analyses of this most universal (yet ultimately questionable) assumption is to be found in Alex Comfort's *I and That* (New York: Crown Publishers, 1979). Many studies now approach this subject in terms of both Asian and Western thought, but few (in addition) draw recent science as ably into the discussion as does this one.

progressively decreasing our lenses' curve—reducing their bulge. The logical terminus of this reduction would be plate glass. Through this we would be able to see things objectively, as they are in themselves in their own right.

This clear plate glass, which for purposes of vision is equivalent to no glass at all, is our sacred unconscious. It is helpful to think of it as an absence because, like window glass, it functions best when it calls no attention to itself. But it is precisely its absence that makes the world available to us: "the less there is of self, the more there is of Self," as Eckhart put the matter. From clear glass we have moved to no glass—the removal of everything that might separate subject from object, self from world. Zennists use the image of the Great Round Mirror. When the three poisons are removed from it, it reflects the world just as it is.

To claim that human consciousness can move permanently into this condition may be going too far, but advances along the asymptotic curve that slopes in its direction are clearly perceptible. When our aversion lens is powerful, bulging toward the limits of a semicircle, we like very little that comes our way. The same holds, of course, for our desire lens which is only the convex side of our aversion's concave: the more these bend our evaluations toward our own self-interests the less we are able to appreciate things in their own right. Blake's formulation of the alternative to this self-centered outlook has become classic. "If the doors of perception were cleansed, everything would appear to man as it is, infinite."

The fully realized human being is one whose doors of perception have been cleansed. And these doors, which up to this point I have referred to as windows, I am here envisioning as successive layers of our unconscious minds. Those that are near the surface vary from person to person for they are deposited by our idiosyncratic childhood experiences. At some level, though, we encounter the three poisons (once again, greed, aversion, and ignorance) that are common to mankind and perhaps in some degree essential for our human functioning. But the deepest layer, we have seen, is really a no-layer, for being a glass door ajar, or a mirror that discloses things other than itself, it isn't there. Even if it were there, in what sense could we call it ours? For when we look toward it we see simply—world.

This opening out onto the world's infinity is one good reason for calling this deepest stratum of the human unconscious sacred, for surely holiness has something to do with the whole. But the concreteness of Blake's formulation is instructive. He doesn't tell us that a cleansed perception discloses the Infinite per se. It finds it in the things at hand, in keeping with those Buddhist stories which tell us that the most sacred scriptures are its unwritten pages—an old pine tree gnarled by wind and weather or a skein of geese flying across the autumn sky.

Description of a Jivanmukta

Thus far I have defined a *jivanmukta*; it remains to describe him or her. What does life feel like to such a person, and how does s/he appear to others.

Basically, s/he lives in the unvarying presence of the numinous. This does not mean that s/he is excited or "hyped"; his/her condition has nothing to do with adrenalin flow, or with manic states that call for depressive ones to balance the emotional account. It is more like what Kipling had in mind when he said of one of his characters, "He believed that all things were one big miracle, and when a man knows that much he knows something to go upon." The opposite of the sense of the sacred is not serenity or sobriety. It is drabness; taken-for-grantedness. Lack of interest. The humdrum and prosaic.

All other attributes of a *jivanmukta* must be relativized against this one absolute: his/her honed sense of the astounding mystery of everything. All else we say of him must have a yes/no quality. Is s/he always happy? Well, yes and no. On one level s/he emphatically is not; if s/he were s/he couldn't "weep with those who mourn"—

s/he would be an unfeeling monster, a callous brute. If anything, a realized soul is *more* in touch with the grief and sorrow that is part and parcel of the human condition, knowing that it, too, needs to be accepted and lived as all life needs to be lived. To reject the shadow side of life, to pass it by with averted eyes refusing our share of common sorrow while expecting our share of common joy would cause the unlived, rejected shadows to deepen in us as fear of death. A story that is told of the recent Zen Master Shaku Soen points up the dialectical stance of the realized soul toward the happiness we are noting. When he was able to do so, he liked to take an evening stroll through a nearby village. One evening he heard wailing in a house he was passing and, on entering quietly, found that the householder had died and his family and neighbors were crying. Immediately he sat down and began crying too. An elderly gentleman, shaken by this display of emotion in a famous master, remarked, "I would have thought that you, at least, were beyond such things." "But it is this which puts me beyond it," the Master replied through his sobs.[1]

The Master's tears we can understand; the sense in which he was "beyond" them is as difficult to fathom as the peace that passeth understanding. The peace that comes when a man is hungry and finds food, is sick and recovers, or is lonely and finds a friend—peace of this sort is readily intelligible. But the peace that passeth understanding comes when the pain of life is not relieved. It shimmers on the crest of a wave of pain; it is the spear of frustration transformed into a shaft of light. The Master's sobs were real, yet paradoxically they did not erode the yes-experience of the East's "it is as it should be" and the West's "Thy will be done."

In our efforts to conceive the human best, everything turns on an affirmation that steers between cynicism on the one hand and sentimentality on the other. A realized self is not incessantly, and thereby oppressively, cheerful—oppressively, not only because we suspect some pretense in his unvarying smile, but because it underscores our moodiness by contrast. Not every room a *jivanmukta* enters floods with sunlight; he can flash indignation and upset money changers' tables. Not invariance but appropriateness is his hallmark, an appropriateness that has the whole repertoire of emotions at its command. The Catholic Church is right in linking radiance with sanctity, but the paradoxical, "in spite of" character of this radiance must again be stressed. Along with being a gift to be received, life is a task to be performed. The adept performs it. Whatever his hand finds to do, he does with all his might. Even if it proves his lot to walk stretches of life as a desert waste, he *walks* them rather than pining for alternatives. Happiness enters as by-product. What matters focally, as the Zen Master Dogen never tired of noting, is resolved.

If a *jivanmukta* isn't forever radiating sweetness and light, neither does he constantly emit blasts of energy. He can be forceful when need be; we find it restoring rather than draining to be in his presence, and he has reserves to draw on, as when Socrates stood all night in trance and outpaced the militia with bare feet on ice. In general, though, we sense him/her as relaxed and composed rather than charged—the model of the dynamic and magnetic personality tends to contain a lot of ego that demands attention. Remember, everything save the adept's access to inner vistas, the realms of gold I am calling the sacred unconscious, must be relativized. If leadership is called for the adept steps forward, otherwise he is just as happy to follow. He is qualified to be a guru, but does not need to be one—he does not need disciples to fortify his self-esteem. Focus or periphery, limelight or shadow, it does not really matter. Both have their opportunities, both their limitations.

All these relativities I have mentioned—happiness, energy, prominence, impact—pertain to the *jivanmukta's* finite self which he progressively relaxes as he makes his way toward his final, sacred unconscious. As his goal is an impersonal, impartial one, his identification with it involves a dying to his finite selfhood. This finite self is engaged in a vanishing act, as Coomaraswamy suggested when he wrote, "Blessed is the man on whose tomb can be written, *Hic jacet nemo*—here lies no one."

But having insisted above that there is only one absolute or constant in the journey toward this self-naughting; namely, the sense of the sacred, that luminous mystery in which all things are bathed, I must now admit that there is another: the realization of how far we all are from the goal that beckons, how many peaks and deserts have yet to be crossed. "Why callest thou me good? . . ." As human beings we are made to surpass ourselves and are truly ourselves only when transcending ourselves. Only the slightest of barriers separates us from our sacred unconscious; it is infinitely close to us. But we are infinitely far from it, so for us the barrier looms as a mountain that we must remove with our own hands. We scrape away at the earth, but in vain; the mountain remains. Still we go on digging at the mountain, in the name of God or whatever. For the most part we only hear of the final truth; very rarely do we actually see it. The mountain isn't there. It never was there.

Notes

1. Irmgard Schloegel, *The Wisdom of the Zen Masters* (New York: New Directions, 1975), p. 21.

13

THE INCREDIBLE ASSUMPTION*

This final selection involves a change of pace. Its different style derives from its having been delivered as a sermon in Rockefeller Chapel at the University of Chicago in 1960. It is thus the earliest of the writings here assembled; but as its thesis pervades them all, it draws them together and rounds them off as a finale.

One hears on all sides that the conflict between science and religion is over. For four centuries the battle has raged: in astonomy over the earth's position in the universe; in geology over the earth's age; in biology over the evolutionary hypothesis; in psychology over Freud's right to "peep and botanize into man's soul." Bitter the struggle has been, and long. Yet (so runs the tale) it has achieved its purpose. Resolution has been secured, concord established. Councils of bishops now speak of scientists as having a religious obligation to follow the truth wherever it leads, and scientists, rejecting the Comptean thesis that religion is to be superseded by science, are busy setting up institutes for religion in an age of science. Occasionally a bible-belt college shows bad form by refusing to allow evolution to be taught, or a Jesuit priest writes an eyebrow-raising book on the phenomenon of man. But these are exceptions. Concord

*Reprinted with negligible changes from *The Pulpit* 32, no. 2 (February 1961).

and good fellowship are the orders of the day. For is not truth one, and are not science and religion but two complementary approaches to it?

In the midst of so much agreement, a demur may sound jarring, but I think it has its place. Several years devoted to teaching religion at one of the leading scientific institutions of our day has led me to see the matter in a somewhat different light.

It's true, of course, that the former battles are drawing to a close. Copernicus, Darwin, Freud—geology and Genesis are not today the war cries they used to be.[1] But the fact that certain battles have run their course is no guarantee that a general armistice has been signed, let alone that a just and durable peace has been established. I, for one, suspect that we are still a long way from the day when lion and lamb shall lie down together, and sages sit, each under his own disciplinary vine and fig tree, in full accord.

As I shall be saying some things about science in the minutes ahead, it is important that I interject a disclaimer. The fact that I happen to be in the employ of an institution polarized around science should be taken to mean no more than just that. A British statesman once confessed that his knowledge of mathematics stopped with a desperate finality just where the difficulties began. I could easily paraphrase that statement in present context; a college major in any of the sciences could step to the board and produce equations that would bring my thinking to instant halt. Still, it is impossible to teach at a place like M.I.T. without encountering certain winds of doctrine, and over the years a vision of the program on which science is embarked has come to take shape in my mind.

It has six parts.

First, we shall create life. Some assume that in a rudimentary way—with the giant molecules, amino acids, and viruses—this breakthrough has been achieved already.

Second, we shall create minds. At this point some of us are likely to suspect a gigantic finesse,[2] but no matter:

with cybernetics and artificial intelligence, the analogy between minds and thinking machines is being pressed to the hilt.

Third, we shall create adjusted individuals via chemistry: tranquilizers and energizers, barbiturates and amphetamines, a complete pharmacopeia to control our moods and feelings.

Fourth, we shall create the good society via "behavioral engineering," a program of conditioning, liminal and subliminal, which through propaganda and hidden persuaders will induce men to behave in ways conducive to the common good.

Fifth, we shall create religious experiences by way of the psychedelics: LSD, mescalin, psilocybin, and their kin.

Sixth, we shall conquer death; achieve physical immortality by a combination of organ transplants and geriatrics that first arrest the aging process and then roll it back in rejuvenation. (See Robert Ettinger, *The Prospect of Immortality*.)

I hasten to insert two qualifications. I have not heard any scientist list these six objectives as parts of a single program, and there are many who discount all of them. But the basic point stands. Each of the six parts of this emerging program commands not just the labors but the faith of some of our finest scientists. Several years ago I invited B. F. Skinner, dean of American experimental psychologists, to discuss with my students the behaviorally engineered utopia he had sketched in *Walden Two*. In introducing him I said that I wanted the students to have major purchase on his time, but I wanted to ask one question and I would ask it at the start. A decade had passed since he wrote that book; had his thinking changed significantly in the interval? Frankly, I expected him to enter some qualifications, to confess that he had been a somewhat younger man then and that things were proving to be a bit more complicated than he had supposed. To my surprise his answer was the opposite. "My thoughts certainly have changed," he said, "This thing is coming faster than I had suspected would be possible."

Perhaps my theology has been inadequately demythologized, but I have difficulty squaring this sixfold program with religion. To the extent that it is taken seriously, God would seem indeed to be dead; to the extent that it is actualized, he will be buried. Instead of a thing of the past, the conflict between science and religion may be shaping up in proportions greater than any we have thus far known.

I have no wish, however, to pursue this prospect further this morning. Instead I should like to reverse the drift I have followed up to this point. Having refused to cry peace where there is no peace, let me now ask whether science, whatever the conscious stance of its practitioners, does not in fact provide us with some clues as to what religion is essentially about.

What is the upshot of man's venture into reality by way of science? Brush aside the details of specific discoveries that are being reported at the rate of two million a year and come at once to the point. From the theoretical standpoint the basic upshot of science is that it has disclosed a universe which in its factual nature is infinitely beyond anything we could have imagined while relying on our unaided senses.

A routine recall of two or three well-known facts will make this abundantly evident. Light travels at the rate of 186,000 miles per second. That's about seven times around the world each second. Now take the time-span that separates us from Christ and multiply it, not fifty times, but fifty thousand times, and you have the approximate time it takes a beam of light to move from one end of our galaxy to the other.

Our sun rotates around the center of our galaxy at a speed of one hundred sixty miles per second. That's fast; how fast we can perhaps appreciate if we recall the difficulty we have had getting rockets to attain a speed of seven miles per second, the speed required for them to escape from our earth's atmosphere. The sun travels roughly twenty-two times as fast as this escape rate, at which speed it takes it approximately 224 million years to complete one revolution around our galaxy. If these figures sound astronomical, they are actually parochial, for they are confined to our own galaxy. Andromeda, our second closest neighbor, is one-and-a-half million light-years removed, beyond which the universe falls away abysmally, range after range, world after world, island universe after island universe. In other directions the figures are equally incomprehensible. Avogadro's number tells us that the number of molecules in four-and-a-half drams of water (roughly half an ounce) is 6.023 times 10^{23}, roughly 100,000 billion billion. It's enough to make one dizzy; enough to make the mind reel, and spin, and cry out for a stop. Nay, more. From the vantage of our ordinary senses the vision is incredible—utterly, absolutely, completely incredible.

Only, of course, it's true.

Now along comes an Isaiah, a Christ, a Paul, a Saint Francis, a Buddha; along come men who are religiously the counterparts of Copernicus, Newton, Faraday, Kepler, and they tell us something equally incredible about the universe in its value dimension. They tell us of depth upon depth of value falling away from this visible world and our ordinary perceptions. They tell us that this universe in all its vastness is permeated to its very core by love. And *that's* incredible. I look at the newspaper every morning and say to myself, "It cannot be!" Yet in my reflective moments I find myself adding, "Is it, after all, any more incredible—does it any more exceed the limits of our normal human experience—than what my science colleagues are saying in their sphere?"

Of course, scientists have the advantage here, for they can prove their hypotheses whereas values and meanings elude the devices of science like the sea slips through the nets of fishermen. But this only leads me to press the analogy between science and religion farther. The factual marvels of the physical universe are not evident to the naked eye. Who, relying only on his own gross, unaided vision, could suspect that electrons are circling their nuclei at the rate of a million million times a second?

Such truths are disclosed to the scientists only through certain key perceptions, certain crucial experiments. The far-flung embroideries of science, and the entire scientific worldview, are based on a relatively small number of such experiments.

If this be true in science, why not in religion as well? If factual truth is disclosed not through routine perceptions but through key or crucial ones, might not this be the case with religious truth as well? The Lord appearing high and lifted up to Isaiah; the heavens opening to Christ at his baptism; the universe turning into a bouquet of flowers for Buddha beneath the Bo tree. John reporting, "I was on an island called Patmos, and I was in a trance." Saul struck blind on the Damascus road. For Augustine it was the voice of a child saying, "Take, read"; for Saint Francis a voice which seemed to come from the crucifix. It was while Saint Ignatius sat by a stream and watched the running water, and that curious old cobbler Jacob Boehme was looking at a pewter dish that there came to each that news of another world which it is always religion's business to convey.

A final step in the comparison is needed. If the universe of science is not evident to our ordinary senses but is elaborated from certain key perceptions, it is equally the case that these perceptions require their appropriate instruments: microscopes, Palomar telescopes, cloud chambers, and the like. Again, is there any reason why the same should not hold for religion? A few words by that late, shrewd lay theologian, Aldous Huxley, make the point well. "It is a fact, confirmed and reconfirmed by two or three thousand years of religious history," he wrote, "that Ultimate Reality is not clearly and immediately apprehended except by those who have made themselves loving, pure in heart, and poor in spirit." Perhaps such purity of heart is the indispensable instrument for disclosing the key perceptions on which religion's incredible assumption is grounded. With the unaided eye a small faint smudge can be detected in the constellation of Orion and doubtless an imposing cosmological theory founded on this smudge. But no amount of theorizing, however ingenious, could ever tell us as much about the galactic and extragalactic nebulae as can direct acquaintance by means of a good telescope, camera, and spectrascope.

I don't know in what direction such thoughts drive your mind; mine they drive in the direction of God. But the word doesn't matter; it's the assumption itself that counts, or rather the reality to which it points. Just as science has found the power of the sun itself to be locked in the atom, so religion (by whatsoever name) proclaims the glory of the eternal to be reflected in the simplest elements of time: a leaf, a door, an unturned stone. And so, for this quasi-religious, quasi-secular age, these lines titled "White Heron" by John Ciardi:

What lifts the heron leaning on the air
I praise without a name. A crouch, a flare,
a long stroke through the cumulus of trees,
a shaped thought at the sky—then gone. O rare!
Saint Francis, being happiest on his knees,
would have cried Father! Cry anything you please

But praise. By any name or none. But praise
the white original burst that lights
the heron on his two soft kissing kites.
When saints praise heaven lit by doves and rays,
I sit by pond scums till the air recites
Its heron back. And doubt all else. But praise.[3]

Notes

1. In 1960 the Creationists were not yet visible on the national scene.

2. See my "Human versus Artificial Intelligence," in John Roslansky, ed., *The Human Mind* (Amsterdam: North Holland Publishing Co., 1967).

3. John Ciardi, "The White Heron," in *I Marry You* (New Brunswick, N.J.: Rutgers University Press, 1958). Used by permission of the author.

INDEX

QUEST BOOKS
are published by
The Theosophical Society in America,
Wheaton, Illinois 60189-0270,
a branch of a world organization
dedicated to the promotion of the unity of
humanity and the encouragement of the study of
religion, philosophy, and science, to the end that
we may better understand ourselves and our place in
the universe. The Society stands for complete
freedom of individual search and belief.
In the Classics Series well-known
theosophical works are made
available in popular editions.
For more information
write or call.
1-312-668-1571